George Cohen was born in Kensington, London in 1939. He only ever played professional football for one club, Fulham FC. He made his first team debut in 1956 and made 408 league appearances. Injury cut short his playing career and he retired in 1968. He won his first England cap in 1964 and went on to make a total of 37 appearances for his country

James Lawton, who collaborated with George Cohen in the writing of this book, is the chief sports writer for the *Independent* and is a winner of the British Sports Journalist of the Year award. He has written eight books, including biographies of Lester Pigott, Malcolm Allison and Lennox Lewis. Most recently he helped Nobby Stiles and Joe Jordan with their highly acclaimed autobiographies.

GW00372363

First published in 2003
by Greenwater Publishing Ltd

First published in paperback in 2005
by HEADLINE BOOK PUBLISHING

1

ISBN 0 7553 1397 6

Printed and bound in Great Britain by
Mackays of Chatham plc, Chatham, Kent

Headline's policy is to use papers that are natural, renewable and
recyclable products and made from wood grown in sustainable forests.
The logging and manufacturing processes are expected to conform to the
environmental regulations of the country of origin.

Typeset in Centaur by Avon DataSet Ltd,
Bidford on Avon, Warwickshire

HEADLINE BOOK PUBLISHING
A division of Hodder Headline
338 Euston Road
London NW1 3BH

www.headline.co.uk
www.hodderheadline.com

GEORGE COHEN
My Autobiography

headline

CONTENTS

Foreword   I

Getting to Sydney   5

1   The Forgotten Five   17

2   'Give it to the Bloody Rabbi'   47

3   'It Was a Rather Good Left Hook   65

4   Thinking and Sweating at the Same Time   85

5   The King of Fulham   III

6   'You're Semi-retired, Aren't You?'   139

7   'Was it that Cliff Jones?'   163

8   Seeds of '66   177

9   Winging It   201

10   Animals and Nobby's Business   217

11   It's Coming Home   233

12   Goodbye, Sir Alf   255

13   Building the Future   277

14   Bitter Pills   295

15   Riding the Storm   309

16   The Kennedys of Tunbridge Wells   323

A Young and Thrilling Vintage   331

Appendix: What the Team and the Manager Said   341

Statistics   349

Index   351

FOREWORD
BY BEN COHEN

I was thrilled that my famous uncle George Cohen made it to Sydney to see me help England's rugby team win the World Cup. It meant so much to me, my family and my team-mates, and there was a special edge to his presence in that he had made the journey despite being seriously unwell; for me that seemed to symbolise perfectly everything he had represented since I had first become aware of what he had achieved that day at Wembley when England won the World Cup of football.

His supreme quality has always been that he is willing to take whatever life offers, the good and the bad, without it ever changing his nature or his view of the world, and I was so proud of him in the days before our final when he talked to the whole team about the challenge we faced against Australia.

He had been where we were now and though he represented a different game, and different challenges, the essence of our situation was exactly the same as that which he and Bobby Moore and Bobby Charlton and all the others had faced when they walked out against West Germany in 1966.

It meant that in our moment of victory in the Telstra Stadium I formed a new ambition. It was to handle the success that had come to me with the dignity and sound perspective of my Uncle George. He has had some major setbacks in his life along with the glory. Three times he has fought off cancer. He has had to come back from crushing setbacks in business. But never once have I heard him moan about his bad luck. He has always taken the view that things might be different, and better, tomorrow.

Such a view of the world, always freely shared with me, was extremely valuable on the downside of victory in Sydney. Since then I've had problems with form, injury and had difficult negotiations with my club Northampton, but always George was there to give the vital advice: be true to yourself Ben, do the best you can and always remember that you are still a young man with so much left to achieve. Keep your pride and your values, he said, and always try to do the right thing.

That kind of advice has always been there since I first began making a name for myself in rugby – and never more so than when we shared with the rest of the family the grief that came with the violent death of my father, and Uncle George's younger brother, Peter, a few years ago. We sat in court together as the men who assaulted my father were given sentences so light we wanted to cry out. In the end we realised we had to handle the pain in our different ways.

Uncle George's presence was so valuable when my emotions were rampant and I was considering playing for England just a few days after my father's death. He said that my father would only have wanted me to do the best for my country and at that time I couldn't be sure of how all the different pressures would affect me. I might suddenly find myself incapable of meeting my responsibilities to my team-mates, my coach, and, ultimately, my country. My father would not want me to make just an emotional response. There were stronger ways to deal with the situation. He would have wanted me to think it through. It was good advice from somebody who both cared so deeply about my father and had operated at the highest level of professional sport – and I took it.

To be perfectly honest there was a little bit of relief for me when I was invited to write the Foreword to this book. For me the inference was that I had finally outgrown my status as the nightmare brat whose visits to his beautiful home in Kent brought so much devastation. The mayhem got so bad that when my parents took me visiting he put away safely all the more delicate trophies and fancy glassware he had acquired in his football career. He has told the story of how, after being cooped up in the back of the family car in a traffic jam on the Kingston by-pass, I strode into the lounge Aunt Daphne kept so immaculately and put to unorthodox use a large cut-class ashtray which had been given to him by the Dutch club Feyenoord.

In all the days I have known him, Uncle George's greatest gift to me has been the word of a man who had climbed to a mountain top of sporting achievement without ever losing his feeling for what was most precious in life. I was reminded of this shortly before I went off to Australia to play in the

World Cup. I was driving along the motorway when a driver was killed after a lorry hit the central reservation and landed on top of his car. I was breaking hard as the accident happened before me and later I thought that if I had put my shoes on a couple of seconds more quickly that morning it could have been my life snuffed out so randomly.

Uncle George has faced that prospect quite a number of times but he has never flinched; he has always tried to get on with his life. It leaves me proud to share his blood, his ambitons, and, now, to some degree, his achievements. He has always shown me that it is possible for a sportsman to fly to the stars while always keeping his feet on the ground.

GETTING TO SYDNEY

As the tension rose in the Telstra Stadium in Sydney my son Anthony put his hand on my old and rather battered knee and said, 'Dad, do you realise this is going the same way as your game at Wembley?'

This was shortly before Jonny Wilkinson dropped the goal that meant that my nephew Ben, son of my tragically dead and beloved younger brother, Peter, became the second member of the Cohen family to help win a World Cup for England. The rain swirled in our faces, mingling with more than one tear of emotion I had shed that night. I squeezed my son's hand and said, 'Yes, I know . . . and it's bloody eerie.'

It was certainly that, as England fell behind, then equalised and were finally carried home by a man wearing the number 10 shirt – and so many other things: pride and joy and a surge of nostalgia for the greatest day of my own life, and then when the ball had flapped over the bar and I picked out Ben dancing with his team-mates down on the field, I thought of something Jimmy Greaves said to us before we went out on to the field. 'Lads, you should know that if you win today your lives will be changed for ever.'

Before the game, at England's beachside headquarters in Manley, I told Ben and his team-mates Martin Johnson, Lawrence Dallaglio and Jonny Wilkinson what Greaves had said, and I added that it was true. I also said that after being around them for a little time, and even though not knowing all the nuances and intricacies of their game, I was confident that they would do it. I felt an energy, an understanding of what was at stake.

But then if I told you this was an uncomplicated time for a veteran of that earlier success, that I was able to put all of my heart and mind into the wonderful prospect of Ben joining me on the peaks of English sporting history, I would be less than honest.

Yes, I could celebrate the possibility of a unique family triumph, something different from, but in its way no less remarkable than, that of the Charlton brothers, Jack and Bobby, playing alongside each other in 1966, but not without a serious tug at my spirit. Even in the euphoria of England's, and Ben's triumph, I couldn't bury a growing concern. It was that 24 years after the second of two life-saving cancer operations, my health was again breaking down.

The day before the final I had done a little shopping with Anthony in Sydney, and suddenly it became an ordeal putting one foot in front of the other. I noted as I walked along the street that we were going slightly uphill, but for a man who had always prided himself on his physical fitness, who had made it the foundation of all his success as a footballer, this was of not the slightest comfort. I didn't know what was happening to me, but whatever it was it didn't feel good. It felt, all over again, as it had on a morning run in the Kent countryside almost 30 years previously when I had come to a gasping, dismaying halt and within 24 hours I was being told by a doctor that he could give no guarantees for my future.

However, in 2003 it was a shadow that for a little time I thought might just be rolled back by the sheer excitement of those days in Sydney. This was not completely so, of course, and as the night of triumph spilled into the early hours in a noisy club in the Rocks district which overlooks Sydney harbour, as the heroes of a wonderful hour, the coach Clive Woodward and all the players, came to me with warm – and very powerful – embraces and said that it was good that I could be there to link two great moments of English sport, I became worried that I might be approaching a state of collapse.

I was bone-tired and it felt as though my body was filling with toxins. The truth was I didn't really know what was happening to me.

So I sipped my Buck's Fizz a little apprehensively while telling myself that this was really quite a refreshing drink and also trying to persuade myself that at any moment I would rally.

Then I tried to move a few steps and I found myself saying under my breath, 'Wait a minute, this isn't happening.' Though it was hard to do, especially with Anthony enjoying himself so much in the glow of his cousin's great success, I whispered that he better order up a taxi. I didn't want to collapse, I didn't want to mar in the smallest way one of those nights which is properly assigned to outright celebration.

Anthony, quite miraculously amid all the partying, conjured a cab and we drove off into the dawn to our hotel beside a beach 30 miles away. I told Anthony that he shouldn't worry too much. I was probably suffering from a rather bad case of jetlag. Then I slept for a very long time.

When I awoke, feeling strong enough to contemplate the long haul home, I went out into the pale sunshine with gratitude that, whatever the next year offered, however difficult it might be to fight off the pain and the weariness that came into my mind when I thought of a return to those days of battling for my life, I had been able to spend this time in Sydney – and, while there, had not given the impression that I had become a complete basketcase.

I managed to chuckle over an exchange I had had with Ben before he flew off to Australia for the World Cup campaign. He phoned me to say, 'Uncle George, if we reach the final and I'm selected there will be two World Cup winners in the family. So what do you think of that?' I made the breezy response, 'Ben, after being wined and dined for 37 years, I'll be totally pissed off if I have to share some of my patch ...' He laughed, after a brief pause, and then I added, 'Ben, this is something you and your team-mates have worked for over a few years now ... I think you'll win, and nothing will stop me being there to see it happen.'

This was owed to Ben and my brother Peter, the nature of whose death will always for me be a matter of great pain and anger and the deepest regret. If Peter couldn't be in Sydney, I could step into his place. I could celebrate my nephew's hard work and ambition, I could welcome him into a sense of achievement that had been with me, through even the most unpromising circumstances, ever since that long-ago day at Wembley.

It was also true that even when I took away all the fulfilment of the Cohen family hopes, I could still put a high value on being in Sydney. Rugby is a game I don't understand at any deep level, but all competitive sport is shaped by certain fundamental values in those who play it and watch it and as someone who has come to despair of much that is going on in football, on and off the field, seeing and being more than a little involved emotionally in the World Cup final of another game, was for me to step back into a much more innocent time.

On the day of the game we went up to Sydney for lunch in one of the restaurants that sit by the harbour. We watched the ferry boats as they passed the Opera House and could hear the laughter of the England and Australian supporters who seemed to be merging into one great mass of gold and white. A football man couldn't but reflect with some pain on the difficulty of creating such an atmosphere in his own game. The ambience was unbroken as we took a train out to the stadium, where the promise of rain had done nothing to take away the sharpest edge of anticipation and where, despite much drinking of beer, I noted later with some wonder, that only three people had been detained by the police, and not one of them charged.

Because of my own experience of big games, I normally don't get too excited as a spectator, but before the kick off I knew that this was going to be quite different. As the game wore on, I found myself moving towards the edge of my seat. We were surrounded by Australians, hugely excited by their team's second half recovery, but aware, also, that their men were against opposition which simply wasn't going to fade. There was a wonderful balance to the game, a bit like England versus West Germany on another day, and when the moment of victory came, when Wilkinson dropped the decisive goal, there was for me an explosion of memory. Faces that had aged down the years were young again, I saw Nobby Stiles, the late Bobby Moore, Bobby Charlton, Alan Ball and our own match-winner, Geoff Hurst, not in golfing weekends and dinner reunions but as they were on the field when the game had been won, laughing and dancing, triumphant and frozen in time.

Wilkinson had not had the greatest tournament until then but like Hurst he had seized his moment so brilliantly. Even someone unfamiliar with the tactics of rugby could see how England were shaping themselves for that kick, and though I believed the experts when they say that, technically speaking, it was far from the best he had ever delivered, he will never do anything more memorable on the pitch as long as he plays rugby. The orchestration of that last minute or so was one of the most extraordinary things I had ever seen in sport. The clock was ticking away but you wouldn't have thought so by the measured way England went about their business. They knew what they had to do, and it was something that couldn't be rushed. It was not a time to snatch and hope. It was a time to execute.

What was so fantastic about Wilkinson for me, with my football background, was that left-footed players are generally most committed to being on their favoured side the greater the pressure becomes. But he took it as it came, impervious to the clamour around him, and in this he was like my old captain Moore, and it didn't matter to me that the ball wasn't going through the air as dynamically as it might have done. It fulfilled its vital obligation. It hit the target.

Afterwards Ben thanked me for being there, said how important it had been for him. He had dedicated his performance to his father, and I was Peter's brother and representative, and now both the footballer and the rugby player would always have their time at the top of the mountain. I said that he had earned his right to step out of my shadow. He had reached his own pinnacle and he and his team-mates, as the great Greaves had said, would always have it. It was tragic that Peter could not be there to see, but I felt his presence more strongly than I had done since the day he had died so unnecessarily. I said to Ben that he didn't have to speculate on how his father would have felt if he had seen the winners' medal being presented, and that part of his pride would have been precisely the same as mine. It would have been strengthened by the knowledge that he would always behave in the right way.

Finally, I congratulated Ben on becoming his own man, the winner of a World Cup and no longer the mere nephew of his Uncle George.

As all the brawny heroes wrapped their arms around me –

I tried to reciprocate but unfortunately I didn't have the reach – Clive Woodward came over to shake my hand and said, 'This, amid everything else, is a wonderful family achievement, thank you for coming down and talking to the boys, we all appreciate it very much.' I was so glad I had been able to get there, to place this memory alongside the other one. Yes, I went into the early morning streets shakily, and with a sense of personal foreboding that I suppose deep down I had never shaken off entirely despite all the support of my family and the brilliant work of doctors. But there was nowhere in the world I would rather have been, not, anyway, in the absence of a time machine and the chance to go out again at Wembley on a summer afternoon.

It was also good that even though my new health problems would make the coming year mostly another harsh trial, I was still able to give Ben a little counsel as he began to learn, as I had done before him, that sometimes the journey down the other side of the mountain can bring more than the odd ambush.

My hope, and strong belief, is that Ben – after some frustrating post-glory days – will be able to reclaim all of the high ground that was for a while taken away. He was carrying a few injuries when he came back from Australia, not serious ones but sufficient to take away that edge of sharpness which every leading sportsman needs if he is to do full credit to himself, and after the briefest of breaks the English season was on again, and then, too soon both physically and psychologically, the World Cup heroes were back on a plane, this time to South Africa. A three-week break after returning from Australia was a most basic requirement if form and freshness was to be easily picked up again.

Ben was noted for his safe hands but in the wake of the World Cup it was said that he couldn't catch a cold. He told me, with a great sigh, 'I'm just not handling my game . . . maybe I've had too much.' Now, as I write this, Ben is coming back to some decent form. He remains in the England squad because basically, I believe, he is simply too good to leave out, but he understands that he may have to be a little patient before he gets another sustained run. I've pointed out to him that my knee – and my football career – was wrecked soon after my World Cup, and he should be grateful for the chance to build himself back up to his old level. At 26 he should know that there is more than enough time for the old appetite to come back.

There were also some contract problems with his club, Northampton, which he discussed with me several times. I was delighted that he didn't need to be reminded of the value of loyalty; he had not forgotten that the club had taken him from school, nursed him through their ranks and had been very good to him when his father was critically ill and then died. At the same time he faced the dilemma of every professional sportsman. He wanted to arrive at his proper value in the marketplace, and I was pleased that he handled this aspect of the negotiations with maturity and in a manner which maintained his dignity.

Now, after the euphoria of that great parade through the streets of London – one that I noted a little wryly was rather more extravagant than the one that my team received, something that a muttering old sweat might have placed alongside the fact that while the rugby boys were granted almost instant, and thoroughly deserved, MBEs, some of us had to wait as long as 34 years – Ben still has a few lessons to learn. He has to grasp that however great one day is, however much fame it imparts, there will always be another one when you find yourself walking alone.

What we all do share, though, is the gift that Ben and his team-mates gave themselves that squally, unforgettable night in Sydney. As long as they lived, they would never be quite invisible.

I was reminded of this recently when I walked down Piccadilly past Green Park. I was feeling as anonymous as any of the shoppers and the office workers – certainly separated by at least one lifetime from the young man who had played for England the first time they won a World Cup. And then a small, ageing guy stepped out from the crowd and offered his hand. 'You're George Cohen,' he announced. Indeed I was. Suddenly I felt a little better about the notice I just had from the Inland Revenue, which pointed out that I would shortly be receiving my old age pension and I should not forget to include it in my tax returns.

No, some things are not wiped away for as long as you live. Some things you can hold for ever. I picked up my stride and thanked God that I was able to do so. Mortality gets everyone in the end, but in the meantime there are few things you can always celebrate. For me, getting to Sydney was one of the greatest. And, as I had thought in very different, and very grand circumstances, four years earlier, quite a lot had happened to me to take me to the point of shaking that gentleman's hand in the centre of London.

CHAPTER ONE

THE
FORGOTTEN FIVE

After the debate, and the vote, we went to the Palace in lounge suits. Roger Hunt, Ray Wilson and I reckoned we could handle top hats and tails. At a push, so might Alan Ball.

But not Nobby Stiles. No, we mulled it over for a few minutes, pictured the absurdity of Nobby marching down the Mall in a morning suit, and agreed there was really only one option.

It was a spring day in the year of the Millennium, 34 years after we had won the World Cup, and after the Queen had handed each of us our MBE she paused, a little reflectively I thought, and said, 'It's been a long time.' A reaction sprang to my lips but I knew enough not to speak to the Queen unless I was addressed directly. The Master of Protocol had been quite strict about that when he gave us our instructions about where we should stand and when and how we should move. So the words were suppressed. They remain vivid enough, however. 'Yes, Ma'am', I thought, 'and quite a lot has happened.'

On that sunlit day when we beat Germany in 1966 it seemed for a little while that the world had stopped. But of course it never does. It didn't for Bobby Moore, who had the gleam of youth when he had accepted the golden trophy from the still young woman in the Royal Box, after carefully wiping the sweat from his hands, and now he was gone.

Nor had it lifted me beyond pain or doubt. Within two years of winning the World Cup, my playing career was over. Three times I had been obliged to fight off cancer.

My mother had been run down and killed by a juggernaut on one of the streets of Fulham through the dangers of which she had always guided my brothers and me with such authority. My kid brother, whatever the deliberations of a court, had been murdered. I had moved up and down the ladder of commercial success, been forced to sell a beautiful home surrounded by banks of flowers in the Kent country-side. I also sold my World Cup winners' medal to fund a pension plan when the bottom fell out of the property market in which I was about to make the coup which would have made us secure for life.

If, however, the Queen had had the time to listen – it was a busy day at the Palace, a thousand MBEs had been struck and my son Anthony had been irreverent enough to muse that maybe it had become more difficult to get hold of a Blue Peter badge – I would have told her I would not have traded anything – at least this side of the love and support of my wife Daphne and my sons – for that little time in the sun at Wembley, when, with these ageing guys who had come with me to the Palace this morning, and like me had awakened with the excitement of schoolboys, we had beaten the world. We had come together so closely under the great Sir Alf Ramsey – who had, after all, received his honour swiftly enough – that we might have been brothers.

I could have told the Queen that although we were very happy to receive the honour, that in truth we felt it was a proper and necessary thing, it was not as though for one single moment down those years we had ever felt unfulfilled.

We had something you couldn't mint, and still less dispense in any honours list. We had a knowledge of ourselves, and something we had achieved, which could hold us against the worst of days. Of course it did not provide any proofing against worry or disappointment, or even despair. It didn't remove the possibility of a little angst – or even envy at the way our old livelihood had become awash with what we might feel, in our grouchier moments, had become easy money indeed. It wasn't such a great help to me when I was twice told that the cancer had come back, or when I had to pick up the broken shards of my life without that vast, all-enveloping reassurance and peace that comes with a shot of morphine.

No, real life is not so accommodating. It tells you soon enough that the shelf life of euphoria is strictly rationed. But then sometimes it gives a gift which cannot be taken away. Only ten Englishmen alive know what it is like to win a World Cup, and, sadly enough, our number do not appear under imminent threat of invasion, at least not if the evidence of Japan and the 2002 World Cup is anything like reliable. Winning that trophy is something to store, something to remind yourself of, when perhaps the going is a little tough.

Having an MBE, quite honestly, didn't affect the sense of that too much, but it was nice to have. It took away a rankle, a little tug of resentment which nobody needs.

A lady from Downing Street called me to ask if I would be averse to receiving an MBE. I said, 'No, not at all, thank you very much.' But there were, I have to say, elements of the comic. She told me that they had had quite a problem finding me. In fact, they had finally got hold of my number from Nobby Stiles, which I didn't think said an awful lot for the Secret Service.

Nobby was terribly excited, a little surprisingly for someone who in moments of great pressure had always struck me as superbly composed, sometimes even nonchalant. Back in '66, before our semi-final game with Portugal, Alf had fretted about the menace of the great Eusebio. He went over all our tactical options, dwelling briefly on individual tasks, and then he said, 'Nobby, I want you take Eusebio out of the game.' All eyes turned to Stiles as he was given this rather arresting command. But the little man didn't blink. 'Do you mean for life, Alf?' he meekly enquired.

I was proud to walk in to the Palace with Stiles. Despite the assassin's talk, his defensive performance against Eusebio was so brilliant, technically and morally, that the great Portuguese player was rendered so ineffective he was forced into taking corners well before the end, and even today the Football Association would do well to seek out the film in the archives and run it as a masterful guide to the art of reading a game. I had the same feeling of pride in all of my companions that morning five years ago. There were perhaps greater stars on that day when we beat Germany. Moore was already a legend of poised defence. Sir Bobby Charlton was beautiful, one of the most liquid movers who ever stepped on to a football field. No-one could have seized an opportunity more perfectly than Sir Geoff Hurst, and our manager had already placed Martin Peters ten years ahead of his time. Gordon Banks was fast being acknowledged as the world's greatest goalkeeper. But Stiles, Wilson, Hunt, and Ball were the heart and the sinew and the superb professional accomplishment of the side that Ramsey moulded with such certainty of purpose.

When I was struggling through one of my bouts with cancer, Wilson, a leading undertaker in his part of West Yorkshire, called to enquire if it was true that Jews were buried standing up so as to prevent the money falling out of their pockets. He also wondered how I was doing. I said not so badly, and that I was giving it a go. 'Oh,' he said drily, 'I was calling to offer you a deal.' Wilson was a superb full-back and the most solid of men.

Hunt worked with phenomenal honesty. Hurst couldn't have happened without Hunt. Ball was quite simply a little marvel of application and skill. In the great ante-chamber where we waited for the presentation of our MBEs, after our crash course in Palace etiquette, I had this overwhelming feeling of warmth that after so long I was back in the company of these tremendous footballers and unpretentious men on the day that we were recognised for an achievement which, among Englishmen, the breed that had given the game to the world, was unique.

I also thought of other things, I thought of those early days at Fulham Central School, where discipline was so keen and the headmaster would come into the classroom with steel in his eyes and say, 'Cohen, are you ready for Saturday's game?' I thought of the simplicity – and the toughness – of life then, of the pang of regret when I unthinkingly told my father, who worked so hard, riding off on his bike laden with his tradesman's tools every morning in all kinds of weather, how my first earnings as a young professional at Fulham had so comfortably surpassed any week's wages he had ever earned. And, perhaps most bitingly of all, how it was when the consultant told Daphne that she should make sure I got my affairs in order, and she said very calmly, but with fire in her eyes, 'George isn't going anywhere.'

There were a thousand memories flooding back. There were the stories of my uncle Len fighting the Blackshirts on Parson's Green. There was my brother Len taking me on his honeymoon – he had had to explain to his French wife Raymonde that as our parents were working there wasn't anyone to look after me. Earlier he had taught me how to ride a bike, and how to dress, and how to look at the world. There was the first taste of jellied eels, an unshakeable addiction.

There was the loss of my mother, who was such a powerful woman her going was so hard to grasp, and of my brother, about which deep down I still cannot be reconciled. I thought about the meaning of this award, and really did it have one? Was it because a few newspaper writers had raised the issue of our absence from an honours list, or was it just an embarrassed reflex action to the fact that my friend Geoff Hurst, who was a leading ambassador for England's failed bid to land the 2006 World Cup, had been knighted two years earlier?

In the end I decided it didn't really matter. It was enough that a great day of our lives had been rekindled, and who really cared if the honour had come so long after the deeds for which it was being bestowed? Perhaps we did live in an age of Big Brother TV shows, and instant celebrity and pop stars who didn't seem to be able to sing, and yes, maybe, there were days when you woke up and felt that someone had turned the world upside down, but we collected our medals in the knowledge that we had indeed done something memorable and that here was something tangible in the way of official recognition. It didn't matter that a couple of years later I would be watching a TV documentary on the honours system and heard a senior civil servant define the various levels of award. 'Now the MBE,' he said, 'tends to be awarded for something achieved locally.' Something extremely worthy, presumably. Something like being a good, long-serving postman or lollypop lady. I certainly don't wish to insult good people in the community, but I did think that winning the World Cup might just have gone beyond the boundaries of winning of local achievement.

Some people say, and it is an argument I find hard to resist at times, that we live in an age of mediocrity. Certainly it was a belief that gathered a little force in my mind three years ago when a newspaper called to check on my reaction to the campaign for a street parade in recognition of England's achievement in reaching the quarter-finals of the World Cup in Japan.

The reporter said that his office had been receiving a lot of calls from fans who said they were disgusted that the team had not been paraded through the streets, and did I not agree that the FA, or maybe Downing Street, should have organised such a celebration? I said, 'Are you sure this "disgust" isn't really originating in your own newspaper?' 'No,' he said, 'we are genuinely getting a lot of protest calls. Don't you think we should put on something for the lads?' I said I was sorry but I didn't. I said back in my time you didn't get anything for finishing eighth. I had an odd, almost surreal feeling when I put down that phone. I knew what Alf would have thought. 'No, blinking way' he would have said in that voice on which he had worked so hard to refine. No way, indeed, for the man who had so fiercely resisted the attempts of some of his players to drag him on to the field at Wembley as Nobby Stiles danced his triumphant, joyous little jig.

In the wake of England's defeat in the quarter-final against Brazil in 2002, I was asked several times where I thought it left our national team. Because you always want to think the best of players representing your country, and strive to be optimistic – quite apart from the desire not to be one of those desperate old guys always eager to knock a later generation, come what may – I was reluctant to rush out an opinion. But sometimes, when you care for the game, when you are just a little too irked by the double-talk and the euphemisms and the refusal to apply any hint of realistic assessment, you are bound to speak what you consider to be the truth.

Apologists for Sven Goran Eriksson's England were keen to point out the draining heat on the day of the quarter-final. Adam Crozier, the former chief executive of the Football Association, claimed a triumph and said that it was the Japanese climate rather than Brazil or our own deficiencies that brought us down. I'm afraid I took a bleaker view – one that in my opinion was confirmed by the more recent and equally threadbare performances in the European Championships finals in Portugal 2004.

My opinion is that the overall performance in Japan, and particularly the effort against Brazil, told us that England then, and frankly now, are nowhere when it comes to taking on the world's best. I had thought, along with a lot of other people, that we had really good youngsters coming through in that summer of 2002, but against Brazil it was clear that we had two major problems. We simply didn't have enough of those good young players and of those we had, two of the most celebrated, David Beckham and Michael Owen, plainly shouldn't have been on the field, and perhaps not even in the tournament. It was painfully obvious that neither was fit. It was a catastrophic decision to take along key players who could not begin to deliver anything like full performances. And to repeat the error with the England captain two years later almost defied belief.

The broader problem, when you looked back over the World Cup, was that at no point did England really exhibit any imagination or flair. We finished eighth, or fifth, however you care to put it, but we didn't separate ourselves from the rest of the pack behind Brazil in any clearly perceptible way. Brazil were not great, it has to be said, but they had something that was beyond the rest of the field, and certainly England. They had a number of players, and notably the young Ronaldinho who has only grown in stature and ability since then, who can make a big play from midfield. When we played them that lack in our team was terribly evident. As the Brazilian game slipped away from us, as Beckham and Owen – despite taking brilliantly the goal offered him by the big defender Lucio – struggled to make any kind of impact in the heat, it was painfully clear that though Ronaldinho had been sent off, it was Brazil and not England who had a real physical advantage. They had ten fit men. We had nine. They also understood what they were doing. We didn't. We didn't have width, we didn't have wit, and I can only believe that my old friend Dave Sexton, one of the greatest football brains I have ever encountered, who was attached to the squad, was not given the chance to supply any input at that vital phase of the tournament. Two years later, in the European Championships in Portugal, it was astonishing that so little had been learned. At the heart of the dismay was something that was really quite unbelievable. England were once more led by a Beckham who was plainly far from fit. This was something that again offended one of the most basic rules of football. You cannot go into a major competition with unfit players; sometimes, yes, there is temptation to gamble, to weigh a supreme talent against the possibility of breakdown in a single-match situation. But Beckham, as captain, was supposed to lead, to set the tone of the English campaign. However, a quick glance at him, either on or off the field, told you he was almost certainly incapable of doing this. Where was Eriksson looking, what was he thinking?

As far as the captain was concerned, we were back in the Far East. In Japan, Beckham had struggled with a metatarsal injury – something which occurs regularly in today's football and which I did suffer once, but then I was walking around my lounge in slippers, not being paid millions to use a customised version of them in a seriously competitive football match.

In Portugal Beckham's face was flabby, far from the chiselled definition you expect from a professional athlete primed for action at the highest level, and on the field he was unable even to match his performances in Japan, which apart from the Argentina game, had been so desperately inconsequential. And it wasn't just the England captain's performances that made Euro 2004 almost interchangeable with Japan two years earlier. There was an inevitability about the performances on the pitch that was almost uncanny.

Against Brazil in the World Cup and France and Portugal in the European Championships England achieved an advantage, and had created the foundations of victory, but on each occasion there was a failure to deliver. In Japan the lack of options, Eriksson's failure to inject new life into the effort, had to be placed alongside the lack of fitness – and leadership – displayed by Beckham. Again, the coach was inert when both France and Portugal, like Brazil, fought back from going a goal down.

Eriksson's faith in Emile Heskey, who I'm afraid has revealed a lack of true international quality for several years but who, incredibly, has been recalled to the squad for the 2006 World Cup qualifiers, was proved disastrous in the French match. His hapless mistake set up Zinedine Zidane's equalising free kick. But deeper than that was the problem of controlling a game, building an edge. Paul Scholes was lost alongside the left of England's midfield, detached from his most effective area just behind the strikers. It was no surprise when this fine, aggressive player called an end to his international career when he got home, deeply disillusioned and frustrated. In the Portugal game, again England yielded the midfield and when Rooney left injured all momentum seemed to disappear. When the Portuguese coach injected new attacking life into his team in the second half, Eriksson responded with Phil Neville. It was not really the answer. Worse still, nor was it anything like a surprise.

During the course of the European Championships, and indeed during the 2002 World Cup, I read, with mounting disbelief, that Beckham was an inspirational captain. But how can you inspire your team-mates when you are so plainly not operating at 100 per cent? Beckham was down to very basic knocks-on and flicks and, of course, he took most of the dead-ball kicks, unfortunately including the penalties.

Looking back to 2002, what did Beckham really contribute then? A corner from which Sol Campbell scored a goal against Sweden. A successful penalty against Argentina? Any competent professional could have done as much. You do not play Beckham for his goals, he scores one in nine matches.

What he is meant to be good at is making goals, but again, if he is not in peak condition he can't work up and down the pitch, which he is so very good at when he is well and in the right frame of mind.

Of course it runs deeper than that. At the level we are talking about, when one moment of breakdown can end your team's chances, full fitness is not some kind of bonus. It is an absolutely basic requirement and Beckham, right from the start, was betrayed by his inability to perform at anything like even mere adequacy.

He really didn't contribute anything of significance to that tournament and I say that with the feeling of someone who will never forget the influence Ball brought to the '66 World Cup. His judgement in getting into the right positions was superb. His running and his sharpness took your breath away. He was always available, always harrying the Germans. He was the piston of the team on that right side. I have to say I would have always had Ball in my side before Beckham. For a start, you wouldn't lose anything. Ball could play up and down the right all day. He played with wonderful energy and craft in the middle. His football brain was like a razor. In the final against Germany he went out wide and gave one of the world's best full-backs, Karl-Heinz Schnellinger, a nightmare. The problem with Beckham is that apart from that beautiful ball-striking with his right foot, he just doesn't have any tricks, and you certainly don't see him going into too many hefty tackles.

And as for being an inspirational captain in the World Cup, the fact is that Beckham supplied a sorry image of his leadership when he jumped over the ball at the touchline shortly before half time, and was then required to watch it flow away at the feet of Ronaldinho and then Rivaldo before it reached the back of the England net and, effectively, ruined England's best chance of winning the World Cup since that day Moore held the trophy aloft.

I think there were two things at the back of Beckham's mind when he pursued the ball into the path of two Brazilians, Kleberson and Roque Junior. One was that he was going to be tackled from behind, which he had every right to think, and the other was that because his opponents were so close to him they were going to take the ball as well as him. So he would jump over the ball and perhaps get a throw-in. But when he did that the Brazilians were ready for it, they knew there was no way Beckham could do anything with the ball because he was running straight at it at speed. If you have a bit of nous you can read this sort of situation quite easily. Beckham couldn't turn either way with the ball the way he approached it, he couldn't turn left or right, and in those circumstances, had I been one of the defenders, I would have been disgusted with myself if I had put the ball out.

In such play all you have to do as a defender is keep your eye on the ball and if you do that you know you are going to get it. What made everything worse was the accomplishment of the Brazilians after Beckham had surrendered the ball, and Paul Scholes had made such a pathetic attempt to recover the situation. Ronaldinho moved beautifully on the ball. He showed great pace and great control and almost effortlessly drew the defenders to him. Rivaldo responded perfectly, he pulled right and, as a left-sided player, opened up all the goal to his best foot. It was textbook lay-off from Ronaldinho because Rivaldo didn't even need to control the ball. He just put it into the net so calmly it made you want to weep.

There was something else astounding, and deeply depressing from an English viewpoint, about that goal. When Ronaldinho made his run he had four defenders around him but no-one dived in front of him. This is a basic demand on a defender in that situation. You thought, 'For God's sake, someone has got to make a tackle sooner or later.' But it didn't happen and at that moment you just knew that we were heading out of the tournament.

The decision to take Beckham to Portugal, and two years earlier to Japan, was highly questionable from the word go. After Euro 2004 he admitted to the press that he had a problem with his fitness and suggested this was because of the training regime at Real Madrid. I could only shake my head and try to imagine Ramsey's reaction to such a statement from Bobby Moore. Prior to the World Cup Beckham hadn't played for seven weeks. When it was announced he would play right at the start of the tournament I couldn't help remembering the agonies Alf went through when he debated in his mind the fitness of great players like Jimmy Greaves and Johnny Haynes. I recalled the time when Haynes, having recovered from a serious injury, had returned to the Fulham team with some typically eye-catching performances. For me Haynes was a god, a player of genius who always knew where to be on the field and always had the time and the vision to make the right pass. One day after an England training session Alf came up to me and said, 'How's Haynes?' I said he was tremendous, he had snapped back into the game with all his old assurance and bite. Alf thought about what I had said, then shook his head slowly. 'I don't think he is quite right,' he said, 'I don't think he has fully recovered from his injury.'

Later, I told Haynes about the conversation. I expected him to be indignant, because to my eyes he had been playing well, well enough certainly to warrant a return to the national team. But, after hearing of the manager's reservations, Haynes nodded, and said, 'Alf's right,' and walked away. I was impressed by the honesty of Haynes and, even more, the shrewd judgement of Ramsey. The idea of him taking a player like Beckham to a World Cup, with such scant preparation and with such responsibilities on his shoulders, is just unthinkable.

All analysis of England's failure in Portugal and Japan has to centre on the fact that it should have been perfectly obvious to the England bench that some fresh direction was needed. We looked as if we were just playing the ball around and with no particular objective other than to keep possession, but it was possession without purpose or insight. We couldn't create gaps in the French, Portuguese or Brazilian defences and even if we had done so you would then have to wonder who would run into them. Here, you have to sympathise with Eriksson, or anyone who is placed in charge of the national team. You have to recognise that there has been a terrible decline in the quality of craftsmanship in midfield.

Watching the laboured efforts of the current England

team, it is impossible not to yearn for the kind of magic produced so effortlessly by a combination like Haynes and Greaves. Greaves loved to play with Haynes because he knew that if he made a break into space, as he did so instinctively, the ball would slide with perfect weight into his path. It was wonderful to see. Haynes was the best of his time in England, but in those days every team had a creative figure, someone like little Ernie Taylor probing away, looking around to see that his team-mates were making the right runs, seeking out the space where the ball could be delivered with most biting effect. Later, Johnny Giles and Billy Bremner had a phenomenal understanding at Leeds. It was as if Bremner was on the end of a string.

Ramsey said one day, 'I regret very much that Giles wasn't born an Englishman.' Players like him had the desire, the football brains and the technique to do all of those things that were so desperately lacking in those last two major tournaments.

Short of Rooney and perhaps Steven Gerrard, the absence of a player with real perception and the nerve, the technique and the judgement to exploit it was the most depressing aspect of all. You feel you are looking into the face of football bankruptcy. Where will we find a Haynes or a Charlton, or even a Glenn Hoddle? I wouldn't rate Hoddle along with the other two, but he could look up and see an opportunity and have the confidence to play the perfect ball. In Japan, I hated to see David Seaman, a senior player who did well through the tournament, cry at the end of the game. When I see a pro crying, especially when things have gone wrong, it just gets under my fingernails. You take the win or the loss and you put a professional face on things. He made a mistake, it happens, and heaven knows it was an extraordinary goal. My first instinct was to agree with Seaman and his team-mates that Ronaldinho's free kick was a freak, but the Brazilian insisted he meant the ball to do what it did, and his captain Cafu, especially, insisted the possibility had been discussed before the kick was taken. As soon as Seaman moved off his line he knew he had done wrong, it showed on his face. But then we heard how England had such bad luck, that they had been denied by a fluke. That wasn't the real story at all, and it made you more than a little ashamed and angry to hear it on the lips of your fellow countrymen.

There have been other excuses, about tiredness and the need for a mid-winter break and how many games the leading players have to play these days and when you hear that it just has to cut into your belief that one day we might win the World Cup again, or even a European Championship. Back in 1966 Stiles played over 60 games. Then England had the World Cup build-up and six games in the tournament. Bobby Charlton, who didn't stop in the final, had also played a lot of games that year, and he had played half of them on an Old Trafford pitch which turned into a quagmire by November. People say how fast the game is today, but you don't play football at 100 mph. It's not about how fast you motor but how quickly you think. The truth is there are quite a few donkeys who get by in the Premiership. The fact is when I played for England I covered 100 yards in 10.3 seconds. That was quick enough.

Perhaps inevitably, over the past few years, in an attempt to paper over the all too apparent cracks, a couple of English performances have been vaunted as evidence of the supposed progress of the national side – most notably that historic thrashing of Germany in 2001. But there were warning signs in the Olympic Stadium in Munich if anyone cared to look a little more deeply than the 5–1 scoreline. I watched the game with Alan Ball and we couldn't believe the frailty of both defences; England's was unconvincing, Germany's was by a wide distance the worst I had ever seen representing a major football nation. When Carsten Jancker scored for Germany inside six minutes, the confusion of Sol Campbell was dismaying. I turned to Bally and said, 'Christ, they're coming straight through the middle.' Ten minutes later, Jancker was free again and it was hard to know how he contrived not to score a goal. Much later in the game, the big, awkward fellow seemed almost to be attempting to break his own neck in an effort not to score. He could have allowed the ball to hit him in the face with a better chance of producing a goal. That was the third time Jancker had been allowed to get free at the far post – a shocking statistic in top-class football.

There was much euphoria in England, and no doubt a degree of it was understandable enough after we scored five goals from five chances. But the pro's view had to be that it was exactly what we should have done, and though it was an excellent example of a team taking all its chances, it did not conceal weaknesses which would resurface quickly enough.

Not dissimilar to the Germany game was the equally

startling 3–0 win over Denmark in the second round in the World Cup. Denmark had beaten the World Champions France in their final group game, but their defence was unbelievably slipshod against England. So England did to Denmark what they had done to Germany. They killed off some lame ducks, but rather than accepting the good fortune, and being grateful for the proficiency displayed in taking advantage, we presumed too much. We saw ourselves as World Cup winners while the truth was that we might have struggled to beat South Korea and Senegal and perhaps even the hard-running United States.

Brazil won a World Cup that was, frankly, sub-standard. In Portugal we saw the great football nations of Europe eclipsed by a Greek team which in terms of talent shouldn't have got beyond the pool games. But they did so impressively and thoroughly deserved to take away the title when teams like France and Germany, Italy and England showed ultimately that in terms of any deep competitive instinct the cupboard was just about bare.

There was no outstanding component in the Greek team, but they were sensible in their approach, they worked hard for each other at every point of a game and none of the basics were neglected. Crosses were covered and headed away, the defence pushed up whenever it could, denying space and making the tackles. Unlike Eriksson's England they kept their heads – and their gameplan. That was enough for them to become the best team in Europe. Their coach, the German veteran Otto Rehhagel, subscribed to the Ramsey belief that if you don't have a sense of a team, if each player doesn't know precisely his place in the overall scheme, everyone is wasting their time.

Some critics said it was boring to watch the Greeks march on but I never saw it that way. Yes, it was true that the big nations were disappointing, that many of them looked jaded, even uninterested – and this was especially true of the French at times – but their biggest problem was that the Greeks were so honest in everything they did. Sad for football? No, sad for the players and coaches of the supposed giants of European football, which in a few weeks were taken right back to the foundations of any team's success: organisation, fitness, and a framework for the best available talent to flourish. This was always the working principle of the man who led England to their only World Cup win.

In all of this, though, you have to admire the tenacity of Michael Owen. He had had a terrible time in a poor Liverpool team and even in Portugal, though clearly struggling, he showed a tremendous willingness to do the work. He scored early against Portugal in the quarter-final which might, if so many other things hadn't gone wrong on the touchline and on the field, just have rescued the team. Since then he has had to battle hard at Real Madrid against the Galactico system which, for all its commercial benefits, took Beckham away from the best of himself.

Owen's ability to produce goals when coming off the bench is a tremendous tribute to a professional character of the highest standard. It seems to me that having lost a little pace through injury, Owen has done a lot of work on the weights. His shoulders have thickened up and he appears to be much stronger in his neck. This, no doubt, has come at the cost of some suppleness, which means that instead of outstripping defences by sheer pace he has necessarily become a bit of a lurker.

So what of the one positive aspect to emerge from Euro 2004 – Wayne Rooney? He is plainly an outstanding talent but one whose subsequent indiscipline in the shirts of both England and Manchester United brought the chilling concern that in the end he, like Paul Gascoigne, might have superb ability deeply compromised by a faulty temperament.

Nothing, certainly, was more disquieting than to hear Eriksson and Sir Alex Ferguson dismissing criticism of the boy's behaviour. They said he was young and he would learn, but what would they be doing to help the process? Would they be significantly punishing the kid, telling him he had to pay for his failure to behave properly? The evidence was worryingly thin.

However, Owen remains a front rank player and one who naturally gains the respect of an old pro, who sees him battling, often against the odds, and inevitably recognises something of a throw-back to another age of football, when reputations were left in the dressing room and every game was a new invitation to prove yourself. The way he has conducted himself at Real Madrid, coming off the bench and scoring goals and always the buttoned-down pro, doing his work without complaint, is maybe the ultimate definition of his character. One example of Owen's dedication is the fact that now he is so much better on his left side. When he first exploded into the big-time this aspect of his game was almost non-existent. But as he says, with legitimate pride, he has done the work required to make himself a much more rounded player.

For those who despair of England's chances to make more of an impression in Germany in next year's World Cup it would be encouraging to believe that young Rooney might sooner rather than later follow along Owen's path. It seems, however, to be something of an optimistic push. When I look at Rooney I cannot help but recall the favourite saying of my old Fulham manager Vic Buckingham, who when asked to give an errant young player another chance would always say, 'You know, the problem is a leopard never changes his spots.' I hope very much that I'm wrong but quite frankly I am far from certain Rooney has the capacity – or the environment – to change. The trouble is that for all his ability, and there is no doubt it is utterly exceptional, arguably the best, and in some ways more complete, than any we have seen coming through in English football since the young George Best, his temperament appears to be quite deeply flawed.

A terrible example came when Manchester United played at Anfield this last season. Now I know Rooney is young and relatively inexperienced, but he wasn't so raw that he could be excused for not grasping the risk of taunting the Kop after he scored a rather fortunate goal, though it should be said that he did much better, in terms of self-control, when he returned to Merseyside to face a much more hostile reaction at his old home at Goodison Park.

There was no excuse for the reaction of the Liverpool fans, especially the one who threw a mobile phone down on the field (something that certainly couldn't have happened in my day!), but inciting supporters is the indulgence of only the most shallow and unthinking of players. Unless you are psychologically challenged – and this is perhaps a bit of a worry in the case of young Rooney, when he isn't making some quickfire decision on the field which comes welling out of natural genius – you know you are risking a riot, which is the last thing your team wants when you have just taken the lead in a vital game. Yes, he had been taking some baiting from the Kopites and no-one would have got too excited, or critical, if he had merely cupped his ear as he ran back to the centre circle to resume the game. But instead he marched towards the Kop, sneering and taunting.

It was stunning that neither Manchester United nor the Football Association reacted in any hard and constructive way. The trouble is that he can now assume he will get away with such irresponsible behaviour, and what does it mean? When Eriksson and Ferguson shrug their shoulders and point out the boy is young they are opening themselves to the risk that a brilliantly gifted youngster is going to spend a lot more time suspended, which is something hard to square with the evidence that indeed this is a kid with the potential for true greatness.

Ferguson may already have decided that the best course is to humour Rooney, get the most from him while he can. This is thinking no doubt tinged with a certain amount of resignation, but I do think the effort of discipline has to be made. Who knows, a penny might just drop. The alternative, I believe, is to watch the boy slip into permanent denial of the need for discipline. Nothing could be more injurious to a talent that has already shown the potential to be the best in the world, something to be placed alongside that of great players like Pele and Diego Maradona. An extravagant assessment? Only if you haven't been able to identify the astonishing quality of some of the boy's work.

The big problem with Rooney's situation is that it typifies a lot of what is wrong with the game today, the indiscipline, the cheating, the constant refusal to take personal responsibility for the image of something which is in danger of destroying itself, wiping away all the wealth that came in such an astonishing and, maybe, disorientating, rush.

To get to the heart of the malaise I really don't think we need go any further than the failure of the two most influential managers in the land, Ferguson and Arsenal's Arsene Wenger, to reach any kind of basic respect for either each other or some of the basic values of the game which conquered the world. The Pizzagate affair, when some of Arsenal's young players were accused – without any convincing denials – of throwing food and soup at Ferguson in the corridor outside the dressing rooms at Old Trafford surely represented a new low. It is impossible to imagine that happening in the reign of Sir Matt Busby. Of course, times have changed and different standards now apply, but certain fundamentals will always be required if football in the long term is to maintain its popularity among decent people of all ages.

I was told by a friend of mine that Wenger, who is obviously an extremely brilliant football man, recently gave a wonderful speech at a sports evening in London. He spoke of his life in the game and the meaning of football. He spoke of beauty and skill and how necessary it is to cultivate a love of the game in those who now earn such rich livings from it.

It was hardly surprising that Wenger made such a favourable impression on my friend. This, after all, is a man of stunning achievement. Not only did he bring success to Arsenal, but he also extended the dimension of domestic football with the artistry brought by his compatriots Thierry Henry and Robert Pires. So why does he so resolutely refuse to take responsibility for the kind of breakdowns in discipline which came that disgraceful day at Old Trafford; why does he turn a blind eye when players like Pires and the Arsenal captain Patrick Vieira are caught in the most flagrant cheating?

Or why does Ferguson, knighted and recognised wherever he goes as one of the most successful managers in the history of English football, only ever criticise wrongdoing on the field when it is committed by the players of other clubs? When Rio Ferdinand was guilty of failing to take a drugs test, Ferguson talked about a conspiracy against his club. Any wider implication beyond his own club's interests appeared to have just gone sailing by. United player Gary Neville was at the forefront of threats of a strike by the England players in protest at the treatment of Ferdinand, who didn't deny that he had walked away from the drug testers. As far as I was concerned, and I'm sure it was true of my old World Cup team-mates, all this might have been happening on some alien planet.

Certainly it is bewildering to see men of such maturity,

and well rewarded success, arguing like fishwives. Every reverse, every decision that goes against them, might be one of a thousand cuts of torture. Perspective is lost in self-interest . . . and self-indulgence.

Ferguson and Wenger might be boys going to war in the schoolyard. We can see easily enough the result of such behaviour from men who are supposed to provide judgement and leadership. It is a fever that seems to grip the entire game and one shocking consequence was the Premiership game at Highbury earlier this year. We didn't get another Pizzagate, but in its way it was equally repellent. Before the kick off we had Roy Keane and Patrick Vieira squaring up in the tunnel, but in full view of a national television audience, and then when the match started it got even worse.

Players dived at will, most outrageously in the case of Ashley Cole, who threw himself down in the penalty area before Keane made contact. This was a game of vital importance in the championship; a match pitting two of the three best teams in England and filled with the highest talent. Yet it was a travesty of football, a sickening demonstration of what happens when the point of sport, full-blooded but honest competition, is pushed on one side.

Now the talk is of technology to combat a wave of referee error. A few years ago I would have dismissed the idea: too time-consuming, too much against the spirit of the game, which should accommodate human frailty with a shrug of the shoulders and the implicit understanding that in the end fate invariably imposes a great levelling during the course of a season. Now it is hard to resist the argument that such a climate is gone forever, that the cold eye of the television camera, in most cases but certainly not all, is the only possible arbiter of the most decisive moments.

Ironically, given all the reservations about the way Roman Abramovich bought his way into English football and proceeded to throw around huge wads of money in pursuit of success, it could just be that the man he appointed, Chelsea's manager Jose Mourinho might be a catalyst for change. He calls himself, rather provocatively, the Special One, but then there is more than a hint that he is capable of imposing a new vision of how footballers should behave, at least on the field. Under the control of Mourinho, which brought such brilliant success at his former club Porto, the discipline of Chelsea has improved dramatically.

Adrian Mutu's lifestyle was swiftly judged to be incompatible with the demands of a highly paid professional. John Terry, who had his scrapes off the field, has become a pillar of his club and for England. Chelsea played tremendously sound football, classically built on secure defence. He may not have been much of a player but it seems to me that he has grasped what is most important: discipline, commitment and a perfectly shared understanding of what it takes to win the big prizes.

However, Mourinho's own conduct on the touchline and his attacks on the integrity of Swedish referee Anders Frisk rightly brought charges from the Uefa authorities. Mourinho has shown dazzling abilities as a coach, but long before the end of last season he too had reason to join Ferguson and Wenger in a long look in front of a mirror.

No, the idea of a triumphant parade in the streets of London and maybe a reception at Downing Street for the England team of 2002 (fortunately no such outcry was heard in 2004) was something that should have been buried at its first glimmer. It is staggering that it reached even the point of a debate. It was, after all, a fact that honouring officially the team, Alf Ramsey's team, which actually won the World Cup, which was put together at the dawn of a new age of football, which was the result of one's man intense employment of his every professional instinct, had been staggered over thirty-four years. The delay affected some of us more than others. Nobby, the least presumptuous of men, ironically had felt the lack of official recognition perhaps most keenly of all. He had felt the joy of the nation that day right down to the core of his being, and nothing expressed it more than his toothless smile and enraptured dance of triumph. He glowed that night when the five of us had dinner with our families in the swanky hotel just around the corner from the Palace.

I said to him over a glass of wine, 'Nobby, that little honour was a long time coming, but isn't it better to savour it now? We can share it with the families that have kept us going, we can share it with our sons.'

In today's game it almost seems that win or lose, it is all just one big party. In '66 the players and our families all worked and fought hard for our moment in the sun.

At the most recent European Championships the wives and children of the England players were installed close to the team headquarters. It was said that when England left after the quarter-final defeat by Portugal there was a certain sense of an evacuation from a holiday camp. When Eriksson was interrogated by the media, he was indignant and said that he wouldn't have done anything differently. An old pro watched and listened in wonderment and dismay.

CHAPTER TWO

'GIVE IT TO THE BLOODY RABBI'

The shout of the supporter cast me in the role of the eager, over-achieving Jewish boy. It has gone down as one of the great all-time terrace witticisms and has long been enshrined in the folklore of Fulham Football Club.

Georgie Cohen was a fixture at Craven Cottage, quick, hard-working, reliable. He always made a tackle and covered the ground. He behaved himself. He did what was expected of him. He was part of the scenery. And so by now was Jimmy Hill, who after arriving from Brentford announced himself as a man who had both a pronounced chin and a willingness to thrust it forward into his new world without any fear of the consequences. This was a time, you should know, when you could talk about a football team like Fulham being a family without running the risk of derision, even if it was true that maybe the great Johnny Haynes was more equal than everyone else, and it was against this tribal background that the fan issued his famous instruction. He might have been talking to the guy next to him on the factory bench or in the pub.

The circumstances were routine at the Cottage. We were battling for survival. Hill, black-bearded (hence, 'the Rabbi') and intense, made a great churning run across the half-way line as our goalkeeper, Tony Macedo, rolled the ball to me in space. Jimmy had not been having the best of afternoons but, true to his nature, he had never stopped trying. He yelled for the ball – yet again. 'George, George, George,' he cried as he galloped on, knees high and elbows pumping, in search of space and as he did so you could hear a swell of exasperation in the crowd. 'For Christ's sake, Georgie,' yelled the fan, 'give it to the bloody Rabbi.' Brilliant – a flash of classic humour from the terraces, for me to pass the ball to my supposed spiritual leader. But it was wrong – I was a Jewish boy strictly in name only. The fact was that my Jewish blood-line ceased to be pure on the last day of February in 1903, when my father, Louis Henry Cohen, was born at Queen Charlotte's Hospital on the Marylebone Road. On another occasion Jack Cohen, the founder of Tesco, was surprised to discover that I wasn't really Jewish, at least not according to the tenets of the Hebrew faith. 'How did a Christian boy get a name like that?' he asked. 'Did you pay for it?' What happened was that my grandfather, Jacob Solomon Cohen, married a Gentile woman, Sarah Mann, of Chelsea, and of course that put him beyond the pale of his family, which had scattered from the pogroms of the Ukraine in the middle of the 19th century, and reached West London around 50 years later via the Canadian steel town of Hamilton, Ontario. Like all those millions of Jews who had to escape persecution in Europe all those years before the arrival of Hitler, my ancestors scuffled for some kind of toe-hold in North America. Some pulled it off, others went down and some, like my branch of the family, regrouped in other places.

For the Jewish people, of course, the family roots are of paramount value. In a hostile world, where so often they are seen as such an inviting target for any society which is looking to vent its frustration, the Jewish family is a bastion – a source of strength and protection. Many years after the breakaway of my grandfather, my elder brother Len asked our father how seriously the marriage had ruptured relationships within the family.

'That finished it,' he was told. Then my father added something that has always haunted me in its sadness and its truth. 'Look, son,' he said, 'we escaped intolerance – and now we're living it.' I think of what he said today when I see television pictures of the bloodbath in Israel and Palestine. I think of my father's despairing remark all those years ago, and I say, 'They've all gone bloody mad and it's got to stop some day.' When I see all the pain and the blood and I think that Israel, despite all the persecution its people have suffered in the past, is part of it I can't help thinking they are all, Jews and Palestinians, as bad as each other.

My father also married a Gentile – Catherine Gibbs, a handsome, powerful woman who was the greatest influence in my life and who I will always remember for the strength that was just below the surface – and the lustrous black hair which flowed down to her waist. She brushed aside my father's concern, which was so common in those days, that if I went into football professionally I should do so only after first qualifying for a trade, maybe as an electrician, a job he thought would suit me well enough. 'No, Harry,' she said, 'if you do anything you should throw yourself into it, give it 100 per cent because that's the only way you have a chance of being a real success. George has a talent for football. He should see where it takes him. Until he has done that, he shouldn't mess about with anything else.'

That is what happened down the road and it is one of my deepest satisfactions in life that just a few years before she died she got to see me playing for England the day we won the World Cup. My father had died four years earlier, but by then I had reason enough to know that he was proud of what I had achieved at Fulham, how I had become part of a football club which had always meant so much in a working-class community which had a strong identity. He never said a lot, but I was always aware of his interest and that intense pride, and when he read something positive about me in the paper, he would slap his side and say, with his brilliant aquamarine eyes shining, 'That's my boy.' It was a wonderful thing to hear.

It had been, heaven knows, a tough and not always promising road for all of us, and though my father had played football for the London Business Houses, as did my brother Len, sport was very much in the margins of the hard-working lives of the Cohens. But then it is also true that when I came to play for England at football, and, thirty-odd years later, my younger brother Peter's son Ben was called up to the England rugby team, and went on to reach the very pinnacle of his sport, we were not the first of our family to be touched by a little sporting fame or, to be more precise in the matter of my father's uncle, Abraham Benjamin Cohen – also known as 'Jewey Cooke' – notoriety.

His wild and disreputable story came into focus for me thirty years ago when one evening I received a telephone call from Pinner Hospital in Middlesex. I was told that a little old lady, a Mrs Cooke, had died of hypothermia. She had appeared to be quite alone and had left a few effects, including an old boxing championship belt, minus the rubies, and she wanted me to have them. The hospital staff had also been given some photographs and newspaper cuttings detailing my football career. Apparently, 'Mrs Cooke' had lived for many years with 'Jewey', but had made no attempt to contact the family after his death in 1948. However, she had followed my career, and had always intended that I should have the mementoes of her partner's life in the boxing booths and rings of England and South Africa. He was the champion of the boxing booths, fought in the halls of East London and, during a somewhat chequered spell in South Africa, won that country's middleweight title. Unfortunately, he was also found guilty of rape and sentenced to eight years hard labour and ten lashes. With the help of my friend, the late Dennie Mancini, the former cornerman, I was able to ferret out some of the facts of this family scandal, and though it appears that Cooke was eventually exonerated and freed, none of the circumstances of the case were too uplifting. His defence was that he had been set up by a prostitute who, having extended her favours, was perhaps understandably annoyed to discover she had been paid in counterfeit money. The alleged victim was a young Dutch chambermaid who – I'm afraid this story doesn't get a whole lot better – was said to have been mentally handicapped.

Certainly Jewey received a bad press. In 1904, two years before he was immersed so desperately in the rape trial, he received one of his better notices in *The Mirror of Life*, an illustrated sports newspaper which claimed to have double the circulation of any rival in the world. A routine career review starts: 'Jewey Cooke hailed from Bloomsbury and had his first lessons in the noble art in Drury Lane, which at that time had a dozen first-class boxers residing in the neighbourhood. He stands about 5ft 8in, and in condition scales about 10st 4lb. We have not got his full record, which consists of nearly 200 battles, though we have a large number of them' Curiously, *The Mirror of Life* then chose to first list his defeats, which included Bill Nolan (in six rounds), Walter Eyles (twice, six and three), Tom Woodley (eight), Harry Webster (twenty) and Jem Holloway (also twenty). Then, almost as an afterthought, a string of victories were listed. This was odd, and not least in that Jewey had been in with some good company, his most prestigious opponent being the great American lightweight champion Joe Gans, who reigned for six years before losing to Battling Nelson in fights which took seventeen and twenty-one rounds to resolve. Jewey lost the fight, but then so did almost everybody who met a man with a record of 120 wins, 8 defeats, 9 draws and 85 knockouts. Apart from that strange juxtaposition of losses and wins – it seems, without stretching the comparison too far, a bit like pointing out Muhammad Ali's defeats at the hands of the likes of Leon Spinks and Trevor Berbick before getting round to his epic victory over Joe Frazier in Manila or his destruction of George Foreman – there was no other hint of prejudice in this article which also spoke glowingly of Tommy Murphy, 'a clever featherweight from New York,' and the legendary cricketer W.G. Grace.

Other newspaper accounts of Jewey, even before the shame he brought upon himself in Johannesburg, are a rather different matter. A report of his victory over Charley Knocke at Whitechapel in January, 1902, illustrates the point vividly enough: 'One decision calls for comment as it was evident that Charley Knocke, whose photo appeared in our last edition, fairly beat Jewey Cooke, but the verdict went in the opposite direction.

'Charley went for all he was worth when they started, and from that point never lost the advantage he gained, and when the verdict went the other way he was almost too astonished to speak. Cooke is no more liked at Wonderland [the Whitechapel venue] than he is at other places, and the uproar was terrific.' This, however, was the gentlest of barbs when compared to the newspaper treatment of Jewey's trial and subsequent flogging. Was it possible, I wondered, to read between these yellowing lines and not feel a touch of suspicion that, however disagreeable a man he was, Jewey Cooke's lack of popularity might just have had something to do with the announcement of his race in his fighting name? Whether or not a whiff of anti-Semitism was present in those unyieldingly harsh judgements, I cannot really know, but they were painful enough to read. On April 6, 1907, under the headline 'Jewey Cooke's Sentence', the editor of *The Mirror of Life* reported, 'Jewey Cooke would seem to have, not for the first time, got himself seriously disliked in South Africa, if the following letter from a correspondent in Johannesburg is to be relied upon, and from the newspaper cutting enclosed with his epistle, I see no reason to doubt his veracity. Writing under the date March 5, this gentleman has the following to say:

' "Dear Sir, You will be interested to know that Jewey Cooke has at last got his deserts, having been sentenced, along with another notorious rascal, Jack Silverstein, to eight years penal servitude, together with ten lashes. The details of the case were too revolting for publication, but I enclose you some cuttings which will give you an idea of the villainy of which this brawny young pugilist is capable.

' "Cooke took his well merited punishment like the miserable cur he is. All Johannesburg regrets that the learned judge did not sentence him to one hundred lashes instead of a bare ten. It is a thousand pities that in these days of faddists and anti-everything's, a pugilist should have been guilty of such an appalling crime, and you may be sure that the spoil-sports [anti-boxing campaigners, presumably] will make the most of this – to them – glorious opportunity. Thank God, Cooke has no prototype in the ranks of South African pugilists, who with this one black exception, are as clean, honest, and manly young sportsmen as their fellows in England, America and Australia." '

One of the newspaper accounts is quite revealing of those

times. 'The case lasted over the whole of last week and on every day the court was thronged with a crowd of the lowest type. On Saturday special precautions were taken by the police, there having previously been wild rumours of an attempted rescue of the prisoners. At the fourth stroke (of his lashing) he (Cooke) wailed like a woman, and begged for mercy, and when the whipping had been completed he bore with him back to his cell unmistakable evidence of his punishment. Silverstein was brought out, but Cooke's groans and shrieks had completely unnerved him, and when taken up to the triangle he collapsed and the flogging had to be postponed.' It would be fascinating to know quite how *The Mirror of Life* reacted editorially to the freeing of the man who had been painted in such unflattering terms. Jewey Cooke may not have been the most admirable of men – among his other occupations were debt-collecting and enforcing – but he was family, albeit a family fractured by the old ways of prejudice, and the little old lady who had stayed with him all those years despite everything, had reached out to me from beyond the grave with her last wish and the ruby-less remnants of her long-gone partner's glory. My brother Len and I went to the funeral. We were the only mourners, and as we stood in the cemetery chapel I couldn't help but think of my own good fortune in life. Jewey Cooke had obviously been a talented fighter, but it seemed that mostly his ears had been filled with jeers, and perhaps, down the years, the sound of his own screams of pain. Not everything in this life, and this England, was perfect, but perhaps a little progress had been made. Perhaps there was a little more tolerance in the air.

We had other relatives more careful of their reputations who had made lives for themselves in North America, where my grandfather had worked as a labourer in his attempt to make a new start. One of my Canadian uncles became a mounted policeman there. Down the years some of these distant kin drifted briefly into my life, and none more fleetingly than the one who burst on to the pitch in Montreal in 1967, when I was playing for an England team in a exhibition match during Expo. 'George, George, I'm your uncle,' he cried, before being carried off by a posse of security guards. Ada Greenberg made more of a lasting impression. She was an aunt who had married one of my father's brothers who had stayed in Canada. During the war she had sent food parcels, which were always greeted with joy. I will never forget the Canadian drinking chocolate, which was laced with sugar and instant milk. It was so rich and sweet it was an almost unbelievable luxury for people getting by on war-time-rations. Ada knocked on our door one day in 1947. She was a grand figure and she brought a waft of perfume and a confident style. She had a gold cigarette case decorated with a Union Jack, and when she saw me looking at it, she said, 'Never, never forget your roots, my boy.' It wouldn't have been easy. My roots ran deeply and still they shape a lot of my thoughts and most of my attitudes. Even today I make regular pilgrimages to the market at Tunbridge Wells and eat jellied eels and journey in my mind back to those days in Walham Green and then West Kensington, a neck of the Fulham woods where people had shoes, we used to joke, and to where we moved, when I was four, into the bright new world of

Clement Attlee's post-war Labour government – a beautiful council flat which had gardens and a janitor who always appeared out of thin air if you ever so much as dreamed of kicking a ball on the manicured grass. Even though I had to share a bed with my brother Peter, the new flat was luxury. It had two bedrooms, a sitting room, a spacious kitchen and a bathroom. I was born in Cassidy Road, Walham Green, which was where we lived with an aunt until we got the new flat, but even after the move I still spent a lot of my time amid the council flats that flanked Cassidy Road. Both my parents worked, my father as a foreman gas fitter and my mother as the stores manager of the Lots Road power station. They paid my aunt Freda to look after me. It was a struggle for everyone to pay the bills, and it was a squeeze at Cassidy Road. I slept with my cousins Peggy and Joan. To be precise, I slept with my head between their feet. But then if life was tough, it was also warm.

There was always food on the table, basic food but it must have been nutritious enough because in the street games we played – one of the most popular was running around the blocks of flats and seeing who would be the last to drop – I always seemed to be a little bit quicker and stronger than the other kids. It may have helped that not only was I able to drink boiled cabbage water without gagging, I actually came to enjoy it. Indeed, I still drink the stuff today in the way of Popeye inhaling a tin of spinach. One of our greatest treats would spread horror among nutritionists today – bread and dripping and plenty of salt and pepper. Food, which is rather taken for granted these days, was a preoccupation back then to a degree which is probably impossible to imagine for someone who has grown up with the sight of well-stocked supermarket shelves. After the street market at North End Road had closed in the evening I would see old women collecting scraps of vegetables, cabbage leaves, that had fallen from the barrows and I imagined they were eking out a very slender diet. 'Oh these poor people,' I thought, 'poking around to find something to eat.' But my brother Len explained that the vegetables were to feed the rabbits which were kept in the little backyards of flats, and were, because of their energetic breeding habits, a wonderful addition to the food supply. You have to remember that in those days a chicken was a rare delicacy. I didn't taste one until I was eleven years old.

However, and thank God, there was no shortage of whelks, cockles, mussels, oysters and jellied eels. They were sold from handcarts outside the pubs and they were gobbled up because they had to be eaten on the day due to the lack of refrigeration – and because they were so good.

The jellied eels were my passion and it was a highlight of my boyhood – along with watching Moscow Dynamo at Stamford Bridge – to eat them down on Petticoat Lane. When I was eleven I earned sixpence – enough for the Saturday morning film show – at Manzies' pie and eel shop on Lillie Road. There used to be another such shop on Walham Green. They sell kebabs there now and when I see that I shake my head and say, 'Bloody tragic.' My job at Manzies' was to make sure the eels were kept moist in steel crates. You had to turn the tap on them and then slide them along to the fellow who chopped their heads off. There was a very strict pattern to the work, as there is in a butcher's shop. I still have Manzies' prices in my head. Stewed eels were ninepence; jellied eels, the real haute cuisine product, were one and sixpence and they came with parsley sauce of a consistency which was never allowed to change. Pie and mash was ninepence. We sold Telford pies, which were of excellent quality even though they were made in a big factory in Earl's Court.

Many years later I was in Brussels on tour with Fulham and I must have mentioned my liking for eels to the manager, Vic Buckingham. Here was a man who knew his way around Europe. He had been the boss of Ajax of Amsterdam and Barcelona and he had acquired some expensive tastes. He said I would dine on the best eels I had ever tasted. He told me to hand out the expenses to the other players and join him for dinner. Mark 'Pancho' Pearson, who had moved to Fulham after stints with Manchester United and Sheffield Wednesday, and was a favourite of Vic's because he had picked up a bit of stardust on his journey through the game, joined us.

Knowing Vic, I wasn't surprised that we found ourselves in a corner of Brussels that was very Bohemian indeed. Vic took us down into a cellar, where he was given a hero's reception. He ordered eels and wine and said, 'George, believe me, this is the place for eels.' They brought a huge pot of eels and placed it on a burner. They also brought three bottles of well chilled Chablis. We ate and drank for three blissful hours. Vic was right. I had never tasted such stewed eels. Back home in Surrey, I returned the compliment, and had Vic and Mark, along with our new young signing Allan Clarke, come out to my local pub where I could introduce them to jellied eels. Unfortunately, Mark came straight to my house, where I was peeling potatoes for Sunday lunch. He was a fellow who didn't even clean his shoes, so his jaw dropped when he saw me doing my chores. Daphne didn't help me too much when she said to Pearson, 'Why don't you go up the pub and see Vic and Allan, and George will join you after he's done the potatoes – and the sprouts.'

Naturally, when I reached the pub, I received more than a little flak. Football, much more than now, was a macho world and players tended not to peel the spuds. Vic was very much the man-about-town – he came to Fulham after getting involved with one of the wives of a director of his previous club, West Bromwich – but we got along very well. He wanted me to join him in Greece when he took a job there after he was fired by Fulham, but that sounded a little too exotic for me. But I had learned a lot from him. He had introduced me to a new and racier world, and one which I had no reason to believe existed when I took my knocks on the streets of Walham Green and, in the plusher reaches of the district, peered through the gates of the Queen's lawn tennis club and St Paul's School, where Field Marshal Montgomery was educated, as though they were located on other planets.

On our planet the challenge was to scuffle along, to get some food on the table and pay the rent. All else was luxury. Running in the streets, playing football and cricket on Eel Brook Common, and the matinee picture show – these were our releases, and we took them with great energy when we could. One claim on our time was the job of hanging around the road workers and collecting the bits of coke they left on the street, putting the coke in an old pram and pushing it around in search of customers. Looking back it seems that there was always one constant – competition, at play certainly, and also when the focus was to get a little job sorted to help out the family finances, like selling the coke. When I eventually got into a football team, I suppose it was just another extension of the instinct to survive, to make some kind of mark.

My father was a very popular man, a socialist who read the old *Daily Mirror* with great diligence but who put everything he had into the task of providing for his family. While his brother Len was a political activist who believed in communism and felt it was his duty to fight the Blackshirts of Sir Oswald Mosley, my father felt he had enough to do around the home. One of my earliest recollections is of him playing cricket on Barnes Common.

He certainly wasn't too good to be true, but when he was brought into the world it was an extremely hard one where the greatest need was to make a living and it was a responsibility he carried until the day he died of cancer. Along the way he received few bonuses. Indeed, some of the greatest days in our lives were when the gas man came to empty the meter and you got a rebate of around 30 shillings – that, and the French coins you had fed into it at the thin times. Thirty bob was a small fortune. The highest point of celebration, though, was when my father won £50 on the football pools. Now that was really big money. He bought himself a suit for £5, from Burtons, which normally would have been considered a great extravagance. The usual rate was thirty shillings untailored, fifty bob tailored.

The bulk of the money went on an eternity ring for my mother. He was completely devoted to her, and this was a rare chance for him to express that. I was always aware of the great respect he had for my mother and though he never surrendered his authority as head of the house, he would always listen to her intently when there was some important family business to resolve, as was the case when the choice for me was between learning a trade and part-time football or full immersion in the professional game. My mother prevailed then, but only after gentle debate, though it was conducted with a hint of steel in her hazel eyes. In effect, I suppose my mother ran the family, but my father was always there, and had always to be listened to and if my mother had her opinions and ideas on what should be done, she never did it at the expense of my father's dignity. They had a love match, that was always clear to me – and she was terribly protective of her boys.

She grew up in Maida Vale, one of a large family who lived on part of an old mews property which would cost you millions now. When Harry Cohen met Catherine Gibbs at a dance, that was it apparently. Her father had been a sergeant in the Indian Army and was then posted to Ireland, where my mother was born. It can't have been the most tranquil of childhoods because her father was drafted into the Black and Tans in the time of the Troubles. Though it was not something she would talk about, she may have experienced a little prejudice when she went to work at the power station after marrying my father. She was, anyway, known there as Kate — or Mrs Cowan — and when I heard that I had to wonder, as I did so many years later when reading those old reports of the notorious Jewey Cooke, how quickly people can be labelled and judged without any knowledge of who they are and what they are.

Whatever the weather my father went out to work every morning on his bike, laden with the tools of his trade. At the weekends he worked an extra job, installing boilers, known as Ascots, in the flats and bed-sitters which were created for the great influx of immigrant labour. Most of this work was around Olympia. Houses were sub-divided in a hurry because you could charge £3 for a bed-sit in those days, and the tenants would have to share a bathroom with three or four other families. I didn't get the impression my father worked for the nicest of people when he was hired to bring a little heat into those mean and chilly rooms, which were mostly occupied by West Indians, many of whom worked at the local Lyons cake factory. But of course he needed the work and like everybody else at that time, he would take what he could and do it honestly.

Occasionally, my father would talk about the lousy living conditions he encountered, and said we should be grateful for our shining new flat. The immigrants were squeezed into every available bit of space, and often they would get up in the morning and give up their beds to the returning nightshift. But if he had socialist instincts, he mostly buried his head in *The Mirror* and suffered in silence. He was the same about his experiences during the war. He had wanted to join the forces, but because of his trade and the fact that he lived in an area of high population with a lot of manufacturing, he was put into a reserved occupation. One of his jobs was to cut off the gas after bombs had hit. I gather he some saw some terrible things, but he never spoke to me about any of that. I was told though that when he talked to soldiers on leave he always had a rather wistful expression on his face. Knowing him, it is easy to believe that it hurt him that he wasn't able to go off to fight.

I never ever saw him drink more than two pints of beer at any one time. He was well respected in the workplace and he always handled himself well. He was quiet, but also hard in the best way. I do believe that whatever success I have had on the football field, and in my marriage with Daphne and the upbringing of our sons, of whom I'm very proud, has flowed mainly, I suspect, from a set of values I was given from the time I first began to walk. My parents couldn't shower my brothers and me with luxuries and until Len left home, they couldn't even provide my kid brother and me with separate beds. But what they could give, they did so each day of our lives. They were hard-working and scrupulous and they never thought of themselves before their children.

'Don't forget your roots my boy,' Ada Goldberg, the provider of drinking chocolate from the gods, had told me as she flicked open her gold cigarette case, and the command had run deeply. It was one that didn't have to be re-enforced by a Rabbi or a priest. The ones laid down by Harry Cohen and the former Catherine Gibbs were quite strong enough.

CHAPTER THREE

'IT WAS A RATHER GOOD LEFT HOOK'

Sometimes I hear people say they have become part of a football club, and how it has come to dominate their lives and shape so many of their emotions, and that when they have to leave – as football men inevitably do – something inside them dies. I listen to these familiar, heart-rending stories but I cannot say that I relate to them easily. This is strange because as one-club men go I would surely have been considered a pretty dire case. Even when the football grapevine shouted rather than whispered to me that I might join bigger clubs something deep inside said that my horizon stretched no further than Fulham.

The fact is, and this may seem strange in the light of what I have just said about my basic contentment in always wearing the same team shirt, I have never been quite so sentimental about the game as the men who make that last, poignant walk away from the place they have come to see as home. But then if I was, the wrench which came to me when I had to stop playing for Fulham would surely have matched that of Bill Shankly when he left Liverpool, and, some believe, promptly began to die of a broken heart.

You hear stories of old players collecting up their gear one last time and going out into a new and suddenly terribly insecure life, and then wiping away a tear when they think of the months and the years that have swept by so quickly, and when I listen to these accounts, and recall the time Bobby Robson stood on the pitch at Craven Cottage and wept after being sacked as manager, I consider myself fortunate that when my time came to go I was more concerned with the possibilities of the future than the call of the past. I was lucky to feel this way because when injury cut me down it meant that, for the first time in my life, Fulham Football Club was no longer the dead centre of my universe.

The umbilical chord that joined me to the club had been attached very early in those days when I looked out of my aunt Freda's window and across the railway line and saw Eel Brook Common, where Fulham FC started its life in the days of gaslight.

Whatever I did as a boy, whether it was running in the streets, filling that old pram with coke, helping to prepare the jellied eels, there was always Fulham – and, to be perfectly accurate, also Chelsea FC But even though Chelsea had one of my great heroes, Roy Bentley, and I was fascinated by the movement of the greyhounds which came out on the track after the match, it was tough to scramble into Stamford Bridge, and Craven Cottage had the big accommodating tree at the corner of Bishop and Thames Streets. It meant you could scale the wall, and drop down the tree – carefully avoiding a fall into the river – and watch the game. You could, for free if you were nimble enough, enter for an afternoon another world filled with colour and drama. You saw the splash of green of the field, at least early in the season before it became clogged with mud, and the brightness of the players' shirts, and the streets outside might have been a thousand miles beyond the banks of the old river flowing by. Afterwards you would tell a policemen that you we're lost and more often than not you would get a lift home. The coppers knew what you were up to, but if they had time they would give you a ride. They were really part of the community then, dispensing rides and clipping your ear, whatever they considered appropriate.

My football career was given tremendous impetus at my school, Fulham Central, which in another life as Henry Compton School would launch Linford Christie into the world, and it was there that I literally ran past the ground staff of Fulham FC. There was a tremendous sports culture at the school – and an extremely high level of discipline. In many ways I was an ideal pupil. I didn't have to be urged to run, and I wanted to better myself. One of the visiting football coaches was Ernie Shepherd, a Fulham scout who had once played for Manchester United. He was a natural winger, fast and with great control and an absolutely immaculate left foot. He was in his late thirties then, but still very quick and he took great pride in his ability to outrun all the boys who came to his training clinics. All of them, that is, except me, who was an occasional visitor to the football training on account of my belief that track and field was probably the place where I would ultimately shine most. When I outran him, he said, 'Why aren't you on this football course, you have great speed, you could be a pro.' I said my father wanted me to be an electrician. Ernie swept that aside. He said he knew that both Fulham and Chelsea were interested in me following my performances for the school – we had won the Star Middlesex Shield – and West London Schoolboys, but Fulham were much the keener. 'Look, you're coming to Fulham,' said Ernie. 'It's far better to be a big fish in a little pond.' It was the first time I had heard the expression and it made a big impression, as did Ernie.

He was part of an attempt to really teach the game in this country, to absorb lessons which were available in the rest of the world. Malcolm Allison had come back from national service in Austria, where he had sneaked a look at the training of the Red Army team in the Viennese woods, and he was campaigning for change within his club at Charlton Athletic. Walter Winterbottom, the England team manager, realised we were lagging behind and he too argued for better, more sophisticated coaching methods. Soon enough at Fulham I would discover the impatience of such as Jimmy Hill and Robson, a future England manager and knight, for a new approach to the teaching of youngsters, and they were joined at Craven Cottage by another eventual England boss, Ron Greenwood. There was also the greatest learning process of all, which I would encounter when I started my career at Fulham – the wonderful example of great old players who were willing to take a kid in hand and tell him what was really important. It was an eagerness to learn your business properly, always look after yourself and always be competitive.

That last instinct, though, was something that had already

been bred into me – at home and at Fulham Central on the Fulham Palace Road. It was a hard school, a forerunner of today's comprehensives, but what may, I just suspect, have been lost down the years is the kind of disciplinary force exerted by two successive headmasters, John Tanfield and E.E. White. In some respects Tanfield came straight from the pages of *Tom Brown's Schooldays*. He wore a winged collar and seemed rooted in the Victorian age. His passion for the school and the success of all its pupils was immense, and it was most keenly reflected in his desire for the school team to always win. When it didn't, he pointedly made no reference to the adverse result when he reviewed the week in the school hall.

He saw the football team as the engine of the school's pride, something that would encourage hard effort on the playing field and in the classrooms. Before a match both Tanfield and White would seek out members of the team, check that they were sufficiently motivated – and fit. 'How are my boys?' Tanfield would ask with a particularly bright gleam of intensity in his eyes. Maybe it is an idea which has had its time, and would not be so easy to apply today, but the principle seemed clear enough to me and most of my schoolmates in those days. The school would provide boys who lived tough lives, in a tough area, with an opportunity to shine in whatever arena they displayed a touch of ability. In the process, of course, they also shifted a lot of testosterone on the training field and the playing pitch, so that when they came into a classroom they were maybe a little more manageable. It was not a time of video arcades and Gameboys. It was a time of personal expression through action. If you did something wrong, if you broke any of the many rules, you would have to write an essay on the unchanging theme of 'Playing the Game'. I don't think this did me any harm.

Nor, probably, did the administration of the 'slipper' – a form of corporal punishment which, while no doubt some way from the exquisite pain administered to my beleaguered great uncle Jewey Cooke, had the capacity to make you think before future wrong-doing. This was especially so when the slipper was wielded by Mel Roberts, a maths teacher and running coach. Roberts, an American, was, when I think about it, one of the key men in my development as a boy of good physical gifts who might just make it as a professional sportsman. He had come from America with a knowledge of the latest sprinting techniques, and in our training sessions he worked me very hard.

When I hear today of how much of sport is being abandoned in our schools, and how teachers are so disillusioned by the pressures on the education system they no longer are prepared to give some of their free time to the youngsters they are supposed to be moulding, I think of Mel Roberts and his breezy American style. He was really years ahead of his time. His emphasis was on interval work and the building of stamina. He took us to the running track at Wandsworth and we knew that by the end of the evening we would be shattered. But we also knew we were getting stronger and I loved it because running was always the thing I did most naturally and with most pleasure. As I said before, I was generally the last to drop when I ran with the kids around the flats in Walham Green, and on the school field I remained just as competitive.

So Roberts was both a teacher and something of an idol, and he retained his status in my mind even after he delivered a particularly painful dose of the slipper. He had caught me malingering on the school bus which was waiting to take us to training some time later. I should have been in Roberts' maths lesson and he had noted my absence and sought me out. He pointed out to me, once again, that through sport you could learn about life, but it was no good being a star on the field and a non-starter in the classroom. It was an approach that ran deeply through every aspect of school life and Roberts, more than even the authoritarian Tanfield and White, was the perfect reflection of this psychology which, I see now, was pitched perfectly for the needs of boys who, because of their place in the economic pecking order, would always have to fight that little bit harder to make a mark. At Fulham Central I learned maths, and technical drawing, which was very useful when I worked for a while in an architect's office, but more than anything I learned the need to set myself standards.

I got to be head boy, but not without a crisis or two. The most serious one involved my younger brother Peter, who was always getting into scraps. The main problem was that he just didn't know fear. But if Peter could be a bit of a tearaway, he did not deserve the treatment one of the older boys was dealing out to him. It was a classic case of the bullying which these days so often seems to bring tragic consequences. On this occasion all that happened was that I took care of the bully. I threw the best left hook of my life.

E.E. White, who had taken over from Tanfield with the blazing conviction that the competitive heart of Fulham Central would not miss a beat, was wearing his most formidable face when I was ushered into his office. I remember the exchanges as if they were uttered yesterday.

'Now George,' he said very sternly, 'What have you got to say for yourself?' I replied, 'Well, I have broken ranks, Sir, haven't I?' 'Yes, you certainly have – and in a big way, but what are the circumstances?' 'An older boy picked on a younger one, Sir, and I attempted to restrain him.' 'This younger boy just happened to be your brother?' 'Yes, Sir.' 'How did you attempt to restrain the older boy?' 'I hit him, Sir.' 'How many times did you hit him, George?' 'Just once, Sir. That's all it took. He went down, Sir. It was a rather good left hook.' 'George, I'm not taking any disciplinary measures against you on this occasion because your victim has been before me in similar circumstances. But remember, you have a lot of responsibilities here – the boys look up to you, never forget that.'

I didn't escape entirely unscathed, however. At the time of the incident I did not realise that the Prudential Insurance man, who collected our pennies each week, lived opposite the lamp-post on which the recipient of my left hook was leaning, rather arrogantly I thought, when I approached him. The man from the Pru told my father everything, and I got a terrible dressing down. Oddly though, my father's chief complaint seemed to be that I had left a mark – a shining black eye, as it happened – on my brother's persecutor. 'What's wrong with the solar plexus?' my father asked, which seemed to me at the time to rather take the moral sting out of his lecture.

This was maybe not a life-changing episode but certainly I think it gives a little feeling of the times. I was quite a successful youngster at sport – the trainer of the amateur boxing club in West Kensington where I had about twenty bouts in the gym, mostly against bigger boys, thought I had possibilities in the ring – but I was never encouraged to believe that any natural gifts I had been given made me at all separate in terms of responsibility for my own behaviour. In fact, as E.E.White pointed out, it was quite the opposite. Again, it is an example of how different those days were back in the forties and fifties.

I suppose the most dramatic memory of boyhood was going to Stamford Bridge to watch the Moscow Dynamo team, who caused such a stir in this country on the tour they made here soon after the war. To be honest, I don't remember too much about the game. The real impact on me was being part of something huge. They reckoned there were 80,000 squeezed into the Bridge that night and the atmosphere was wonderful. The crowd heaved and roared with excitement. The thrill of it all went into my young bones. My father lifted me over a fence, into the hands of strangers and I was placed along with other kids on the greyhound track which went around the pitch. Can you imagine a father willingly parting company with his son in such a crowd today? Another striking memory is of the presence of women in the crowd. There is a feeling today that in those old days the big football crowds were exclusively male, but that was far from the case. Women were there, and it was remembered that they were women. I recall one fan shouting a fairly mild swear word and he was hushed by the cry, 'Ladies present.' It was something I thought of recently at Craven Cottage when, at the start of the game, a middle-aged man walked up one of the aisles shouting, 'Arsehole, Arsehole, Arsehole.' I had five children sitting near me. The guy was eventually told to stop, but he didn't like it and the really extraordinary thing was the look of bewilderment on his face. He really didn't know what he was doing wrong. On another recent occasion, when Martin Peters invited me to White Hart Lane, the official Wendy Jones was running the line and making some very tough but good calls. At one point a fan shouted, 'Oh, for tits sake love,' and everyone, man, woman and child, roared with laughter. It was depressing to think that that this woman who had conducted herself so well under great pressure was, in the 21st century, being judged not on her performance, which was so far ahead of that of many male 'assistant referees' I see at work these days, but on her sex. I report this not to labour a point, but just to underline the place where I am coming from, and perhaps make it a little less mysterious to another generation who have grown up without such pressure to behave in a certain, universally acceptable way. For myself I continue to believe that if times change, it is not always for the better. If someone can explain to me how it is that the authorities can live so easily with public obscenity, that terrible coarseness which bombards the ears of any kid who is taken to a football match, I might just find the watching of an average game a little less of an attack on the spirit. Maybe someone can say why it is we have to endure crudity and filth as we watch the national game. But I will not hold my breath.

For a while, the pull of boxing was strong indeed, and it was based on something more than the one punch KO administered underneath that lamp-post on the Fulham Palace Road. Though I didn't have much in the way of reach, I had a natural quickness and I didn't mind taking a punch, and the trainer told my father that I could very well have a future in the game. My father was unimpressed. He said, finally, 'I'll tell you one thing George isn't going to be, he isn't going to be a fighter.' It was one argument he didn't have to worry about getting past my mother.

But if I was not to be allowed to take my chances in the square ring, I had developed a taste for the sport that I have never lost. I loved the honesty of the young lads who came to box, their dedication and their basic courage. It is not everybody who wants to take one on the nose and so you develop a certain *esprit de corps* in the sweaty confines of a gym.

I also had the friendship of Dennie Mancini, whose family had strong links to the professional fight game and who would emerge as one of the outstanding 'cuts men' in the sport. Indeed, I've been told that he is certainly the best in Britain, and probably Europe. He would later manage a decent stable of fighters, but when I first met him I was a gauche under-aged kid trying to buy a drink in his family's pub, the

Lord Palmerston, which was just around the corner from Fulham's ground. Johnny Haynes was a regular there, but when I made my fumbling attempt to get myself a drink I had still to make the first team. Dennie knew me because he was one of the many young local sporting types who casually came along and trained with the team. Fulham was always that kind of club. He was four years older than me – a man of the world. His first tip to me was not to bother with a pub that had windows which hadn't misted over. The beer and the ambience just hadn't drawn enough people.

Whenever I went into the Lord Palmerston, Dennie and his mother treated me like a long lost brother and son. 'George, you are too thin,' she would say. 'Come and eat some good spaghetti.' Dennie took me to the fights, particularly the ones at Manor Place Baths in south London, and when this continued into my marriage, Daphne became a little restive. She insisted on being taken to one of the fight halls so that she could get some idea of why I was so compelled to so regularly give up the chance of spending a night at home with her. I said I didn't think she would enjoy it, but she was adamant in rather a foot-stamping way. Dennie supplied an extra ticket and we duly found ourselves in the front row. Even on a night of the most tepid action, the front row of ringside can be a gory place. Naturally, on the night that Daphne came the crowd in the front rows were quickly made to feel like extras in a Sam Peckinpah epic. In the first round, of the first fight, one of the fighters was backed up into the corner of the ring where we were sitting. The man under pressure promptly took a fierce cross right on the end of his nose. The blood spurted about eight feet in a great arc and it seemed as though it was happening in slow motion. The torrent of blood landed at Daphne's feet.

She was absolutely appalled. She said she wanted to go home. I said, 'Listen, Daphne, there's a bench outside, why don't you go and have a coffee? I want to watch this fight — and the next one. It was your idea to come here and I'm not going home right now.' To be fair, Daphne went out for a coffee. Nor was it altogether a surprise that she never again asked to spend an evening with the fight crowd. I kept going along, not for the blood and the gore, but the unique edge of excitement a good fight can create in a crowd who know what they are looking at, who can recognise craft and courage, and who so quickly get caught up in the drama of two men giving it everything they have. The best fight I ever saw in the flesh was between Bobby Neill, who was challenging for the British featherweight title of Terry Spinks. In the last round, all Spinks had to do to keep his title was stay on his feet. But he couldn't do it. They say that styles make fights, and this was a classic dispute between the fighter, Neill, and the boxer, Spinks. The crowd became totally involved, and I will never forget the ovation they finally gave Neill. But first there was a terrible silence when Spinks went down and you knew that he wasn't going to beat the count. The crowd were gutted.

Terry Downes was another great favourite of mine. He didn't have a lot of science, well, hardly any at all to be honest, but he was a natural fighter. He didn't seem to think about it, he just went in there and banged.

Another memorable night was at Wembley, when George

Eastham, who was then playing for Arsenal after fighting so hard in the courts to lift what were categorised as conditions of 'slavery' facing the English professional footballer, invited me to be his guest at the fight between the then Cassius Clay and Brian London. This was soon after the World Cup win, which was why we were called up into the ring after the fighters had been introduced. George, a fellow northerner, knew London and we walked over to his corner. George asked, 'How are you Brian?' and the fighter said, 'Fine.' But he didn't look fine. He looked rather concerned, an impression that was confirmed by the fact that he was sweating so hard he might have just come out of the shower. 'I'll take Cassius,' London said. But you couldn't help thinking, 'Where?' When we went over to Clay he looked so casual he might have been waiting for a bus. He said, 'Congratulations, gentlemen, on winning that big game – that was absolutely wonderful.' It was amazing to get up close to his extraordinary man. He cut the most impressive figure I have ever seen.

I thought, 'Jesus Christ, this is a god.' Everything about him was so perfectly sculpted. His features were so even and then, when you got back to your seat and they rang the bell for the first time, the feeling of awe increased yet again. He moved beautifully, and I counted roughly three dozen punches thrown by London in what could only be described as a frenzy of anxiety. Not one of them came within six inches of its target. Next to me, George was getting a little hysterical. He said, 'Clay's going to kill him.' In fact, that seemed the last thing on the great man's mind. In the second round he seemed to land every punch he threw, but they were light blows. I really believe to this day that Clay didn't want to hurt him. He knocked out London, it seemed quite effortlessly, in the second round. Then he sauntered out of the ring. He was untouched. He had just strolled through the evening.

For me it meant that I would always be fascinated by this man who mesmerised the whole world along with his opponents. I have seen all the great footballers of my time, and played against most of them. I have marvelled at the skill of a Puskas and a Charlton, the nous and the passing genius of Johnny Haynes and like everybody else I have knelt at the altar of Pele's amazing gifts and character. But never have I been in the presence of an aura to match that of Cassius Clay that night at Wembley, so soon before he became so much more than a mere fighter. My only regret is that I didn't see him on a night when somebody other than poor Brian London was able to offer more in the way of a serious challenge. I would have liked to have seen Clay when he became Muhammad Ali and bestrode the world after beating George Foreman in a clearing of the African jungle, and if I could get hold of a time machine I would most appreciate a battle between Ali and one of the great mythical figures of my youth – Rocky Marciano.

I would listen to the fight reports from America, straining to hear through the static. I remember when Marciano fought Don Cockell, who was a polished fighter in his own league here in Britain, but was never a match for a man as hard as Marciano. I'm sure Marciano was a bully, and a very unscrupulous one. It certainly didn't help Cockell's cause that Marciano hit him below the belt about a dozen times.

Watching the fights over the years – and to a degree it is also true of football, in the matter of the viciousness of the tackling – you realise how much crueller it was back in those days. The fighters were allowed to take so much more punishment. I recall the old film of Joe Louis. He was the prototype of Ali in some ways, and he punched so hard – with those lighter gloves.

These were things I thought about a lot in those days in the gym in West Kensington. How would I absorb a real beating, the kind of systematic mashing of the body and the spirit that can come if you have a bad night or find yourself over-matched? I never experienced that because I had a decent technique and the natural speed and reflexes to keep out of trouble. It also helped that the gym was well supervised, but sometimes you did see a kid who had stepped in a little out of his depth and when he nursed his wounds, and put his gear into his bag and walked out in the night, often alone, you did wonder how you might handle such a set-back.

Such speculation did not last long, however. My father insisted that I should put away the gloves. He may have given ground on his conviction that I should become an electrician before I gambled on my football talent in the professional game, but he was unswerving on this one. Of course he was absolutely right. I shaped well in the gym, I knew that. I could also tell myself that, with enough work, I might just make it as a professional fighter. But my destiny, when I really thought about it, lay elsewhere. It was to walk through the front gates of Craven Cottage rather than shinnying up the wall and on to the tree and sliding down through the branches.

Today, of course, the debate over a young footballer's career route is somewhat more serene. A 15-year-old of promise who has a few clubs interested in him, as I did back in the mid-fifties, has only one agony of choice. It concerns precisely which club he joins with a guaranteed contract to be signed at the age of 17, one which these days I'm told can add up to as much as £150,000 a year. Imagine that. It would have been impossible to do so back in the fifties. Back then, Johnny Haynes had still to break through the £20-a-week barrier, and when he became the first £100-a-week player there was astonishment within the game. It seemed like a fabulous wage, at least if you didn't measure the gap between a big club's take at the gate and its payroll, and begin to make comparisons with the world of, say, showbusiness – or, if you thought about Brian London's reward for his futile performance against Cassius Clay. London picked up £35,000 for not landing a punch. In those days you could have bought five substantial houses in decent areas of London for that amount. It was seven years' salary for Haynes, a genius of the most popular game in the world.

I was happy to go to Fulham FC because I thought it infinitely preferable to clocking in at a factory or working as an electrician or a gas-fitter. I loved the game – and I loved to run. But if I was pleased to be called to the professional game, I couldn't divorce that pleasure from a deep uncertainty, the one that had been voiced by my father in those fierce, quietly conducted, family debates about my future. What if I failed? What if I got some serious injury? There were no safety nets then. There was just this imperative to finish up among the winners.

Today when I hear of some kid being besieged by scouts, and of his family hearing sweet talk of riches that was beyond their dreams before little Johnny started to kick the ball with some promise, I have to wonder what is happening inside the youngster's head. How hard will he work at his game when he knows that the future is more or less financially guaranteed. How can he have that gnawing feeling in the pit of his stomach which came to the young players of my generation when they looked at the team sheets which measured the flow – or the ebb – of their career hopes, when they looked desperately for signs of warmth from the old manager or the coaches and collected like moths around a light when an old player, who knew all the secrets of the trade they hoped to master, offered the encouragement of a little advice? Would I have hung on every word of a Bentley or a Haynes if I knew that whatever happened I would leave football a wealthy young man? Because I was a child of my times, probably, but how long would that earnest respect have lasted? Would I have thought that the almost impossible dream of playing for England one day, if it was ever going to happen, had to be carved out over a number of years in which you could never afford to forget that someone a little younger and a little better might suddenly appear at your shoulder? Those certainly were the feelings I carried into Craven Cottage that first time, and they would never leave me. Of course you acquire confidence with achievement in any circumstances.

But achieving in professional sport without hunger, without the fear that you are always one step away from having to make another living in another walk of life in which you have no natural edge over your rivals, well, that is a challenge which I cannot relate to so easily.

At Fulham, at 15, the challenge in front of me could not have been more basic. I had to run harder than ever before, and that was just to survive.

CHAPTER FOUR

THINKING AND SWEATING AT THE SAME TIME

Dugald Livingstone was a classic, wry old football manager, who long ago had learned the limits of his power when dealing with the businessmen and local traders who inhabited the boardrooms of the game, in the belief they knew more about it than the professionals they employed – and fired – in such a random, imperious way.

He had a soft Scottish accent which lightened the effect of some of his remarks, if only for as long as it took to separate the velvet from the steel. He had been in charge of the Belgian national team. He guided Newcastle United to victory in the 1955 Cup Final against Manchester City, a talented team marshalled by the subtle inside-forward and future managerial giant Don Revie. Later Livingstone was asked what Newcastle gave him for winning the Cup. He rolled his eyes and said, 'The sack.' He had raised in the boardroom the possibility of dropping 'Wor Jackie' Milburn, which up on Tyneside was akin to demoting God. He was told he couldn't do it. So Livingstone packed his bags and moved on to Fulham, where he raised a few eyebrows with one of his early pre-match team talks. 'Okay lads, get an early two-goal lead today,' he said, 'before they realise what a terrible team you are.' A ghost of a smile crossed his face when he said that, and the old sweats in the team chuckled grimly. Livingstone didn't have to exert the heavy hand of discipline. He treated players – most of the time – with respect. His approach was that if they had talent, and a sense of responsibility, they should be dealt with as men rather than overgrown schoolboys.

I was in that last category, a 17-year-old ground staff boy working away at my cleaning chores, including the scraping of dried mud off the boots of the senior players on a Friday afternoon, when I was summoned to his office. 'I have a wee outing for you, George,' he told me. 'You're playing against Liverpool tomorrow – at right back. Good luck.' At first I thought he was joking, but then I looked at the expression on his face, and I knew he wasn't. He was an old pro passing this off as a routine situation, but of course to me it was astonishing. Robin Lawler, our Irish full-back was injured, and Livingstone obviously felt that I had done well enough in the reserves, among the old pros hanging on and the young contenders, to warrant this early chance in the first team. I knew I had been playing well enough in the reserves, but the thing that really attracted attention was my ability to run with wingers, to match them step for step, swerve for swerve. It wasn't a routine attribute of full-backs in those days. Full-backs tended to be hard rather than fast, and often with a streak of brutality in the tackle. But, as Ernie Shepherd discovered on the school training field, I could run with anybody, and I suspect this was why Dug Livingstone had a broad smile of satisfaction when he told me I was in against Liverpool. He had seen, before anyone else, that when I arrived at Craven Cottage I was miscast as a wing-half.

This point of discovery, which changed my football life and gave me the possibilities on a wider stage which might otherwise never have come, was in a reserve match against Portsmouth. Livingstone had promised me a run-out with the 'stiffs', saying that from time to time 'mere children' were injected into the action usually dominated by old pros, some of whom were mean enough to physically discourage the bright-eyed youngsters tearing about the field in the hope of making a big impression. So I went into my first rite of passage as a prospective pro, playing at right-half. The crucial break was that our right back Norman Smith was injured early in the game, and had to go off. Livingstone, who was watching the match with that intensity which comes with the need to always know what you have in reserve in the event of the injury or catastrophic loss of form of one of your first teamers, marched to the touch-line and told me to take over from Smith. I protested that I was a wing-half, but in those days when substitutes were not yet permitted there was no time for such self-indulgence. 'Right now,' said Livingstone, 'you're a full-back. Go and do it.' This pitted me against Pat Neill, a young England amateur international who had a big reputation as a rising star in the game. He later moved to Wolves, after getting a degree at Cambridge University. Somewhere along the line Neill must have lost that edge of ambition, or nerve, which carries a young player to the front rank of the game, but when I faced him he was considered a definite comer, a flier and tricky on the ball. Yet I didn't find him a problem. I matched him for speed and I read his moves. At the end of the match Livingstone said, 'George, you are now a right back.' Again I protested, but I could see that I was wasting my time. 'You're never going to be a right-half, son,' he went on, 'so just take it. You're going to be a full-back – and a bloody good one. We're going to make sure of that. Every evening from Monday to Friday you're going to come back with me out on the pitch. You're going to be taught everything a full-back needs to know – how to kick, how to take the right positions, how to tackle – you're going to work with me and Joe Bacuzzi.'

Bacuzzi was a great old pro, a hard, knowing full-back and he took me through all the nuances of playing the position. The work was based on the 'Swivel Defence' in the old W-M formation of two full-backs, a centre-half, two wing-halves, two inside-forwards, two wingers and a centre-forward. Fashions change, of course, but certain fundamentals don't. I received a barrage of fundamentals over the next few months, and every one of them is as relevant today as it was in the mid-fifties.

Sometimes now when I'm watching a Premiership game I turn to Daphne and say, 'Oh my God, look at the position the full-back is taking up – hasn't anyone taught him the basics?' I have to wonder if the young man making the crass error, and who is probably earning in a week more than the liberated Johnny Haynes did in ten years, has spent five minutes, let alone five nights of a week, in the company of a Joe Bacuzzi. One weekend a couple of seasons ago Dennis Bergkamp, Arsenal's beautifully talented forward, was being hailed as a genius for setting up a marvellous goal for his team-mate Freddy Ljungberg, but the fact was that Bergkamp had played the ball between two centre-backs and Ljungberg had picked it up completely unattended. Bergkamp's skill was exceptional but it was inflicted on suicidal defence. An utterly fundamental rule had been flouted. You stay with your man, at least until alternative cover is in place, or until a situation has broken down.

Football is a simple game, but a lot of hard work has to go into making it so. I groan and moan and cry out phrases like, 'oh no,' when I'm watching football now because if you have been educated thoroughly in the demands of a certain position, you see disasters waiting to happen all over the place. Livingstone and Bacuzzi hammered home the fact that often you can save yourself as much as ten yards by anticipating trouble, reacting, as it were, before something bad happened. When you were confronting a player of great creativity, someone like a Haynes or a Giles, you had to know you were involved in a game that, like chess, can suddenly leave you utterly out-thought and defenceless. When a player of the quality of Haynes, who is always going to try to make the telling ball to feet, draws back his foot your instinct is to head for the area of interception. Perhaps a Haynes would try the ball, anyway, and maybe it would be intercepted. But Haynes would log that. Giles would log it, and the next thing that would happen was that the ball would move on to the right foot of the great midfielder and he would look out to the left-wing. Then in a stroke it would be switched to his left and he would put it inside the full-back. Today, frankly, I see full-back play that appals me, at every level of the game, and not least on the international stage. I see a young star, somebody as talented and quick as England's current first choice Ashley Cole, showing a basic ignorance of positional play. I see him still looking at the ball when his winger has gone inside. The requirement, constantly, is to keep everybody in focus. One moment you may have discouraged an opponent from making a certain pass, saving yourself a lot of wasted effort, but then suddenly the point of attack is switched, and you have to take up still another position, and in a split second you have to ask yourself if it is the right one; have you kept close enough to your man, or passed him on to a team-mate and is everything still covered? These are the mechanics of the job which you have to learn, and, if you have done so, it means that during a game you always know you have to keep asking yourself a score of those questions. You have to have the right answers – and the vision and the flair and the nerve to say, 'Oh, I can go there and make that play' and save yourself ten yards – five yards to go in there, and five yards to get back.

The most important thing is not letting your man get away. Football will always be about time and space and so at the start of any game you know that you are going to be man to man as long as your man wants to be in your zone and the moment he runs out of it you have to know whether you are passing him over to a team-mate, or going with him.

You might be facing a rotation system which has someone running across the pitch, and one of his team-mates coming into what he hopes is unguarded space, with a full-back drawn out of position. The defender has to have the wit to make a snap decision and get it right. If he goes, is the position behind him covered? Have responsibilities been exchanged, is everybody paying attention? It is not rocket science or advanced calculus, but it is a lot of hard work and a lot of concentration, and if you don't learn to think and to sweat at the same time you're going to be in a lot of trouble.

Month after month, Monday to Friday, I had these questions and answers drilled into me, and I have to presume I had got enough of them right by that Friday morning when Dug Livingstone found that Lawler wasn't fit and he realised he had to use a young, untried full-back. Against Liverpool I faced an England international, Alan A'Court. One of his greatest strengths was that he could go right down to the goal touchline and then cut back dangerously after it had seemed impossible for him to retain control of the ball. On one occasion I decided there was just no way he could get his body around the ball and get it across. But he did, and I had given up running because I was so sure the ball was running out of play. But he got the bloody thing over. Fortunately it didn't result in a goal. However, that didn't excuse me from a tongue-lashing. Livingstone wasn't happy and Gordon Brice, our big centre-half, came over to me and said, 'Look, you can't give up on any ball. You have to see everything through, you have to stay on the job.'

He was giving me an early warning against any form of cheating. He was saying that maybe you can cheat 99 times and get away with it, but the 100th time it is going to cost your team a game, and it could be a huge game, it could be one on which a whole season, or a whole career, hinges. He was saying you have to do all the hard work irrespective of how tired you are or how good or bad you feel. You have to get through all the work you have been taught to do. You have to remember that it is just not for you but the whole team and if you do it for them you can expect them to do it for you.

Players cheat for various reasons. Most seriously, it is a flaw in their nature. Or maybe they don't have the confidence to play honestly, to always go to the limit of their ability. Perhaps they are too afraid to do that, and hope they can get by, and that no-one will notice their lack of moral courage. But the good pros do not miss a thing. The good pros watch a game impassively and afterwards they will comment on something which may have gone quite unnoticed by the casual fan. They will say, 'Did you see what so-and-so did under pressure – wasn't it brilliant?' Or they may say something quite different about a moment of professional betrayal, something that has shocked them to their core.

Evidently, though, my lapse against Liverpool was not considered killing – even though it was ten months before I returned to the first team. I felt that but for the one occasion I had allowed A'Court that little bit of leeway, I had accomplished what I had set out to do. I'd played with great concentration, kept everything as simple as I could, and never consciously forgotten for a second the overwhelming need not to let anyone down. I certainly sensed that the people in charge of my career had been pleased with what they had seen. After the game Livingstone didn't say anything to me. He just smiled in my direction. Frank Osborne, the general manager, normally didn't watch the match. He would busy himself with various duties, but on this occasion he had watched the game with a particular interest. He wanted to see how the local kid shaped up, and he said he was pleased. It was a statement he underpinned with a wage rise a few days later.

For me it was the start of a surge in popularity in the district, especially along the North End Road. I would be handed vegetables and fruit and the affection would grow down the years. Later, when my mother walked my young sons down the street people would come out of the shops and say, 'Oh, Georgie Cohen's boys.' The boys would come home laden with toffee apples and sweets and oranges.

When Osborne called me into his office I was earning three pounds a week. He said, 'Georgie, my boy, you played very well. I think we're going to pay you another thirty shillings a week.' I rushed home to Mum to tell her the news and she was delighted. I said you could take a girl up the West End by taxi, have a steak, go to the cinema, get a taxi back – and still have change out of two quid. We agreed it was rather wonderful.

Life was opening up for me splendidly. I didn't have to scrape together a few pennies to go the cinema. I could do it in style, sit back as a man of means and watch the elegant James Mason, the tough Humphrey Bogart and our great actors Ralph Richardson and Alec Guinness and come out into the street with the price of a taxi and the feeling that I, little Georgie Cohen, might just be somebody. That wasn't the greatest thing, however. The best of it was the training. I loved the training. I loved the feeling I had in the morning when I woke up and felt that I was going to make myself a little stronger. I learned then, as I would know much more deeply in bleaker times, that there was nothing quite like being fit. In my case, of course, it was utterly essential. My game depended on great fitness more than most, and I was beginning to acquire a reputation for being one of the strongest young players around. My fitness was so much part of my technique, it was a most valuable tool of my trade, but I have to admit I was particularly delighted to be told that Dusty Springfield thought I had a great body. She was one of the showbusiness crowd who regularly appeared at Craven Cottage. Others included the actress Honor Blackman, Pussy Galore of the Bond film, the famous creator of Alf Garnett, Johnny Speight, and the actor Tony Booth, who would eventually become a prime minister's father-in-law.

It was also true that the dramas of Fulham were increasingly the staple of our professional comedian-chairman Tommy Trinder, though not always to the universal approval of the dressing room. At one time of struggle he told a national audience watching *Sunday Night at the Palladium*, 'Did you notice Fulham did a lap of honour yesterday? They won a corner.' But that was just one jarring moment at a time when we had our first inkling that football was on the way to becoming fashionable. Footballers were still, relatively speaking, poor, but though it would take another forty years or so before their financial rewards would make them fully paid-up members of the Ferrari classes, it was becoming clear they were beginning to be touched by a little glamour. But before the glamour, such as it was, there was always the work and the learning. Already I had acquired a formidable list of teachers, and then when I finally broke through as a regular first-teamer, in March 1957, I found a new advisor and an old but still shining icon. Roy Bentley had gained that instant status in my young mind when I first watched him perform for Chelsea at Stamford Bridge. He was so strong and composed. He looked untouchable. He was England's centre-forward and everything he did on the field told you why that might be so.

Now, in his mid-thirties, he had dropped into the Second Division with Fulham and moved back to right-half – just in front of me. He was a marvellous guide, taking me through the thickets of professional football. He geed me up and steadied me down. Sometimes in the tension of the game your hackles might rise a little with the stream of advice, but never to the point where you were tempted to snap or pout. Always you were aware that this was a great footballer and a generous heart. Today, now in his eighties, he is still a wonderful companion and when we play a round of golf I can still see in him the natural grace and athleticism of a great sportsman. He and another tremendously talented player, the Scottish international winger Graham Leggat, never tired of encouraging me, and also advising me that sometimes my enthusiasm to be first in the tackle and to play the game at the highest possible speed could overreach itself. Leggat took me aside one day and said, 'George, it's brilliant the way you get forward, I love it, but you don't always have to operate at that speed once you're clear of your marker. The skill factor tends to dwindle the faster you're moving, so slow down a little and work a little more on your accuracy.' Bentley had some similar advice, and was particularly keen on refining my sense of when to go and when to stay. It helped that he was a master of such judgement.

Certainly I appreciated their advice more than the comments of another senior team-mate, Bobby Robson. Bobby was a great enthusiast but as a player he never struck me as being quite as altruistic as either Bentley or Leggat, or the great Haynes. I was irritated to read Robson's comments on my early progress. They seemed unnecessarily barbed – and patronising. He said, 'We used to say about George Cohen that he's hit more cameramen than Frank Sinatra. George was quick and broke up the flanks exceptionally well, but his final ball was rarely on target. Usually he would hit his cross into the crowd or the photographers. George was a nice type of boy, a whole-hearted player with a sense of humour and good social habits. Fulham always produced players like that.' It was true that by and large Fulham exerted a wholesome influence on their young players, and if boys will from time to time inevitably be boys, overall there was a good set of values at Craven

Cottage. Still, I felt Robson had rather skewered me with faint praise and my response was a little bitter. I said maybe it was true I put in a few off-target crosses, but then it was also right that I got there up more than most, and that included him.

Roy Bentley was always a little more inclined to step down from the mountain top, and in a way that wasn't so apparent in another veteran player, Ron Greenwood. I never felt particular warmth from this knowledgeable football man who would eventually manage England and made such a vital contribution to Ramsey's World Cup win with his development of such key players as Bobby Moore, Martin Peters, and Geoff Hurst. When he took over the England Under-23 team my run at that level of international football came to an end. He preferred the Burnley player, John Angus. I remember getting a lift from the airport with my friend Ken Jones, the sportswriter, at the end of an Under-23 tour and saying, 'Well, I suppose that's the end of my England hopes.' Ken, who had played professionally before becoming a journalist, was aghast. 'Not at all,' he said. 'You've come a long way doing the right things, and that's not wasted. Don't be so bloody stupid, push on now.'

It was the best of advice, of course, and I decided that Greenwood, like everyone else in the game, had his own perspective on the game and in my case it didn't have to be a final judgement. However, there was no doubt Greenwood was an exceptionally good football man and maybe I was caught a little in his general frustration with what he perceived to be rather the happy-go-lucky chaos at Craven Cottage. In his autobiography he was certainly withering about the only football club I would ever know.

Greenwood wrote, 'There was no discipline at all at Craven Cottage. The players were excellent but the set-up was abysmal. Everything was horribly lax and sloppy. Fulham deserved much better because basically it was a smashing little club. It was friendly and homely and full of good humour. So much was against the manager in those days. I do not think Fulham were really knocked into shape until Alec Stock went there in the 1970's. It was surprising Fulham achieved anything on the field but they did because of the quality of their players. They were capable of beating almost anyone on their day. It is impossible to say why so many ultimately successful men wore the white shirt of Fulham, or why the club produced so many colourful characters or earned itself so much affection. Perhaps the answer is in its happy spot beside the Thames or in the history of the club. But if the club was exhilarating in one sense, it was endlessly frustrating in another. I could see the club was not going anywhere and I vowed that many of the things that went on at Fulham would not happen if I ever got hold of the club.'

Greenwood came from outside and maybe he had broader vision on how a truly competitive club should be run. There was no doubt some of his points were valid, and certainly I was shocked when in 1964 the board agreed to sell Alan Mullery to Spurs for £72,000. The problem was that the bank was pressing for repayments on a £30,000 loan, which even then didn't seem too much of a mountain to climb.

Spurs offered £80,000 for me at the same time but the board turned down that offer, possibly on the grounds that I was part of the furniture. Mullery was a foreigner from Notting Hill, and it may have been that he was a more prickly customer to deal with than me. Later, he revealed that on the advice of Bentley he had asked the club for £1,000 in 'readies' before signing a new contract just when our team-mate and crusading chairman of the Professional Footballers' Association, Jimmy Hill, had broken through in the fight to lift the wages ceiling. Frank Osborne reacted angrily, threatening to report 'Mullers' to the Football League and have him thrown out of the game. Perhaps some of the acrid smoke sent up by that affair still lingered when, a few years later, Spurs made their move. But whatever the thinking of the board, it was an absurd decision. Mullery had some feeling for the club – he reported how he and his dad had got off a bus from Notting Hill and had felt immediately at home when they walked into Craven Cottage for the first time. He was also an excellent player, intense and skilled and very aggressive in his thinking. He took over from Bentley, playing just in front of me, and as I grew in experience, under the promptings of such as Bentley and Leggat and Haynes, I was able to contribute to a very effective partnership with Mullery. We worked hard on launching attacks from the right, but never at the expense of defence. In fact we developed our own system of 'passing on' attackers, with Mullery challenging for the ball with the awareness that I was lurking in support. There was a risk factor involved, but it was limited by my ability to move quickly from a standing start.

When Mullery was sold it seemed like a terribly short-sighted response to a problem which with a little business imagination could have been smoothed away against the knowledge that Fulham were a team of talent with a good future, a team that was hugely enhanced by the presence of such a strong, talented and hard-edged player as Mullery. It was, looking back, some vindication of Greenwood's blistering assessment of the club's general philosophy of muddling along, but, as he also said, there was always an extraordinary capacity at Craven Cottage to pluck out results which could, at any time, turn the power structure of the old First Division upside down. There was always a touch of charisma, even genius, waiting to leap out of that old dressing room and, at least for a day, completely transform the horizon.

Haynes was the supreme example of that, but he was much nearer my own age and for a while his brilliance, though obvious to the rawest kid, took second place in my mind to the aura of my hero Bentley.

One morning early in my life as a first-teamer I had a knock on the door of my room in the team hotel. We were in Bristol for a Second Division game with City. I looked at my watch and saw it was 7am. I wondered who on earth was disturbing me at such a time. It was the great Bentley. 'Get dressed, son,' he said, 'I want to show you something.' He then walked me through the empty streets of Bristol and out to the Clifton Suspension Bridge. It was awe-inspiring, and a little scary, as the great bridge seemed to sway in the wind. 'I thought you should see this,' said Bentley, 'and see what men can achieve when they put their minds to it. I thought it might help you put the pressures of football into a little bit of perspective.' Roy, like a lot of those older players who had lived through a war, could look easily beyond the touchlines of our game. He had served in the Navy. He told me about riotous shore leave, how when the sailors left the ship they held out their hats for the obligatory issue of condoms. He was a man of the world who said you wouldn't come to too much harm if you remembered to take at least one bottle of Mackeson a day – and he was a wonderful footballer. When he briefly played centre-half in the last phase of his career, the England manager Walter Winterbottom saw one of his performances and took him aside and said, 'Roy, you're the best centre-half in the country at this moment, but unfortunately you are thirty-six and I can't pick you.' But before he went striding off into an honoured place in the halls of football history he had one last run at glory and it took him to within a few minutes of the FA Cup final. I went along with him, an 18-year-old acolyte, following his lead, accepting his promptings, and quite often dashing into the open spaces he had so deftly created. Before the fifth round game at West Ham – we had earlier beaten Yeovil and won a replay against Charlton at the Valley with Bentley scoring one of our two goals – we were lucky to escape from a car crash without serious injury. Les Austin, who ran the old Warnes Hotel in Worthing, where Fulham sent us for mid-season breaks and special training, was driving us back to town in a big Humber Pulman. The weather was filthy, with icy roads and freezing fog, and while passing through the village of Washington we went into a skid and finished up in a ditch. Eventually, a breakdown man winched us out of the ditch. Unfortunately he did it with a little too much force as we sheltered in the car, bruised and shaken. He got us out of one ditch only to see us skidding into another one at the other side of the road. Upton Park filled us with little terror after that experience, and we always had the beating of West Ham, a feeling confirmed elegantly by Haynes, who scored the decisive goal in a 3–2 win.

Bristol Rovers came to Craven Cottage for the sixth round and were beaten comfortably, 3–I, in front of a crowd of 42,000. We were in the semi-final of the FA Cup, but when the draw was made on the Monday morning, as we huddled around the radio in the way beloved of every Fleet Street sports editor in those innocent days, we found out that we faced something more than an important football match. We had been cast as the 'other' team in a story that was gripping the nation with an emotion never before experienced in all the days of the national game. We would play Manchester United, who had been so terribly ravaged in a snowstorm at Munich a few weeks earlier, at Villa Park. I was playing snooker with Frank Osborne when the news of the air disaster broke across the nation with a sickening force. Frank put down his cue, gave a great sigh and tears came to his eyes. It was a shock for anyone, but I suppose an old football man who had spent so much time attempting to assemble a great team, would have felt particularly the loss of the flowers of the English game. Roger Byrne, Tommy Taylor, in time

Duncan Edwards, and the others were the hope of our game, challenging Real Madrid; they were a dynasty taking shape in front of our eyes and suddenly they were gone. Now we stood between a shattered legend and its first stage of resurrection as they strove to reach that very special place – Wembley.

We had to beat a team backed by the spirit of the nation and one which, because of the unique situation, had been allowed to step beyond the usual FA Cup regulations and sign more than half a team of players who would normally have been Cup-tied. Matt Busby's right-hand man Jimmy Murphy worked feverishly to piece together a team as his boss fought for life in a Munich hospital. Murphy had drafted in the guile of little Ernie Taylor, who five years earlier spoon-fed the ball to Stanley Matthews in the most emotional of all FA Cup finals, the hard tackling and high energy of wing-half Stan Crowther, and the speed and touch of the Welshman Colin Webster, who would be my responsibility.

United had another shining asset, of course. It was the home-grown one who had emerged almost unscathed from the ashes of that horrific night in Bavaria. It was the young hope of Old Trafford and England, Bobby Charlton.

Maybe it was because of my age, I was still only 18, or because of a touch of single-mindedness that was part of my nature, but a lot of the pre-game emotion passed me by. I looked around our dressing room and I felt that we had enough talent and character to do a good job, at least good enough not to be swept away in some gale of national wish fulfilment that a tragic story should rush to a sentimental uplift which would wipe out, however superficially, some of the pain. In Tony Macedo we had one of the best goalkeepers in the game who, under today's international qualification regulations, would surely have been a prime contender for a place in the England team. But he was born in Gibraltar, which meant that he was effectively stateless in the international game. Macedo had kept us on the road to Wembley with some brilliant saves. He was bold, too bold, some critics said, but he had oodles of moral courage, without a fair measure of which no one in that position is going to amount to much, and superb reflexes.

My full-back partner was Jim Langley, who played just three times for England but was hugely respected in the game. He was particularly good in the air and he never lacked for confidence. He was cool in the Villa Park dressing room. It was something you would expect of a player who always had the ability to shrug off a mistake. A few years later he would bring roars of laughter to a team meeting which had been called to discuss a sharp dip in form, particularly that of our colourful centre-half Bobby Keetch. The manager, Bedford Jezzard, had laid into Bobby, and whenever the player tried to defend himself somebody else chipped in. At one point Langley said, 'To be honest with you, Bobby, I remember when I had a bad game, about two years ago . . .' The half-back line was solid and had wit: Bentley, tough old Joe Stapleton and Lawler, a versatile player who had been bought up by Frank Osborne as part of an Irish job lot when the old Belfast Celtic team was breaking up. On the right-wing we had Roy Dwight, a good, orthodox winger whose musical nephew would find such great fame under the name Elton John. One year after our match with United, Roy would have a tumultuous day of his own at Wembley with Nottingham Forest. He scored a goal, broke his leg and won a winners' medal in the defeat of Luton Town. The Rabbi was at inside-right, having persuaded the club that his best talent would never be seen at half-back, where the club expected a little more caution than was permitted by his bold spirit. At centre-forward Arthur Stevens was a formidable worker who could score goals and brought with him a fierce loyalty. He was, in his love of the old place, the definitive Fulham player, but he was minus the madness. He said, 'I regard Fulham as a fine club but it is not just my experience since I signed here during the War that causes me to praise them. We must be the envy of the Football League because we are not just names on registration forms. We are members of a family. If we have a problem off the field the club try to sort it out. They understand the value of happy players.' Haynes was at inside-left, which meant that in one area of the field at least United had no reason at all to feel superior.

Haynes was the enabler from Edmonton, a man who could read a game like an open book and touch every member of his team with the sense that anything was possible. On his left was Tosh Chamberlain, who stood outside the ground on match days and called everyone darling. He could kick the leather off the ball, he was quick and inventive, more than slightly mad and if a full-back forgot to kick him up in the air in the opening minutes of a match he was flirting with a terrible nightmare.

All in all, then, we were not fodder for some tortured football dream. I was calm enough in the minutes before the game. I had been in the team for the best part of a year now without being scarred by serious mishaps. I had been learning my business, making my way, and it was going pretty well. However, the moment I walked out on to Villa Park I sensed that this would be a different kind of afternoon. The pitch was heavy, as was usual anywhere in England at the end of the winter. What was most striking though was the atmosphere in the ground which was filled by nearly 70,000 fans, of whom about 311 appeared to be neutral. There was an enormous buzz. I thought, 'Christ, this is a huge place – and a huge crowd.' Even in the Second Division big crowds were not rare. I'd played in front of 62,000 at Anfield, but here was a new level of intensity. I had to catch my breath.

We played well, exceptionally well, and even though United had this vast pool of sympathy, we had a sense that the emotions up on the terraces might have been a little more complicated than was imagined before the kick-off. You could detect a growing feeling that here was a Second Division team who could really play with craft and bite and the reality of this impression was confirmed soon enough despite a Charlton goal designed to smash the spirit of any team. Ernie Taylor fed the boy wonder an exquisite through pass. Charlton swivelled brilliantly, and beat Macedo from the edge of the box with a superb shot. This was discouraging twelve minutes into the game but Haynes, particularly, was not about to surrender. His response was a string of telling passes and with every one of them you could feel a surge of confidence in our team – and a growing uncertainty in United's defence. Langley created the momentum for the equaliser, charging down the left flank as defenders scattered before him, and when his shot-cum-centre flew into the box Stevens was the first to make contact, side-footing it into the net.

United had been pushed back on their heels, and then brought to their knees. Haynes, who was quite masterful this day, broke up a United attack on the edge of the box and sent a pass wide to Dwight on the right. The winger's cross was precise and Hill controlled the ball despite fierce challenges before shooting coolly past Harry Gregg. The big Irishman had displayed tremendous courage on the airfield in Munich, but he was powerless against the sweep of a goal which matched the splendour of Charlton's early strike.

We thought we were home, and we might have been if Langley had not been reduced merely to nuisance value by a collision with United's big striker Alex Dawson. Langley was carried off the field and by the time he returned United were level, Charlton having struck again. But we fought on well. Haynes continued to be the most influential player on the field and Gregg remained the busier goalkeeper, despite the fact that Macedo once had to fling himself unavailingly at a drive from Charlton which crashed against the cross-bar. There were no goals in the second half, which meant that we had to do it all over again, this time at Highbury. After the first match Charlton, who was only a year older, came up to me and said, 'Hard luck, son.' Though you put on a defiant face in such circumstances, I knew deep down that this was commiseration from an opponent who knew we had done well, better than anyone imagined we would, but that we had missed our chance. Macedo, who had done so much to carry us through the campaign, had a disaster at Highbury and we lost 5–3.

The comfort was that we were a team who had showed some quality and had the ingredients for a decent future. I could be pleased, in a modest way, about my performances so near to an early arrival at Wembley. I hadn't had too much trouble from Webster. I had done a lot of running, and if some of it might have seemed unnecessary to a casual observer, I knew, and more importantly the manager and my team-mates knew, that I had played a solid part in the effort. I had discouraged a talented player from making too much mischief. I knew, too, that my father, who said so little about his deepest emotions, had been made enormously proud. I knew that because a few days before the game at Villa Park he had gone to a fancy dress and circus outfitters shop on the Hammersmith Road and bought a top hat. He brought it home and promptly painted it in the black and white colours of Fulham. He would always be a Chelsea man because that was in his blood but he was happy to break ranks on this occasion. When I played that first game against Liverpool I learned later that he had gone to see the game without telling anyone. My mother said, 'You know, your father saw your game.' I asked her if he had said anything. She said. 'No, but I think you can take it he was pleased and very proud.' I had also learned a little more about the important matter of absorbing defeat, of picking from it the valuable lessons it always offered. For this I had to thank some good colleagues who took a little time to point me on my way, both on the field and – most memorably – on an early morning walk to a beautiful bridge that, like the certainties of my game of football, from time to time seemed to sway a little in the wind.

CHAPTER FIVE

THE KING
OF FULHAM

Naturally, being Fulham, we didn't punish ourselves for our failure on that last step to Wembley. Whatever happened to us out on the pitch, I learned quickly enough, we were the last football team on earth who needed to be told the sun would still come up in the morning. Our chairman, a professional comedian, might make bad jokes at our expense, and we might reach out for disaster from the jaws of glory as easily as picking a grape, but it never interfered with our belief that one day we would do something to shake the world.

So we brushed off the barbs of chairman Trinder, who in the wake of a 9–0 defeat at Wolves told the newspapers, 'I was listening to the radio and I heard there was a sensation at Wolverhampton. I thought, Christ, we're winning.'

We said that the world could laugh at us a little if it liked, but we would prefer that it laughed with us. We said that because if we knew our weaknesses, we also knew our strengths. A year after frustration at Villa Park and disaster at Highbury, we had claimed the right to play on such grounds before great crowds by promotion to the First Division. Under our new manager, Craven Cottage hero Bedford Jezzard, we won the first six games of the new season. 'Beddy's' first signing, Leggat, proved an instant success, and one of the last of Livingstone's, Maurice Cook, from Watford, scored three in the opening day slaughter of Stoke City. We won away at Sunderland, in the inaugural First Division match played at Roker Park, and then Swansea. When Sunderland travelled to Fulham a week after losing to us in front of their disbelieving crowd their rage for revenge was quickly turned to despair. We over-ran them 6–2. We took 19 points out of a possible 20.

After some mid-season wavering, we surged back into the race with a 6–2 win over Sheffield Wednesday – a performance which showed that in all the whimsy there was from time to time a touch of steel which on this occasion was best expressed by Jimmy Hill, who was fighting for a new status for footballers and his own career at Craven Cottage in the face of some heavy barracking. In that game, our captain Johnny Haynes, the idol of the terraces, turned on the crowd and shouted angrily on behalf of Hill, 'Give him a break, will you.' In the end Hill fashioned his own survival. He scored a tumultuous hat-trick.

It confirmed that we had some resilience, a touch of class and not a little talent and, also, something more. Something which for any connoisseur of football was sublime. We had Haynes. This meant we had one of the greatest footballers who ever laced up a pair of boots. I had five managers in my fourteen years at Craven Cottage – Dugald Livingstone,

Bedford Jezzard, Vic Buckingham, Bobby Robson and Bill Dodgin Junior and they were all, in their different ways, excellent football men. I played alongside men of character and great talent like Roy Bentley and Graham Leggat. I rubbed shoulders each day with Hill, someone who had the passion and the thick skin to fight effectively an injustice which had blighted the lives of so many of the greatest practitioners of our national game. Sun-kissed youngsters like Allan Clarke, Malcolm Macdonald, and Rodney Marsh passed through. No-one ever had a more engaging – or eccentric – team-mate than Trevor 'Tosh' Chamberlain. Bobby Keetch was a hard-tackling centre-half who eventually went into the antique business, still, I always suspected, frustrated that he wasn't born to be a Regency buck. There was, however, always one supreme point of focus in this essentially happy but some-times convulsive little universe. The cast changed frequently, as it does at all football clubs, but while I was at Fulham there was always Johnny Haynes. He played his last game for the club in 1970 – two years after I was forced to quit through injury, and in a way that was a blessing for me because even though I supplanted him as captain during the reign of Buckingham – I always felt it was an honorary title at the first whistle of every game – I could never imagine being at Fulham without Haynes.

He arrived five years before me, a small boy who needed some building up. He was well established when I first saw him on the training field. I had read of him being a future star of the game and already he was on the fringes of the England team, and you only had to take one glance to see that he was an outstanding talent. It was wonderful to see his timing on the ball. Frank Penn was the trainer, a lovely old guy, and I would watch him chipping balls in to the young Haynes. They would spend hours working on this, with Haynes getting into such a groove his body was always in the perfect position to volley.

We talk about great players so freely these days, but great, I often wonder, when compared to whom? Alfredo di Stefano and Ferenc Puskas were great players by any standard. When di Stefano ran through the Eintracht Frankfurt defence to score for Real Madrid in the 1960 European Cup final everyone who saw it felt that the football world had stopped for a few seconds. And later, at a European Union celebration game at Wembley I had to catch my breath when Puskas, in front of the Royal Box, put a ball inside Jimmy Armfield which will live in my mind forever.

It is of this standard of performance I am thinking when I say I have a hundred individual memories of the beauty of Haynes's play. One stands out for the sheer perfection of his skill. It was a charity match which, but for this one second, has faded completely from my memory. The ball came to him at speed on a wet, slippery surface but with the slightest of adjustments, one that was almost imperceptible, he played it inside a full-back and into the path of the on-running winger. I looked at Dave Sexton, who was sitting on the bench, and he caught my glance and shook his head as if to say fantastic. Haynes could give you goose bumps on a wet night in a match that didn't matter.

Sometimes now, so long after he played his last lacerating

pass, I watch a match and wonder what he might have done, say, alongside Patrick Vieira at Arsenal; Vieira devouring the opposition with his power and his tackling, Haynes killing them with a hundred delicious cuts. I think of him orchestrating Manchester United, releasing Ruud Van Nistelrooy with those smooth surgical strokes. Some might say that the problem with this speculation is that Haynes operated in the career-long 'comfort zone' of Fulham, a club that had its highs and lows but never found itself on the edge of ultimate competition for any sustained period.

Could Haynes have been so consistent on a permanent knife edge? Was he too happy to unfurl his brilliance in his comfortable little empire by the Thames? We cannot really answer that question because Fulham always said they would never part with Haynes, and if it is true he might have fought that declaration if he had had a fiercer ambition burning inside, you still have to remember the way club–player relationships went in those days. A player might propose, without any contractual underpinning, a course of action but inevitably the club disposed, as we saw at Craven Cottage when Alan Mullery stuck out his bowl in the style of Oliver Twist.

I also think of what might have happened for him if four years before England won the World Cup, and after he himself had played in the 1962 World Cup in Chile, he hadn't been driving a MG Midget on a windblown Lancashire road when he should have been back in the team hotel in Blackpool. Johnny, who was a single man at that time, broke curfew for a night out with a 'family friend,' and he might have got away with it if the little sports car hadn't been blown off the road. Haynes broke his leg and was out of the game for a year — and never played for England again.

I don't know whether, if Haynes had managed to fight his way back into the England set-up after his accident, he would have been first choice ahead of Bobby Charlton in '66, but I do think he would have raised a challenge because he was too good, too perceptive not to intrude into the consciousness of a judge as shrewd as Alf Ramsey. However, Ramsey's priority was always the assembling of a team of perfectly complementary parts and ultimately Haynes's lovely game might have been deemed less relevant to England's needs than the graceful, endless running and pulverising finish of Charlton, the brilliant functionalism of Nobby Stiles, the drifting menace of Martin Peters, and the firecracker bustle and sharp skills of Alan Ball. It was something condemned to the footnotes of speculation the moment, in my view, Johnny Haynes was removed from the crumpled MG and carried off to hospital. He took the blow of being out of favour in the England camp philosophically enough, and when he came back it was a wonderful relief to see that his game had not been diminished one iota, at least not in the scale of his imagination or his ability to rip open a defence in one peerless stroke. You didn't see Haynes bursting past a defender in the manner of Charlton. That wasn't his game. Haynes by-passed his marker. He was constantly on the move and when he received the ball it was at the moment that he had created the space. A Fulham player knew that the moment he won the ball Haynes would want it, and that he would be free. He wouldn't be standing in space signalling for the ball. He would be moving into it, and like all the great players he was very quick over five yards. Movement was Haynes's greatest asset. It was liquid, subtle movement and so many times it was found impossible to cover a player who was so intelligent and so constantly mobile. He much favoured his right foot but he could use his left when necessary, which wasn't so often because of that knack of always being in the right place at the right time. He could do anything with the ball – chip it, drive it, bend it, whatever the situation demanded. There were plenty of tough guys around who wanted to blunt Haynes's sharp edge and some of them could be seriously nasty sods. But even with their freedom to tackle from behind, their opportunities were rare. He always knew where he was on the field, and where everyone else was, and on top of everything else he had an innate ability to shield the ball and, while so close to it, change direction in a completely unpredictable way. Recently I heard how John Giles, who built such a vast reputation as a midfield general of the sixties and seventies, was hugely influenced by watching Haynes at Maine Road on a night when Manchester City beat us, despite the brilliance of the captain's performance. Giles, who was playing wing or inside-forward for Manchester United at the time, went along with Matt Busby's knowing number two Jimmy Murphy. Apparently as they walked away from Maine Road Murphy said, 'That was the best midfield performance I have ever seen.' And Giles thought, 'Yes, and that's how I would like to play, not in any set position but moving around the field, finding space, always being in position to receive the ball and move the play along.' A play-maker's baton had been passed on.

Haynes, who in most other ways was the mildest of men, couldn't stand bad football. He was quick to praise good play in a colleague but when a chance was missed, when a ball was played thoughtlessly, his anger was quick and hard. Off the pitch Haynes didn't play the senior pro, the captain. He said to me once, 'These are grown men, they have kids and responsibilities and off the field we're all the same. But if you are captain, on the field you have to take responsibility – and you have to set some kind of example.' So it meant that on the pitch he would often shout the odds, but off it you wouldn't know he was in the same room.

Down all those fourteen years we played together I had just a couple serious run-ins with him on the field. On the first occasion we were playing Preston North End at the time when the great Tom Finney was over the hill but still full of skill and knowledge. Most of the time in that game he was an old, cornered fox, but you couldn't take your eyes off him for a moment. He couldn't really run any more, at least not as he had so brilliantly down either wing, and Preston had him at centre-forward, where his basic move was to take a pass with great touch and then put his body between you and the ball.

As a centre-forward Finney wasn't my direct responsibility, but the play shifted quickly and Finney was left unmarked. As Bill Shankly might have said, you wouldn't leave Tom Finney unmarked if he was sixty and wearing an overcoat, so naturally I moved to cover the danger. It should be said we were not playing well at the time, and for once this also included the great Haynes. He was very frustrated and a couple of times he had held up his arms and shouted, 'What the bloody hell is happening here?' When he saw me in the unfamiliar ground of central defence, he snapped again, yelling, 'What the hell are you doing there?'

For the first time I spoke back to the great man. 'I'm marking Tom Finney, John – look, do your own bloody job and I'll do mine.' I felt a little uneasy about the exchange as the game wore on but as we walked off the field he came alongside me and said, 'Are you coming for a drink?'

That was the definitive Haynes style. He cared passionately about football while he was doing it, but when it was over he wasn't going to let it dominate his life and that, when I think about it, may have been one reason why he settled so happily for life at Craven Cottage. But then he certainly could be cutting on the field. The whole team was reminded of this when we struggled one afternoon against Chelsea.

It was an early season game on a hot afternoon and Chelsea were firing through some long balls and running hard. We were a goal down and under pressure, and Haynes was getting increasingly impatient. Again he demanded of the defenders, 'What the hell is going on?' I said that the problem was that the ball was coming back the moment we got rid of it, and added 'Why the hell don't you hang on to it?' Back in the dressing room the temperature rose again, and their was a lot of shouting and barging. Jimmy Hill walked in and was appalled by the scene. 'This is absolutely disgraceful,' he said. But by then the tension in Haynes was uncoiling. When he came off the field it seemed that he regained his understanding that some players simply were not as talented as others, and if it was something he could forget in the heat of the game it didn't take him too long to regain his perspective. Certainly in all those years of struggle against superior forces, he never publicly criticised his team-mates. He closed that row after the Chelsea game in familiar fashion. 'Let's go across the road to the pub.'

It was, I suppose, just another of those days when Fulham was both his trial and his joy. Basically, he liked the feel of the place and the warmth it extended to him. He loved the atmosphere of the ground, and he adored his mate Tosh Chamberlain. Tosh was probably the most beloved of all the Fulham characters and his exploits thrilled the fans as much as they so often exasperated his friend the captain. I used to call Tosh the 'Fucking King of Fulham,' because in his stream of Cor Blimey consciousness that particular expletive was never far away. Johnny and Tosh were always an odd couple, but they would invariably finish up having a couple of lagers together even after the exchange of some very hard words indeed. One of Tosh's problems, and it was really quite an horrendous one to have at Fulham, was that he couldn't read Haynes on the field. John would often be left so nonplussed he would hold up his hands and shake his head. He would deliver a beautifully weighted ball into space, perfect for a quick winger who had anticipated the pass, but Tosh would be nowhere in sight. Then Haynes would try to anticipate Chamberlain's next move, a risky business at any time, and he would see the winger charging off in an entirely different direction. Stand-up rows would occur at roughly the rate of one per match.

The rows would happen on the field, in the dressing room, all over the place. Yet they always patched up things before Tosh went off to his family. He liked a lager, he loved the buzz around a match and the routine of a football club, with all its opportunity for laughter and bonhomie, but it was never allowed to interfere with his family life. He was strict about that – and also his unwillingness to take too much physical punishment, which could be something of a problem for wingers in those days of brutally callous full-backs. This was especially so when you were playing an away game at Bolton. Of all those rugged full-backs Tommy Banks of the Wanderers probably inhabited more of the nightmares of wingers than any of his rivals. There was an unforgettable occasion when Tosh had a flash of both inspiration and high courage. He rolled the ball between the legs of the formidable Banks, scampered down the wing and crossed perfectly for a goal. Unfortunately Chamberlain didn't have too much time to savour the glory. Before the restart Banks stepped up to Tosh's ear and said, very calmly, 'If thy do that again lad, I'll break thy fucking leg.' Tosh's courage, as it sometimes tended to do, vanished. 'No, you won't, I'm pissing off to the right-wing.' Haynes was not impressed. 'Where do you think you're going?' 'Where do you think? I'm getting as far away from that bastard as I can.'

In a way I suppose that summed us up a bit as a club. We were happy and we had some good days along with the bad but you wouldn't really say that our lives depended on success.

When I read that somebody like Sol Campbell just had to leave Spurs for a winning club like Arsenal, it is still a little bit of a shock to the system. In my day, a player wouldn't have dreamed of saying something like that, and when you think of Tottenham's tradition, and all the great players it has had wearing its colours, Mackay, Blanchflower, Greaves, my tormentor Cliff Jones, the quickest, most combative winger I ever played against, Campbell's defection from White Hart Lane was even more amazing for someone with my background. But of course it is the way it is now – and a way Johnny Haynes could never be.

Haynes's reward for his skills and his loyalty was to become England's first £100-a-week player but if that looks paltry now, he had reason to believe that he was blessed by the greatest of good fortune. Certainly he was lucky in the way that Tommy Trinder and the Fulham board were more or less obliged to lift his wages to that record mark. Just a few days before his team-mate Hill and the Professional Footballers' Association had finally smashed through the maximum wage barrier, AC Milan made a £100,000 bid for Haynes. Trinder said that Haynes simply was not for sale. He was a fabulous player and if the club had the power they would pay him a £100 a week. Suddenly, Fulham had that freedom, however unwanted if the truth be known, and Haynes was on the kind of money that mere tradesmen and factory workers could only dream about. I happen to think Haynes would have had a magnificent career in Italy. His game was so subtle I'm sure it would have thrilled the football cognoscenti. But he had no real yearning for fresh horizons. He had a nice house in Epsom, a good car when most of the population were still travelling by bus and tube, and he was close to his parents. He was an only child and devoted to the lovely couple who had done all they could to give him the best of everything as he grew up in North London. He had made for himself a pleasant, self-contained world in which he was a beloved and somewhat indulged citizen.

His response to his good fortune was generous. Parties in Epsom were frequent and lively. Haynes had his old pals at the club, notably his sparring partner Tosh, and new ones like the man-about-town Bobby Keetch, and though Haynes's first two marriages failed he never showed evidence of a broken heart – especially at those parties which stretched to the dawn and which more than once left me sleeping on the Haynes carpet.

It was at one of those all-nighters that I first met Keetch. He turned up at the club as a centre-half from West Ham. He was an extremely good looking guy with long flowing golden hair and a real presence. Johnny obviously recognised a fellow night owl, and one determined to pursue his relaxation in some style, though with a discretion notably absent in some of today's football stars. Keetchy was, in those days, a rare pro footballer in his liking for some of life's fancier refinements. He dressed in suits of Edwardian cut complete with waistcoat. He talked enthusiastically and knowledgeably about vintage wines, painting, fine furniture – though maybe not always quite so knowledgeably about opera, which I happened to know something about. His cultural instincts declined quite noticeably, however, when he went on the field. He was quick and mean – invaluable qualities in the middle of defence – and when the manager Buckingham moved him on to Queens Park Rangers I was rather surprised – not least for the fact that in an attempt to improve Keetchy's footwork Vic had taken the trouble to provide him with dancing lessons out on the pitch. Always the dashing figure, Vic had led the dancing, but without dramatic effect. Haynes, who had been removed from the captaincy by then, was far from thrilled when his friend Keetch was sold. Buckingham's instinct, I suspect, was to tighten discipline that had been so notoriously lax for so long at Fulham, and sensed that Keetch might not have been the most willing recruit to such a crusade.

That was not the most unreasonable presumption. Bobby would become a much more responsible character when he met his wife Jan – indeed it was a remarkable transformation and made his untimely death a few years ago all the harder to bear for all those of us who loved him for both the man he had grown into and the devil-may-care young tearaway he left behind – but back in the early sixties you wouldn't have fancied him to last too long in one of the more sedate football establishments. His death was a terrible blow to a great crowd of friends from inside and out of the game, who filled the church for his funeral as many had his 'Football, Football' memorabilia restaurant in the Strand. Once I took some of my own mementoes down to the restaurant. I just bunged them into a plastic bag and took them up to town. Bobby was shocked. 'You should have told me you were coming, I would have sent a car – what if somebody nicked the bag?' I said that I felt pretty safe because I was the only one who knew what was in the bag. You could always have a laugh with Bobby.

I remember the dramatic effect he had on me, a blissfully happily young married man, when he rolled up at the team hotel in Italy at the start of an end-of-season tour. Keetch had managed to talk his way out of travelling with the team. He had told the general manager Frank Osborne that he would be visiting a lady friend in France and would drive down to Italy. Somehow he managed to get permission for the arrangement. We knew he had arrived by the screech of brakes and the skid over the pebbles of the hotel driveway when he brought his Lotus Elite to a stop. He presented an enormous image, but it was not that of a professional footballer.

He was wearing a fisherman's sweater frayed at the edges and the first pair of faded washed denims I had ever seen. He was bronzed from the Riviera sun but looked absolutely knackered. He carried a little bag which I hoped contained a few toiletries and I remember Osborne asking, with a slight tremor in his voice, 'Where's your suitcase?' He didn't have one. So we had a whip-round and bought him some clothes. He and I were completely different characters – and he had the little black book to prove it – but I always loved his company and rather admired his style. I certainly liked the way he played football. Despite the wild impression he often created, he was thoughtful and very competitive. He wanted to get something out of life, things that might pass the average footballer by as he travelled to exotic places and never looked much beyond the next hotel lobby. He was a regular member of the card school that Haynes, Jimmy Langley and I automatically formed when we boarded a bus, train or a plane. Surprisingly, he wasn't particularly good at cards but, as he said, no-one could excel at everything.

I suppose part of the difference between Bobby and me was simply a matter of years and environment. I was older and had perhaps been through a slightly tougher school. I was brought up in a small flat with just two bedrooms and that didn't permit too much space in which to misbehave. Bobby demanded – and won – a bit more breathing room. What he had, more than anything, was a desire to be really somebody, if not as a footballer, though he would give that all he had, then maybe as a businessman, an importer, or perhaps an entrepreneur. Until he died Bobby was committed to his quest, as you knew he would be as he packed up his gear and headed off to QPR. Craven Cottage, I always thought, was a poorer place for his departure. The old place could never govern all his dreams, but while he was there he brought great commitment and terrific honesty.

I would, frankly, have liked to have seen a lot more of his attitude in another, younger Fulham player who I thought, when I first saw him work, had enough talent to be a truly great player. He had wonderful, original skill, Rodney Marsh, but he was one of the greatest disappointments I have ever known in football. He could have taken the game by the throat, but instead he played at it.

He was a very confident young fellow. Perhaps, looking back, too confident for his own good. You could hear him all over the place. He said he could play on the right-wing, the left, anywhere you wanted him, and the early evidence was that he was right. I thought to myself, 'Crikey, this kid is phenomenal.' He was a big boy and looked older than his sixteen years. He had a lot of definition in his body, but then it is also true you got the impression that he wasn't training full out. He always seemed to have a lot in hand. His running wasn't so good but he did such marvellous things with the ball.

But for all his superb touch he just couldn't make it with Haynes, and if you didn't make it with Haynes at Fulham, you just didn't make it. Haynes would play good balls into him, but he never got anything back. It seemed that Marsh just wanted to play on his own. So of course he had to go. Vic Buckingham, who loved star players, naturally tried to sort him out, but he saw quickly enough he was wasting his time. It was a terrible shame, everyone felt that. Here was a kid who had all the quality for a terrific career, but it just didn't look as if it was going to happen.

I tried to encourage him in training, you do that with every young player, but I didn't feel I was really getting anywhere. I sensed that this was a kid who was always keeping something back and there was no encouragement to sit him down and try to get to the bottom of it. It felt as though it would almost certainly be a waste of time. Training should be a pleasure and you should give everything you have because you know then, for sure, what you can do on the pitch. I tried to get this over to Rodney, and in a way that didn't suggest I was just leaning on him, trying to kick the cockiness out of him. You don't want to do that because that can be a prime ingredient in the make-up of a great player.

Certainly I never contemplated the action of Gordon Brice, the big centre-half who had given me that little pep talk about the need to go for everything in my debut against Liverpool. During training I questioned the way Brice was doing something and he came back to me and grabbed my shoulder – his big hand felt like a clamp – and said, 'Don't you ever tell me what to do, kid, I was playing this game when you were still in nappies.' Marsh never provoked me into saying anything like that. It was more a case of putting a little wall around himself. Frequently, he would emerge from behind it to do something extraordinary on the training field. He was a great fan of Denis Law and he became famous for emulating some of the great Scot's skills. He had a knack of hitting the cross-bar from the corner flag – a considerable skill by any standards.

After training one day I was sitting in the stand listening to some ground staff boys chattering away. Rodney was one of them. I heard him talking excitedly about the fact that Law had apparently hit a post from the right-wing – with his left foot, and then struck it home before it bounced out of the area. I wanted to go down and tell him that such skill was brilliant, but it was only part of what Denis Law had to offer. Law was a dynamo, a slight little fellow who made himself huge. Rodney was a big, powerful kid who was in danger of going in the other direction.

When he left, like Keetchy for QPR, I did speak to him. I liked the kid and I told him that, but I also said I was very disappointed in him. I said that when I first saw him with the ball at his feet I thought he was heading for the stars, but he had to work a lot harder if he wanted to turn things around. Of course he was a star at QPR. They called him the Sheikh of Shepherd's Bush and eventually Malcolm Allison, who had won a First Division title for Manchester City but wanted to add the flourish of Marsh – and a little glamorous competition for the Georgie Best show across town at Manchester United – moved to sign him. Malcolm later admitted it was a terrible mistake that cost City the title and you heard stories that Rodney had desperate trouble meeting the fitness standards demanded by a very good and highly competitive City side. Rodney did get a run with England as Alf Ramsey's time began to ebb away, but he wasn't really a Ramsey player – no more than other highly gifted contemporaries like Stan Bowles and Peter Osgood. The truth was that Ramsey didn't trust such players. He might, like all of us, be thrilled by their skills, but he wanted more. He need the sustained commitment of players who wanted more than anything to win, and to keep on winning.

Rodney never conveyed that as a priority, and it is a great sadness to me that within the game he acquired the reputation of a dilettante rather than a masterful player. I understood that he had a certain showy streak in his nature, but I hoped that element would dwindle as he developed his skills and learned to inflict them with the discipline of a properly trained professional. Various good football men tried. Certainly Vic Buckingham was ready to celebrate his talent, but the right level of effort was never forthcoming. Rodney had unique skills but too often they were merely ornamental. He didn't respond to the promptings of the old pros who knew a few things he refused to, or could not, absorb. The harsh bottom line was that he was a potentially great player who simply lost the plot.

Allan Clarke, who was signed by Vic Buckingham from Walsall, was not generally well liked and certainly he did not slip naturally into the easy ambience of Craven Cottage. But I liked him a lot and saw in him things that I didn't in Rodney Marsh or, for that matter, Malcom Macdonald, another outstanding young talent who just happened to miraculously appear at Fulham. What it was was a deep ambition. He was a little difficult at times, easily upset, and London wasn't his natural environment. The fact is you can't bring somebody down from the Black Country and expect them to behave as if they grew up in Sloane Square. But though he ruffled quite a few feathers right through his career, I found him to be a good professional who would fight hard for success.

When Don Revie wanted to take him to Leeds, he was reluctant. He said that he liked the Leicester City manager Matt Gillies, and so he turned down Leeds and went to Leicester for a record fee of £150,000. That was typically quirky. I told him that Revie was building a tremendous football empire at Leeds. They had Giles and Bremner and a flock of brilliant young players. Clarke was adamant however. He would move to Leicester.

Twelve months later, with Gillies gone, fired, Clarke finally arrived at Leeds. I was happy for him, felt sure he had arrived in the best environment for his driven nature, and I allowed myself a wry smile. Clarke was a good young pro and I knew he would not waste his time at Elland Road. In fact he became the famous 'Sniffer', a deadly marksman around the goal who formed a superb, if sometimes ruthless, partnership with the hard-working Mick Jones, and inevitably he received the call from Ramsey. Ramsey could relate to Clarke. He could see that behind the brooding, waspish manner there was a fire going on. Of course, like most football men, he had his good times and bad, and his stints as a manager at Leeds and Barnsley, after some promise, ended in disappointment. But of course most managers are putting their heads in a noose the moment they step into the job, and the good thing was that as a player Allan Clarke achieved most of his goals. He was prepared to do the work that was required to get to the top – and then stay there. As for his being unpopular, well, I just don't understand it. I wouldn't, however, because whenever I see him he greets me as though I'm a long-lost uncle.

And while the young players came and went, some flashing a little too brightly, and deceptively, others finding new momentum when they left – Macdonald became a much better player when he moved to Newcastle and then Arsenal, where it became more apparent that it was better to play balls into space for him to run on to than to his feet – there was, of course, always Haynes.

As always the fortunes of Fulham were erratic; we got to another semi-final, against Burnley, but with the same result as before, and though we finished tenth in the First Division one year, there were no illusions that we would not be fighting for our top-flight lives soon enough. Never, though, did we do it more gallantly than in the late winter and spring of 1966. We were five points adrift at the bottom going into the last thirteen games. We beat Shankley's Liverpool 2–0, won 5–2 at Villa Park and 1–0 at Elland Road, where Bremner was sent off. Vic Buckingham was hailed as the Great Houdini of football, but he was the first to admit that a crucial role had been played by his new coach Sexton. I was just one of the players who flourished under Sexton; he was brilliant, intense and deeply knowledgeable.

It was sad, though, that by that time both Dugald Livingstone and Bedford Jezzard had both left Fulham – and football. Jezzard's parting was particularly jarring. He was a man who earned great respect, in the dressing room and on the terraces, but he left the club with a disgusted sense that after giving the best of himself, both as a player and a manager, he had been betrayed in the boardroom. It was, I'm afraid, a fairly familiar story in football, and one that we still hear today. Beddy eventually left after pondering through much of 1964 why Mullery had been sold to Spurs above his head. In fact it was Haynes, to whom Mullery had whispered the news in the dressing room before a match, who passed the word on to Jezzard. He demanded an explanation from the board and they told him it was business. He said they could stick their business.

Jezzard didn't need Fulham, or football. His family were in the pub business and he went into catering. He never looked back at the sport into which he brought a lot of passion – and great honesty. He saw beyond the sentimentality of football in the end. He saw its random cruelty, and how it used up the dreams and the best efforts of grown men who found themselves trapped in the allure of a boy's game.

Livingstone had grown old in the game and the tormentingly close run thing at Villa Park, and the anti-climax at Highbury, persuaded him that it was time to go. When things went wrong he used to say, 'Don't worry, boys, it will come right next time.' But the man who was fired after winning the FA Cup for Newcastle decided there would be no more next times for him. I thanked him for everything he had done for me, how he had so carefully evaluated my ability, and made sure that I had every means of fulfilling my potential. I couldn't have asked for any more from my first manager.

The truth was that I understood that all of them, Livingstone, Jezzard, Buckingham, Robson and Bill Dodgin Junior in so many ways faced an impossible, if not unique task.

They ran a famously relaxed 'family club' for a boardroom which enjoyed that reputation but which was as keen as any other set of directors for a winning team, and of course winning teams require money and investment and a lot of nerve when a bigger club comes in for a key player like Mullery. Jezzard saw the futility of his task when Mullery was sold to cover a debt that represented not even half his value in the transfer market.

When the news broke, I took the firing of Buckingham hard because I thought that if anyone could create a competitive culture at Fulham it was him, and this was particularly so after his appointment of Sexton. I played my best football under that regime and in 1967 came in second behind Bobby Charlton in the voting for Footballer of the Year. Vic was considered arrogant by some senior players, but I always felt this had something to do with his unwillingness to tolerate the old view of Fulham as a glorified comfort zone for players of talent who really could have offered more if they had taken a good look at themselves. Buckingham tried to change the mentality of the club in a big way. He was appalled when the famous Billy Wright, captain of Wolves and England and manager of Arsenal, refused to use the visitors' dressing room at Craven Cottage, saying it was unhygienic.

Buckingham apparently went berserk in the boardroom over the issue and the building workers came in within days. He couldn't tolerate people that he believed just didn't measure up. He no doubt also made himself a lot of enemies when he picked a fight with Haynes and did the unthinkable, dropping him and taking away the captaincy. He obviously had a huge regard for Haynes's talent but he got it into his head that he wasn't really doing it for him. I tried to convince him that he was wrong, saying that in my opinion Haynes pulled his guts out every match. But if Vic formed an opinion you just couldn't shake it out of him.

So, inevitably, he began to isolate himself and when Sexton, who supplied the driving intelligence and passion in the 'Great Escape' moved on to Arsenal, Buckingham found himself on an irreversible slide. His contract was not renewed as Fulham plunged towards the Second Division, and in retrospect it is hard to believe that he really ever had much of a chance – his nature and Fulham's were, in the end, just too far apart.

Bobby Robson, who would have so much success at every level of the game as both a player and a manager, was also doomed. He lasted just ten months, failing both to check the slide towards Division Two, which he inherited from Buckingham, and prevent another one which would leave the club in the third. He was extremely bitter when he left, complaining that a club he loved had fallen into the hands of Eric Miller, a controversial businessman and property developer whose motives Robson openly questioned. He also said that he had lacked support from senior players, but I have to say he never confided such worries to me. I was always there – and I can say that I was always playing to my limits.

Haynes took over briefly as player-manager, but though the board pressed him hard, he was emphatic that he had no taste for the job, and was happy to step down in favour of Bill Dodgin Junior. Haynes said that it was hard enough imposing his values on the field once or twice a week. But he couldn't do it day-in, day-out. It was true that sometimes Haynes had a short fuse when dealing with players who he felt had slipped below acceptable professional levels.

For example neither of the two ambitious youngsters, Clarke and Macdonald, had much to say for their relationships with the great player when they left Craven Cottage. Clarke said, 'We didn't always get on, and it may have been as much my refusal to bow to his fame and reputation as anything else. Perhaps to him I was a young upstart too ready to open my mouth with so many experienced players around. On the other hand, Johnny was in my eyes too impatient and not only refused to suffer fools gladly, but also declined to suffer the human mistakes of any player very gladly.'

Macdonald had similar complaints, but to his credit he recognised in Haynes a searcher after excellence which sometimes some of his team-mates simply couldn't match, neither in talent or the seriousness of their application. Macdonald said, 'It was the beginning of the end for me at Fulham when Johnny was appointed caretaker manager. Haynes loathed me and at the time the feeling was mutual. Haynes was the King of Fulham. He wielded more power than anyone at the club except Tommy Trinder. He was renowned for impatience at the shortcomings of other players and no-one experienced this side of the man more than I did. I was hopeless then. I could score goals, but as far as other aspects of the game were concerned I was so bloody naive it wasn't true. I now understand Haynes much better, and have a lot of sympathy for him. I still think he said and did some rotten things to me, but I did react to them – and they did make me a better player.'

In me there is absolutely no ambivalence about Johnny Haynes. He never demanded from a team-mate any effort that he wasn't prepared to put in himself. Others may have seen an ego. What I saw was a relentless need to deliver the best he had, and so when I left with my injury to try to make a new life outside of football, it was a great sadness to leave Haynes, the peerless Haynes now in his mid-thirties, having to bed down into the mediocrity of the Second Division.

There was just one escape route for him but it was blocked by Trinder. Spurs came in with a bid that would have enlivened the last hurrah of a great player – and put him in the company of another who had known his disappointments. Jimmy Greaves was drawing close to the end of his magnificent reign at White Hart Lane, and together they might have given football a few poignant glimpses of what might have happened if, in the prime of their days, Haynes and Greaves had become a regular working partnership. It was still a mouth-watering prospect and I urged Haynes to talk to the board and tell them that he wanted, after all the years on the Fulham helter-skelter, a challenge that might freshen his last days in the game. Haynes was intrigued by the thought. He said to me, 'Do you really think it would work? Do you think they would let me go?' I did, but they wouldn't. They had one of the greatest players who ever lived finally a prisoner of a romance he had done so much to create. He shrugged his shoulders and played on for a little while, before moving to South Africa. His last hurrah therefore ended up far from the little ground by the Thames he had entranced for so long. But he did find some happiness. After two failed marriages, he returned from Durban and got together again with a girlfriend of his youth, Avril. She is a lovely girl and I was happy for that. He had spent a professional lifetime giving pleasure and finding it for himself hadn't been quite so easy. It is sometimes like that when you spend your life looking for perfection.

Daphne and me at our engagement party in the Red Lion. My mum and dad are on the left and Daphne's are on the right.

I obviously didn't disgrace myself at the Red Lion. Our wedding, 1962. Over 40 years later and we are still just as happy. In my darkest moments, it has always been Daphne who has provided the most compelling reason to fight to live.

My mother and brother Peter in 1966. I wonder who Mum is supporting?

With Daphne and the boys (Andrew and Anthony) in 1967.

Three heroes heading to the emotional 1958 FA Cup semi-final against Manchester United. L-r Johnny Haynes, England's first £100-a-week player and a footballing genius; Jimmy Hill, whose passion and determined fight against the injustices within football made the game better for everyone; Roy Bentley, my first footballing hero, who guided me so marvellously through the thickets of the game and who is still a wonderful companion.

Typical 6os line-up. Back row, l-r: Langley, Robson, Keetch, Macedo, Me, Callaghan. Front row, l-r: Key, Metchick, Marsh, Haynes, O'Connell.

Guarding a post against the 'Lawman' Denis Law. Standing room only at The Cottage demonstrating the immense popularity of the game then and how right Jimmy Hill was to fight for players' rights.

Over page: Johnny Haynes (l), the idol of the terraces and one of the greatest players ever to lace up a pair of boots, congratulates the young Allan Clark on a goal.

October 1966:
in full flow,
concentrating
hard on the ball.

Presentation to me after the World Cup by the Fulham directors.
L-r De Amato, Trinder, Walsh and Tony Dean.

Over page: the inscription reads: 'George, "late as usual",
warmest regards, Geoff Hurst.'

CHAPTER SIX

'YOU'RE SEMI-RETIRED, AREN'T YOU?'

Johnny Haynes took a roundabout route to happiness. I came upon mine a little more directly. She was called Daphne and she was sitting in the picturesque Cottage Stand. I thought she was rather picturesque herself. We were nineteen years old.

She had been brought to the match by Angela Craggs, the wife of one my club-mates, Ken, who never established himself in the first team but proved to be a brilliant scout. Angela and Daphne worked together in the Millbank building in London for a travel agency serving ICI. Angela was telling Daphne about Ken's life as a footballer and wondered if she might like to see a match. Daphne was a Sunday School teacher from Southgate and she wasn't sure it would really be for her – all that shouting and possibly questionable language. But Angela insisted that Fulham was a bit different. You could sit in the Cottage Stand and watch the world go by. You could look out and see the flow of the Thames.

Daphne was persuaded. So when I walked up to the Cottage, where directors and guests and players used to congregate after the game, she was there. I was introduced to her – and instantly smitten. I was usually quick to make a joke but not on this occasion. It didn't help that I got the impression she hadn't been smitten with me. I wasn't exactly a ladies man and – my romantic training was limited. My older brother Len had taught me a lot – how to ride a bike, use a knife and fork and even how to dress – but none of it seemed particularly useful at this moment. But Daphne had made a very big impression on me indeed and I got up the nerve to ask Ken to get me her telephone number. Then I got up more nerve to make the call. I asked her if she would like to see a show, and she said, 'Yes, George, of course,' which was very gratifying. I took her to see the Crazy Gang at the Victoria Palace. It was one of their farewell performances. Like Frank Sinatra, they staged one every few years.

I had been up around Victoria on jaunts with Dennie Mancini and I knew a nice little restaurant near the theatre. It must have been a decent restaurant because the TV celebrity Lord Boothby was there. He appeared to be sucking up lamb chops. It wasn't the most romantic start to the evening. Nor did it help when later, up on the stage, Chesney Allen asked Bud Flanagan what he was going to do when he retired. Flanagan said he was going to open a betting shop or a butcher's shop or another kind of shop and then burst out laughing. Daphne, being a good Sunday School teacher, nudged me and asked, 'What does he mean?' I said, 'Well, a knocking shop.' Naturally she then asked, 'What's a knocking shop?' I was thinking, well, I'm from Fulham and she's from

Southgate, and this might be a little difficult. But, anyway, I had to explain the term knocking shop. She was most unimpressed.

Naturally, I was a little bit fraught. We were not yet at the holding hands stage. I took her all the way to Southgate on the Piccadilly Line, and saw her to her door and said goodnight. Of course my last train to West Kensington had gone. So I got a taxi from Park Grove. The driver said it would be £3 and demanded the money up front because he didn't believe a kid like me would be carrying such an amount. On our next date I joked that we had to get married because I couldn't afford to keep taking her home.

Daphne would never learn much about the intricacies of football, though she always seemed to know whether I had played well or not. She was not fascinated by football tactics but early in our courtship she admitted to being a little intrigued by some aspects of my working life. 'What,' she asked, 'do you do when you are not running around the field?'

I gave her my routine. I woke up in plenty of time to get a little breakfast and be at the ground for 9am. I would then change and chat with my team-mates before going out to training around 9.30. We would train until lunch-time, then go back again until around 4pm. Usually, I was home by 4.30. I would then go to bed for a couple of hours before calling my good friend Dennie. We would then arrange to go off to the cinema or perhaps a restaurant. There was, however, one unbending rule. I had to be back home for bedtime at 11pm. She absorbed this information, looked quite thoughtful for a second or two and said, 'You're semi-retired, aren't you?' I'd never really thought of it like that.

Three years later we moved into 88 Rhodrons Road, Chessington, as Mr and Mrs George Cohen. We had a back garden that ran 200 feet. It was a jungle but it had apple trees, and I thought, 'My God, we own an orchard.' You could wake up at 5am in complete silence. There were no trucks rolling down the North End Road, the churning thoroughfare which runs from Hammersmith to Chelsea. You could hear a dawn chorus unimpaired by coughs. I was so happy I wouldn't have called the King my cousin. I had lived most of my life in a flat, albeit a nice one with well kept gardens, but this was something beyond my experience. Like most young couples settling in we had a few teething problems. When I cleared the jungle and made a bonfire I set it too close to the wall of the garage and narrowly avoided burning down the house. Daphne's first meal when I returned from training was not the greatest success. The chops were fine but the apple crumble refused to crumble. I chewed away, patiently, and did not complain. I was in love, and I'm happy to say it would prove a permanent condition that, because of all the qualities my wife brought to our marriage, proved capable of withstanding even the most terrible pressures.

As in most lives, quite a bit of rain would fall into mine in between the bouts of sunshine, but Daphne would always be there to pick me up and set me going again, and then, when I needed the most compelling of reasons to fight to live, she provided the ultimate one.

Back then in 1962, however, everything was before us as I

contemplated my good fortune on landing amid the suburban glory of Rhodrons Road. For Daphne it wasn't such a change of lifestyle. She had lived in a more polite society than the one I had known, and she came down to Surrey from one of the more salubrious corners of North London quite happily. She understood and shared my excitement at setting up house in this new, serene world – and the pride I took in my evening inspection of the 'orchard' and the lawn on to which a zealous janitor could no longer suddenly appear to bark out my marching orders.

Right from the start she made it clear she put a high emphasis on family life. Her father had served in the Eighth Army. She described how it was when she saw him for the first time at the age of six after responding to his knock on the door. She recognised him from the photographs he had sent from North Africa and Italy, and she remembered so well yelling, 'You're my daddy.' I'm always touched when I hear that story. It makes me wonder how many times that scene was enacted in all kinds of homes up and down the country – and how many thousands of homes didn't hear that knock on the door?

It is amazing to think of how many were separated from their loved ones for so long, and also that if the Americans hadn't dropped the atomic bombs on Japan the Eighth Army would have been expected to head for the Far East after slogging through Africa and a big slice of Europe. There might have been a riot if that order had come through. Daphne strived hard with me to lay down solid foundations of family life, and she worked on after the birth of our first son Andrew, finally becoming a full-time housewife and mother when Anthony came along a few years later. When Anthony arrived I was earning, with my England money, the best part of a £100 a week, which was way beyond the national average. But before that we were getting along well enough. We could cover the mortgage and still buy a shining new Vauxhall Viva, which cost us £599 and was parked proudly on the drive and polished quite religiously every night. We never had enough to go mad – there was no *OK* magazine then and footballers weren't so fashionable or sexy that anyone would pay big money to photograph their weddings or christenings. However, if you asked nicely, the local paper would send you a copy of the relevant edition.

I paid £4,000 for my house in Chessington, £1,000 down and mortgage payments of £22.15 shillings a month. I was quite a formidable saver and I think my new wife was impressed by the way I had salted away what was left of the money I hadn't lashed out on taxi rides across London.

There was one drawback for Daphne, though, in our first few months in Chessington. She didn't enjoy the commute up to London and decided she would look for a job locally. She found that easy enough as a graduate of Pitman's Secretarial College and landed work at a detective agency in Kingston. This proved something of an eye-opener for me and, ultimately, much more so for Daphne. When she first told me about the new job I thought, 'This is something, a girl who not so long ago didn't know about the existence of knocking shops is going to work for the local Philip Marlowe.'

In fact it was a big operation staffed by lawyers and former policeman.

As Daphne worked as a secretary, and didn't have to track down misbehaving husbands or embezzling treasurers or perform late-night stake-outs, I was a little surprised to take a telephone call from the boss of her firm after she had been working there for just a few months. He invited us around to dinner at his big house in Worcester Park. The couple were charming and after an excellent meal Daphne's boss said to me, 'George, would you join me in my study, please.' I thought this was rather odd, especially when he started talking about what an excellent secretary Daphne was, and that he was anxious to widen her responsibilities. I suggested he should be talking to Daphne about this, but he said no, there was an aspect of the situation he wanted to discuss with me first.

He said his wife had been documenting the more difficult cases but that she wanted to scale down her role in the company. She thought Daphne would be a perfect replacement but, well, there might a problem. 'For example she would have to prepare reports like this,' he said as he handed me a file. 'You better read it.' *Lady Chatterley's Lover* had recently been published but it had nothing on this. There was a photograph of one of the least handsome men I had ever seen, who nevertheless had been visiting practically a whole block of housewives while their husbands were at work.

From the descriptions of some of the things he had been getting up to he was in a position, if you will excuse the expression, to write his own version of the *Kama Sutra*.

Would Daphne be prepared to work on such material? I

said she was twenty-three years old, very bright and had a mind of her own, he had better ask her.

She took away the report and read it and afterwards she was subdued for quite a while. Not so long ago she had been a Sunday School teacher and now she was reading about what happens out in the world, and the things people do, including putting plastic bags over their heads, to get their kicks. She said she wasn't sure she could do the job; some of it would obviously be very nasty and troubling. I said that if she felt she couldn't do it she should say so. But in the end she decided she would give it a try, she liked her office and the people she worked with, and she got used to dealing with the seamier side of life that no-one had told her about at Pitman's Secretarial College. She became very good at her job and might still be doing it if Andrew and then Anthony hadn't happened. She then had the enduring challenge of her life, bringing up her sons, with a little help from me, in a way that has always filled me with pride.

So things were generally going well in my corner of Chessington but, inevitably, there were some dark moments. My father, the most fastidious of gas fitters, who so lovingly installed our central heating, died two years after our marriage, and though he would not see my finest hour as a footballer, I know he was happy that I had made something of a name for myself, had found a lovely young wife, and was set up in a way he couldn't have imagined as he worked his overtime in the human warrens around Olympia.

My life in football had been a wonder to him — and a banishment of all those fears he had nursed when my mother argued strenuously that, for a little while at least, I had to give the game everything I had. Part of my father's relief, and the big reason for my well-being, was the winning campaign of my team-mate Jimmy Hill as the impassioned and inspired chairman of the Professional Footballers' Association.

He showed the nerve and the imagination and the sense of purpose that beat down the establishment of football; he took the game to the brink of a strike, but his arguments were so strong, and his use of publicity so brilliant, that the old guard led by Alan Hardaker, the tough old ex-Navy man who as secretary ran the Football League as if it was his personal fiefdom, simply ran out of threats and bombast. Jimmy took on the businessman and professionals, and famous comedians, who believed they could indefinitely keep down the footballers who filled the stadiums but received such a small percentage of the income.

Not so long ago I heard Alan Hansen having a serious go at Hill on the television. I don't remember quite what provoked the argument, and of course I realised TV pundits are supposed to liven things up a bit, but there was something in Hansen's tone which rather shocked me. Here was a famous former player, far more distinguished in his achievements on the field than my old team-mate, expressing something which seemed pretty close to contempt. I thought there was a shortfall in respect and I also wondered if Hansen quite grasped how much he and his generation had benefited from the passion and the sheer brightness of this man who was now being spoken to as if he didn't really know a lot of what he was talking about.

Now I know that Jimmy Hill can be exasperating and contentious, that he can fly away with the latest idea that has jumped into his head. But I also know the value of Hill, I know the depth of his feelings for the game, and I know what he did to change it for the better. He took the trouble to fight and I will never forget that. I was there when he did it and I'm not sure that there was anyone around at the time who was capable of beginning to match his performance. No doubt the football dinosaurs would have been brought down eventually, but how long would it have taken, how many young men would have been denied rights that were accepted as a matter of course in almost every other walk of life?

Hill seized the moment and accelerated the process quite dramatically. He was willing to put himself out. I switched off the TV with some irritation – and I thought about Hill, who could be so many different things: outrageous, preposterous, ambitious, irritating, but with a mind that was always on the move, and plenty of guts.

I remembered the buzz of excitement when he came into the dressing room that morning in 1961 at Craven Cottage and said that the wages ceiling had been smashed – to what extent he was still not sure, but he knew that Hardaker and his pals had buckled and were about to crack.

He said, 'I think we will get up to £50 – the £20 a week maximum is dead.' But within two weeks the ceiling had collapsed. John Haynes got his £100 and, after talking to Jimmy, I went into the general manager Frank Osborne's office and demanded £50 a week.

Osborne was a wily old guy who knew his way around

football and had seen a lot of things, but he was stunned when I made my request. He came back with an offer £40, which was a staggering amount of money at that time. I had been a first team regular for three years, I was on the ladder of the England team with appearances in the Under-23 team, but my earnings had stopped at £20. Of course I did get a bonus. It was £1 for a win.

It's astonishing to me when I think about it now. I think of the huge crowds – we got 42,000 for a home game with Bristol Rovers on that run to the semi-final game with Manchester United – but we got £1 extra for a win and were told that we couldn't change our employers without their permission, we couldn't get more than a certain amount of money each week, and that we should behave ourselves. It wasn't even bloody legal, for heaven's sake. This was a fact which was established quickly enough when George Eastham, backed by the PFA, went to court and won the agreement of a judge that footballers had the same rights under the law as any other workers in a free society.

Illegal it certainly was – and immoral quite definitely. That was abundantly clear when you realise that a brilliant player like Wilf Mannion could play for England in front of 120,000 at Hampden Park and then come home sitting on his cardboard suitcase in the corridor of a third class train carriage, or that the young genius Stanley Matthews had to wait at the bus-stop as the club directors drove by.

But it was Hill who had the nerve and the fight to act upon this knowledge. Cliff Lloyd, the players' craggy, knowing old union secretary who had been battling for so long against Hardaker's reactionary forces, knew straight away that the players had found a real champion. Lloyd was an ex-player and quite a hard case himself. He fought these tremendous battles with Hardaker, and sometimes apparently he wearied of the job of imposing fairness and logic into their arguments. When Jimmy came along, Lloyd had the suspicion that Hardaker, for all his bluster, might have found himself a little more than a match. Lloyd was certainly confident that Hill could win the battle with the man who was fighting so hard to keep the players in their places. Lloyd, reviewing Hardaker's style and tactics, told a colleague, 'That bastard belongs to Jim.'

Hill got hold of the players and nagged them out of the ignorance trap – and the 'Slave Row' mentality. We really didn't have much of an idea about anything. We lived in a dream factory. We played football and we loved to do so. We were happy in a very insecure kind of way. Someone might say to a player with a grievance, 'Go to a solicitor,' and he would think, 'Jesus Christ, I'm a footballer – footballers don't go to solicitors. Footballers play football, doff their caps, and say, "Thank you very much, sir."' Footballers didn't look up at the packed terraces filled with all the swaying and cheering supporters and wonder where the hell all the money was going. They didn't really grasp, even though some of them had fought in wars, that they had been condemned to membership of an inferior class. They didn't look around and see that in the minds of the directors they were not a whole lot better than the fans who, up north particularly, were often crowded into the most appalling conditions.

But Jimmy Hill, who got the thick end of Alan Hansen's tongue, made them look and think and fight. He wasn't an Arthur Scargill. Though he could get very angry, he didn't want to break football. What he saw in the threat of a strike was, at last, a real chance to make the League chiefs think seriously about the issue. Until then, the Hardaker gang thought they could always keep the players at arm's length. It was a master–servant way of thinking. Certainly I didn't have a problem with the possibility of a strike. I remember that as a schoolboy I had read that fifty million watched English football in 1950. They got 100,000 at Wembley for amateur cup finals between teams like Bishop Auckland and Pegasus, and some of those 'amateur' players, with their 'boot' money, were earning more than the big stars in the Football League. Sixty thousand crowds were routine at places like Anfield.

Hill didn't want to stop the game even for just a few weeks. That would mean he couldn't play. He couldn't go chasing around the field, laying the law down, disputing every decision, and never getting discouraged when the ball didn't run his way, which quite often it didn't. He warned us that morning in the dressing room: 'Look, the money isn't just going to start tumbling down on us. We have to negotiate. Some clubs might struggle to keep everyone happy. But what it means is that we have some basic rights. They can pay us money we think we're due, or at least something a lot closer to it.' At the same time George Eastham was having his own fight to leave Newcastle for Arsenal. He went to court, with the help of his friend Ernie Clay, a northern businessman who would later try his hand at guiding Fulham, and when he told a judge about the terms of his contract, how he had no option but to play in one place and await the discretion of his bosses, it was agreed that this was indeed a form of employment that had a big element of slave labour. Football was being dragged into the twentieth century. It could no longer own a player's body and soul; it could no longer easily assume the dictatorial powers that were applied to Charlie Mitten, the fine Manchester United player, who broke his contract at Old Trafford and went off to play in Bogota for a wage he considered much fairer than the one he was receiving in England. Mitten was banned for six months when he returned from South America. It was one of the most dramatic examples of football imposing restraints on players' freedom with powers it had granted itself without any references.

Hansen's scathing dismissal of the man who had confronted these injustices so strongly made me angry – and may well have hurt Hill, who beneath the extrovert personality has always been a man of some sensitivity. But I knew that as long as he lived Jimmy Hill would have the capacity to take a few blows – and bounce back. His greatest asset, apart from the extraordinary knack of being able to fill his mouth with mashed potato and carry on talking without spitting out a morsel, is his energy. He displayed it both on and off the field. Once I saw him digging a hole on an Italian beach, which seemed an odd activity for an adult on such a hot day. He explained that he was doing it for his pregnant wife Gloria. This way she could lie face down and tan her back without any discomfort. On the same trip, which had been arranged at the time of the Italian centenary celebrations, we were in Florence at the height of the festivities. Part of the programme was a series of matches between various districts of the city played out in the shadow of the castle. They put two big nets up at either end of the square, which they covered in sand. We were asked to dress up in costumes from the fifteenth century, which was a bit embarrassing for some of us, but of course not Jimmy. He strode out into the square in all his finery, the chin with its nobleman's beard thrusting out proudly. Rampaging 'Rabbi' of Craven Cottage, union agitator, transforming manager and architect of Coventry City, the trend-setting First Division club, TV personality, now he had another role. Of course he threw himself into it.

It had been a rare day at the Cottage when Hill didn't have some new scheme buzzing away. As long as he was involved in football his commitment would be fierce. He was friendly with Walter Winterbottom, the England manager, and got involved in coaching courses at Arsenal's ground, and he was always saying that young players needed a lot more help on and off the field. But for all his devotion to football he was aware that there were other things in life. He made a few moves into the property market, which I gathered were not so successful, but he took those blows in his stride. Sometimes he suggested we get involved in some business plan or another, but I rather ran for cover. I wasn't so bold back then. I set myself on a steadier and (I liked to think) less risky course.

Of course life always imposes its own risks, but the difference in Jimmy Hill was that while most of us tend to try to duck away, he embraced them.

I first knew him in 1954 when I arrived at the Cottage as a ground staff boy. He had signed from Brentford two years earlier, apparently breezing in full of ideas and telling the club that he would always be happy to be put on coaching sessions. Unfortunately, the old guard tended to suspect his motives, saw someone who was maybe more interested in self-advancement than the general good. But this reaction was always something of a mystery for me. He was a lively guy and he always tried to help someone if they were in some kind of corner. I didn't see a hint of anything destructive in his nature.

He did however have a rather turbulent personal life. While Daphne and I were setting up the foundations of our life together in Chessington, Jimmy was faltering in the first of several marriages. I can't remember the first time I met him. He just always seemed to be there, and he always had time for me. I never understood why, but it may have had something to do with the fact than unlike some of the others I was always eager to listen to what he had to say, which was quite a lot. As a tongue-tied and extremely impressionable seventeen-year-old, I fell in love with his first wife Gloria. Like Jimmy, she always had a word and a smile for me. She was a very good-looking lady – and very talented. She had a lovely voice and was a tremendous pianist. I was sad when they parted, and I thought at the time that he was a little mad, but then when you live at his pace, and attack so many things on so many fronts, I suppose sometimes something gives.

It has to be said that as a player Jimmy was never more

than a journeyman but his redemption was that he knew it. He always tried to do the right thing on the field. He never tired of supporting team-mates when they had the ball, he never shirked a tackle and was always looking for a bit of free space with that intensity which persuaded the fan that I should 'pass it to the Rabbi'. Because he tried so many things on the field, as he did off it, he accepted a much higher failure rate than most of his team-mates. It was typical of him that after suffering some lean times as a right-half he elected himself to the role of inside-forward and though again he had his off days, he did score plenty of goals.

Johnny Haynes used to laugh about the time Hill was having a particularly bad day and was attracting more than his usual ration of boos. He went up to Haynes and said, 'It's terrible the way the crowd is booing – it's really going to hit the confidence of the younger players.' He simply had no idea that he was the sole target of the barracking. But then maybe he did have an inkling and decided to dismiss the idea as just too improbable.

Inevitably he led a revolt against the chairman's regular use of the team as key material for his comedy act. Perhaps we were guilty of a little over-reaction, but when you're doing your best, and feeling that sometimes you are fighting fairly heavy odds, it can be more than a little demoralising when your boss is constantly putting you down by way of entertaining the nation. Jimmy and Trinder had quite a serious set-to, which is another indicator of Hill's willingness to put himself on the line for his team-mates. He told Trinder that the constant routine of mockery was not particularly helpful when you're trying to fight away from the bottom of the table and at the same time wondering if the board will ever make a move to strengthen the team.

A few of the boys complained one Monday morning about the chairman's comments that had been reported over the weekend and Hill said, 'Right, I'll have him.' He angered Trinder by asking the basic question, 'Where is all the money going?' and then adding, 'It certainly isn't going on the team – or the ground.' He gave Trinder a lecture on the realities of football, he told him that sooner or later you have to face up to the facts. Maybe you can get lucky for a while. You can bring on a few youngsters and if you have enough older players of the right type of character and ability, you can get by for a while. You can even make the occasional splash which excites the ambitions and hopes of the fans. But it is not a formula for long-term success. You just can't get enough good young kids to keep you going indefinitely because the failure rate is high and the competition for them was getting more intense. In this sense Trinder was compounding an injury, said Hill, and would he please desist. Trinder was getting a cheap laugh – and, in terms of investment in First Division status, a cheap football club.

Even then Hill was engaging the basic issues of football, the need to bring on young players in a more thoughtful way, and the development of clubs. He put some of his ideas to work quite brilliantly when he transformed Coventry City. He left there when the chairman Derek Robbins refused to give him a ten-year contract. Jimmy knew what he had done for the club, and knew that keeping Coventry at the top would be a hazardous job. He felt he deserved security if he was going to tackle it, and I imagine his old confrontations with Tommy Trinder played powerfully through his mind when he made his stand. Many years later, he would fight off the bailiffs as they circled around Craven Cottage, keeping the show going with the help of another old Fulham player, the right back Tom Wilson. The hand-over to the current owner Al-Fayed wasn't so amicable, but I've never delved into the details. What I didn't know wasn't going to worry me. What I do know is that when the life of Fulham was in jeopardy, a man who hadn't always been treated as a hero at the club, indeed had often been cast as villain, and not least on the terraces, was one of the first to respond to the crisis. Knowing him, it shouldn't have been much of a surprise, but it was still impressive.

Eight years on from Al-Fayed's first intervention in the affairs of Fulham there is still a groundswell of doubt about his motives, but for someone like me, who played for just this one club, and for whom it became such an integral part of my life and the foundation of all my success, I can only see him as a kind of saviour. A controversial, enigmatic one, no doubt; somebody who says and does what he likes without considering too heavily the possibility of resulting mayhem, maybe, but there is no question that the old club's future was in extreme jeopardy before he drove down the river and draped himself in a black and white scarf.

The solution to the stadium crisis after the return from Queens Park Rangers' Loftus Road remains problematical. The Cottage has been refurbished and is a much brighter place to be, but the reality is that a capacity of 23,000 is still at least five thousand short of what the club needs, assuming that it maintains Premiership football, for a healthy financial future. There are various estimates of Al-Fayed's investment in Fulham, but a guess of £100 million doesn't seem unreasonable. What many of his critics in the stands have to consider is the possible alternative to the Fayed regime. It might just have been oblivion.

What we've had in its place has been, heaven knows, fairly tumultuous — Kevin Keegan's defection to England, the sad and litigious end to the reign by Jean Tigana which was filled for a while with high promise and some fine football, and now the battle for Premiership survival. But then however fraught at times, it has been comfortably superior to all of the other options that were in place when Al-Fayed said he was willing to become involved.

It seemed in the end that Tigana had to go, and this was quite apart from the issue of his £11 million signing of compatriot Steve Marlet. There was clear evidence that Tigana, whose own cultured playing career was nicely reflected in some of the team's more fluent performances, had lost the dressing room, and when that happens there is only one end to the story. Whatever the details of the Marlet saga, there was no doubt an £11 million fee was excessive. This is not to say he was a bad player; indeed, there were times when he produced some excellent performances, but I always thought £11 million was an extraordinary valuation for a player who did things well but rarely supremely so.

The truth is Al-Fayed bankrolled a stream of expensive

signings and with the striking exception of Louis Saha, a player of great class and potentially high achievement who Manchester United have yet to see the best of, it was clear enough most of them were overpriced. Plainly Al-Fayed, who let's not forget long ago proved himself a rather good retailer, reached the point where he had to ask, 'Wait a minute, am I really getting value for money here?' The short answer is that he was not.

The 2004–5 season was one of struggle but it has to be said that Chris Coleman dealt with his problems with a certain toughness and nerve. Sometimes in football one injury is quite pivotal; its effect goes beyond the loss of one accomplished player. This was the case in the long term injury of the fine defender Alain Goma.

He is a centre back of great presence and good vision, and before an injury which all but took him out of the game from October 2004 until the following February, he was confirming, and now continues to I'm delighted to say, the assessment given to me by Jack Charlton before the Frenchman moved down from Newcastle. Jack said, 'If he stays free of injury, he'll do a hell of a job.' You have to wonder how many managers might reasonably have that sentence emblazoned across their football headstones. Goma has that precious ability to hold a defence together however intense the pressure. He has a good heart and a good head, and both assets were sorely missed as Coleman and his team were fighting in the middle of the season to avoid dropping into the relegation zone.

As the season wore on, an old truth surfaced once again. It

is that the manager's biggest challenge is to maintain a healthy level of confidence in the dressing room. For Al-Fayed there was another inevitable reflection. His expensive investment in name players was at times beginning to look like so much wasted money. For him, like everyone else running Premiership football, the greatest challenge of all is to prepare for a time when the largesse of TV money might, for one reason or another, be withdrawn, or at least sharply reduced. Then the economy of Fulham and so many other clubs will be in extreme peril. The fear must be of a devastating financial drain, something far more dramatic and life-changing that what is beginning to develop at this point. Fulham are a classic example of a club who have gone to the edge in fighting for top-flight football, have spent a lot of money improving their historic ground but at the same time have acknowledged the need to find a new piece of ground where they can build a bigger stadium.

For me the imperative is much greater investment in time, money and organisation in the development of young players. This, I'm convinced, will soon enough be the point of separation between clubs who have anticipated the future, seen its potential for ambush, and made their plans accordingly, and those who keep desperately forking out big money for players of questionable talent and character.

Meanwhile, as a committed Fulham man whose life for so long revolved around the passions and the warmth of Craven Cottage, I can only celebrate the fact that the worst fate has so far been avoided.

Al-Fayed may not be the easiest man to understand; he

can be volatile, angry and bitter, but it shouldn't be forgotten that he brought down from Knightsbridge something more than quick profit and a lot of easy publicity. Maybe somewhere along the road the profit will come along with the publicity, but anyone who cares for the future of the club which touched so many hearts, and represented for so long so much of what was best and most charming in football, is bound to have a degree of respect – and gratitude. Hero or villain, there is no doubt Al-Fayed brought the kiss of extended life.

In the old days some of Jimmy Hill's Fulham team-mates thought he had too many crackpot ideas, and that generally he had too much to say for himself. But they couldn't hold him down – and he didn't hold grudges. Nor, in my opinion, was he too bad a TV pundit. Sometimes he went out on a limb. Sometimes he said things which didn't seem entirely logical. But he was always nagging away at what he considered wrong in the game, and how it suffered too much at the hands of people who were in it for reasons other than a simple passion for football for its own sake. The Rabbi had always been prepared to lead from the front, and I thought that Alan Hansen might just have reflected on a little of that before he launched his withering attack. As far as I was concerned, Jimmy Hill was good for the game and was somebody I am glad to call a friend. Certainly there is no doubt in my mind that football would have been a much worse place if he hadn't come along.

For the record, Daphne heartily agreed. When I told her that Jimmy Hill had won a great battle of principle, how he had led the footballers of England out of their chains, and that I had just received a 100 per cent wage rise, she said, 'George that is wonderful. I've just seen a lovely dress by Louis Feraud.'

CHAPTER SEVEN

'WAS IT THAT CLIFF JONES?'

Jimmy Hill pushed opened the gates to the football good life but he couldn't claim for his generation the riches that are heaped on today's stars. That awaited upheavals in all walks of life and a massive change in values. It means that a player of the past has to think about that, and count to at least ten, when today he reads of reserve players driving around in Ferraris.

For myself, I have to remember how happy I was in my suburban 'castle' in Chessington, and how good it was to be playing football for a living and driving home to Daphne in that gleaming Vauxhall Viva, which sometimes I liked to think was going at about a hundred miles per hour. Back then, I could only congratulate myself on my good fortune, and if I ever wavered on this, if I ever got frustrated with the fact that despite the progress made by Hill and George Eastham, a footballer was still in many ways at the mercy of his employer, there was never a shortage of reminders that in the past the footballer's life had been so much worse.

There were so many times when you met or heard of great

footballers down on their luck. Men who had held great stadiums in the palm of their hands but who had finished with nothing, partly no doubt in some cases because they hadn't been very good with their money, but also because they had never had enough of it, not by any decent standard, in a game which had claimed the hearts of the English working class. Not enough money, or the dignity which can come with it, anyway, to live in any style or celebrate that you were at the top of your field.

Probably the classic example was Wilf Mannion, one of the greatest footballers in the history of the English game, a magnificently skilled inside-forward who some critics say was a member of the finest forward line England ever knew: Matthews, Mortensen, Lawton, Mannion and Finney. Mannion played eighteen seasons for Middlesbrough and was then accused of being an ingrate when he refused to sign one last contract, and attempted to pick up his career with Hull City. He was banned from the game for revealing, while working briefly for a Sunday newspaper, all the illegal inducements he had received from clubs attempting to draw him away from Middlesbrough.

In his middle age Mannion worked as a tea boy in a Teesside factory. He once told of the time he played for Middlesbrough against Arsenal in front of a crowd of nearly 70,000.

Babe Ruth, the great baseball player, attended the match and told his hosts that he had never seen such a vast crowd. 'How much do you guys earn?' asked The Babe. He gasped when he was told that all the players on the field drew the same amount: £8. 'You guys are bloody idiots,' said the American demi-god doing the Grand Tour of Europe while even the most gifted of his England-based sporting cousins couldn't afford to buy their own homes.

Roy Bentley told me about Mannion. He talked of his beautiful balance, his quickness in seeing an opening, his velvety skill. Then one day I happened to find myself on the same pitch with this player of the ages. It was a testimonial game in Hull. We were on the same side. Our goalkeeper rolled the ball to me across the rain-slicked grass. I looked up to see that Mannion had drifted into the inside-right position about thirty yards away and I hit the ball to him all along the ground because the surface was so wet. As I hit the ball I realised I had really got hold of it and it shot to him at a high rate of knots. He took it with his right foot on the half-turn and just killed the pace off it. He shielded the ball with his right shoulder and he was exactly where he wanted to be. Here was this frail little guy with such beautiful control, and I thought, 'Christ, that was majestic.' He was small and white haired and into his fifties but I knew in one flash that all the things Bentley had said about him were true. His fate was to end up a tea boy in a factory, where so many of his co-workers didn't even know his name, but that night in the rain in Hull he was Wilf Mannion and proud of it, as he had every reason to be.

Hearing players today talk of 'having' to move clubs for the chance of winning big prizes – and, no doubt, big money – still sounds strange to me. And it certainly would have to Wilf Mannion. For both of us, I suspect, playing for one club all those years was a little bit like being married. Most of the time you know it is right for you, that probably outside of it you would be lost, and, anyway, you couldn't imagine another form of existence. But occasionally, for one reason or another, you speculate on other forms of life and in my case that happened one night at home in Chessington when I took a phone call. The caller said he was acting as a third party for Everton Football Club. Would I like to play for them?

This was a little curious, and exciting, because of all the clubs in England, Everton was the one that excited me most. I always said that if I ever moved from Fulham I would like Goodison Park to be the destination. There were several reasons for this. One was the prestige that Everton still carried in the fifties and sixties. They would have their share of success later under Howard Kendall, but when I took that phone call they were still heaped in glamour. They had the marvellously skilled blond-haired Scottish centre-forward Alex Young, who was known as the 'Golden Vision' and, some thought, was moving in the footsteps of Dixie Dean and Tommy Lawton, and already I had fought some tremendous duels with their fine left-winger Derek Temple. It also so happened that I always played well at Everton. Indeed early in the World Cup year of 1966 I probably played my best game for England in a 1–1 draw against Poland. The match is rooted in my memory mainly for two incidents – and the fact that sometimes you feel perfectly right out there on the field. You sense that it is your match, a time when you just can't do anything wrong. It was a heavy pitch and it was as though I had found some extra strength from somewhere.

Either of the incidents would have made the night unforgettable. First I fashioned a goal scored by Bobby Moore. Really, it was a wonderful goal. Moore brought the ball out of defence and played it to me on the right side near the half-way line – and kept running. I took the ball past two Polish players and all the time I could see Bobby moving forward. I played a ball to the far post. It was a driven chip and it was perfect. Bobby had shaken off the cover and he headed in with great ease. After that match Vic Buckingham went rather overboard, said I was the best right-back in Europe and of course I wasn't going to argue with him. My friend Ken Jones also had a kind word in the *Mirror*, writing of my contribution to the goal, 'Cohen was hunting hungrily and characteristically along the touchline.' But even more gratifying was the compliment paid to me by the Leeds United full-back Paul Reaney, who was one of my rivals for an England place. Reaney was a tough, quick and hard-tackling defender making his name with the new power in the land, Leeds United, and a big part of his reputation had come with the impressive way he had handled the threat of George Best in some big matches. He was ambitious and, as I would have done in his position, he coveted my place in the team. But he came up to me after the match and shook my hand, saying, 'That was terrific, George – a great performance.' He was a lovely kid behind the professional front and I thought his gesture was, in the pressure building around the fight for a place in the World Cup, really magnanimous. When something like that happens you forget all the needle and the disappointments that come in the game, and you feel good about yourself and the other lads on the field. It makes it all seem that little bit more worthwhile. So when the man on the phone said Everton, I had to keep the excitement out of my voice.

In fact, I was rather businesslike. I said I wasn't going to talk to just anybody over the phone like that. The call could be coming from anywhere. I was given a Liverpool number to call. Harry Catterick, the manager, came on the line. I recognised his voice immediately. He said he would very much like me to play for Everton. I said that a player would be out of his mind not to think carefully about the chance to move to such a successful club. It was a first rate 'tap-up' because Catterick got straight down to details. We would be able to keep our house in Chessington. Everton would find us one in Southport, near a golf course. There would be an 'under-the-counter' payment of £5,000 – precisely the cost of our house in Rhodrons Road.

Despite all my affection for Fulham, all those feelings of being at home, I told myself, 'George, you've got to have a go.' Daphne agreed. She said we would be out of our minds to miss out on all that money – and for me not to get a taste of football with one of the biggest clubs in the country. Of course there was a lot of wrestling in my mind. Fulham were in my blood and, by the general standards of football, they had treated me very well. But the game was opening up it seemed, to new horizons, new opportunities, and here was one of the top clubs in the land, who just happened to be my sentimental favourites, coming in with an illegal approach and the promise of more money than I could hope to save in years. In those days you could get intoxicated just thinking about something like that.

The problem was that Fulham said no. Just like that. Not to my face, of course. They didn't have to do that even after a judge had talked about slave labour and Hill and Eastham had won their victories, great ones, but, as it dawned on me, incomplete ones. They didn't even report the approach to me. As far as they were concerned I was their property, their local boy favourite, and I could just damn well get on with it. As I established myself in the England team, and my confidence grew through 1965 with the increasing likelihood I would play in a World Cup, it was maybe inevitable that I would come to the attention of some of the bigger clubs. There was another illegal approach and it came on the plane flying the England team back from a tour of South America. Alan Bass, the Arsenal and England doctor, asked me if I would like to move to Highbury. Again, it was the old story – the tug of new territory, and an injection of money into the Chessington economy, against the pain of cutting the cord connecting me to Fulham. But the result was the same. Arsenal proposed, Fulham disposed, and I kept marching on. Arsenal offered an attractive deal; Don Howe, the good, experienced former England full-back and a cash bonus. But, like Haynes, I was obviously deemed part of the furniture.

Jimmy Greaves reckoned I would have been a great favourite at White Hart Lane if the Spurs manager Bill Nicholson had persuaded Fulham to part with me as well as Alan Mullery. We were playing golf together when, just before he made a putt, Jimmy said, 'You know George we've had some wonderful games together, but the one thing I haven't enjoyed about playing your lot is that we have so many Jewish supporters at White Hart Lane it means that when you come to play I always think we're away from home.'

It was true that we almost always played well at Tottenham. There was something about that wonderful Spurs team which brought the best out of us. Haynes's passing was invariably acute. The Rabbi ran his socks off, and perhaps it was because of that support from the terraces – which might not have been so forthcoming had it been known that my branch of the Cohen family had been Church of England for the best part of a hundred years – I tended to put in some of my more powerful performances.

However, Fulham being Fulham, there was the occasional lapse. Probably the worst came one afternoon when we were playing rather well and leading 1–0. Bobby Keetch went to meet a rather speculative through ball, saw there was no danger and let it run through to Tony Macedo. Instinctively I looked over my shoulder to see where their left-winger Cliff Jones was. I was going to break out wide and call for the ball. But while I was doing this I heard a great roar of 'Goal . . .' I looked at Keetchy and he said, 'George, he just threw the ball to Greavsie – I wouldn't have minded any other player in the world, but can you believe it, Greavsie.' Later Jimmy said he was so surprised he thought the whistle had gone, but he just kicked the ball into the net automatically. As he would. It was the kind of small catastrophe we knew how to endure better than most and I have to say such pratfalls where mere specks on my horizon. By the early sixties I was moving confidently towards my football prime, the years of hard work and good fitness were drawing dividends match by match and the moves made for me by Spurs, Everton and Arsenal increased my self-confidence. There had also been an overture by the great Stan Cullis of Wolves.

Cullis, the dour but brilliant master of Molineux, had won three titles in the late fifties plus two FA Cups and had led his team to spectacular victories over Moscow Spartak and Honved that created a groundswell for European club competition. He was a legendary taskmaster, famously only interested in players he considered of the right competitive character, and his teams were noted for phenomenal fitness, a reputation they underlined when putting four goals past the Russian team in the last ten minutes of what had previously been a ferocious deadlock.

Fulham gave to Wolves the same reply they had given all the others and of course once again I was not consulted. In a way I was having the best of two worlds. I could enjoy the emotional comfort zone of Craven Cottage and still make my mark on the wider game. It was also true that if I had been noticed by such as Bill Nicholson, Harry Catterick and Stan Cullis there was every chance that Alf Ramsey, the freshly appointed national team manager who pledged to carry English football into the new age, would confirm my place in his plans. I was lucky too that in Vic Buckingham, my Fulham manager, I had somebody who been around the football world, and who had been exposed to both Continental methods and the early stimulation of seeing Arthur

Rowe's revolutionary push-and-run work at White Hart Lane, which was the starting point of all Nicholson's brilliant achievements at Tottenham. Buckingham was maligned and in the end driven away from White Hart Lane, but where some saw mere arrogance I saw the streak of perfectionism in many of his attitudes.

It meant that I was receiving a pretty thorough football education based on the fundamentals of Dugald Livingstone and carried forward by some of the refined insights of Vic Buckingham. Of course the sharpest and most deeply absorbed lessons were administered out on the field. Some of the most dramatic, and often painful, of these were delivered by that man I was looking for so keenly when Macedo made his extraordinary decision to throw the ball to the feet of Greaves. Cliff Jones was quick and hard and wonderfully skilled and was the winger who gave me the most trouble. It is an assessment which takes into consideration the amazing talent of the young Georgie Best, who of course had a habit of turning up everywhere, and the thoroughbred Bobby Charlton, whose first and not always comfortable ride into football was along the left flank. It is the oddest thing to recall, but I remember hearing the name Charlton booed when it was announced in the left-wing spot on the public address before a game.

Buckingham gave me a daunting appraisal of Jones. He said, 'If he comes at you with speed with the ball you are in trouble, you're on a loser. If he is just running to get free you have more of a chance.' Naturally at the start of our first encounter he came at me with the ball on his left foot. He was going at speed. He then changed feet and balance and moved the ball on to his right foot. He was making room for himself out wide. Fine, I thought, I can deal with this, but then I couldn't be sure he was going to do it. He didn't.

He hammered the ball with his right foot. He could use either foot and play, at speed, on the left- and right-wing. The moment he knocked the ball past you, you knew you had a problem. The difficulty with Clifford was he never stopped moving the ball in his determination to deny you any kind of chance. He rather persecuted full-backs, which was of course his job, and one he was superbly equipped to do both in terms of talent and competitive instincts. Inevitably, he scored goals against us, but to tell the truth I never had to nurse those particular wounds for too long. I knew from the first moment I played against him that he was a great player, and though you were always at your limits against such a competitor, always desperate to shut him down, at the back of your mind you recognised the law of averages. It said that from time to time a guy as good as that was going to do you. My mother wasn't quite so philosophical after some of my early battles with the Welsh flyer. When I went home to West Kensington after a match with all kinds of bruises, she would say, 'What's that on your neck — was it that Cliff Jones?'

I heard that for a while after he finished playing he had, like so many old players, some problems of re-adjustment and that, like his team-mate Greaves, he had to come to terms with the effects of some heavy drinking. But I was delighted that, as Greaves did eventually, he got over that difficult phase of his life. It is always a joy to see him now and recall those sparkling contests out on the field. He invited me to his sixtieth birthday party a few years ago. His grandchildren were making a video and inviting opinions on their grandfather from former team-mates and opponents. I told them that in the end I was quite pleased with the overall result of our battles, but then I had never realised he was quite such an old man.

George Best, unfortunately, didn't start his ageing process off the field until his powers as a player had dwindled beyond recall. When he finally engaged his problems, his career had long been a memory. They are thrilling memories, no doubt, but anyone who played against him, who saw up close the extraordinary talent and courage, know that they are too few. Best was the shooting star of football.

The way to mark George was to let him try to beat you. You were better off inviting him to go a certain way because if you happened to win the ball off him and tried to get away you knew he would be snapping at your heels. He was tremendously tenacious and when he had the ball he did unbelievable things. He never wanted to lose anything, and sometimes that instinct spilled over into a problem for his team-mates. I always imagined that playing with him was one part delight, one part nightmare because you would be running all over the place trying to make positions and deep down you had to suspect he wasn't going to give you the ball. Basically, he had one idea in his head. He wanted to score and that was it. Given his problems off the field, and all the celebrity that weighed down on him, George was always going to make it difficult for himself and the people around him.

When you look at it in that light, it was astonishing that he achieved so much.

Bobby Charlton was electric over fifteen yards but he had a little characteristic which gave you a chance. Bobby would come to you with that lovely flowing action but you knew when he was going to push the ball past you, get round you and go for the cross. He gave a little skip, and that's when I went with him. I had quite a lot of success. Had he eliminated that skip, and gone inside me, I suspect I would have been completely lost. The skip had the effect on me of a starting pistol, and when I reacted properly he would disappear into the middle. I was very happy for that. Because of his beautiful talent he was never easy to mark, but, as I said, he did give you a chance. The truth was he wasn't a winger in the way of Cliff Jones, and nor was Bestie. They were magnificent players and so naturally I was happy that they would prove it mostly away from my little patch.

The set of credentials I was trying to put together were heavily dependent on my ability to deal with talent of the highest order, and whenever you went out against one of the great players you had a lurking fear that this might be the day you would get ambushed and have your nerve seriously damaged. Your reputation could not stand too many such invasions. So I worked slavishly to cover a Jones or a Charlton or a Best. I would go to sleep thinking about the menace such men represented and what I had to do to stifle it. This was especially so when the World Cup of 1966 came into focus and I knew that whatever I did there was a very good chance Alf Ramsey might be watching.

CHAPTER EIGHT

SEEDS OF '66

Alf Ramsey was very sure about his likes and dislikes, in and out of football. He liked footballers he could trust, who shared his commitment to getting everything they could out of whatever ability they had been given. He liked Westerns, retreating to the quiet of his modest home in Ipswich, and the care of his devoted wife Vicky.

He was also very keen on celery hearts. Once he had some served up to him with great pomp in a rather stylish restaurant and it seemed from his look of pleasure that he would scarcely have been happier if John Wayne or Gary Cooper had pulled up a chair and asked him to explain the intricacies of the old Swivel Defence.

At heart he was a simple, rather shy man who didn't expect too much from life beyond the achieving of a little respect and the acceptance that he had always done what he could. Certainly his greatest demands were on himself. He fought so hard to remove the traces of a poor background, even to the point of taking those elocution lessons, and if he was conscious that from time to time this provoked a little mockery, well, it was something he was prepared to suffer. He knew how he wanted to be. He wanted to be improved. He was, no doubt, a product of his times and when those times had passed few men would ever have had more difficulty in adapting to a new style – and new values. His marriage to Vicky was a perfect reflection of this. He worshipped her but he also expected everything of her. She served him, as so many women did their husbands in those days, and in return he adored her. If ever anyone walked in a man's shadow it was her. She had that Victorian attitude that he would live his life, do what he had to do, and she would make sure that he had his meals and that his shirts were washed and ironed immaculately. It is not easy to imagine him as a particularly romantic lover. His great passion, you had to suspect, was reserved for his country. He would go down drain holes for England, and if that sounds strange today it was the reality he lived – and something he never ceased trying to instil into his players.

I have a feeling that if he was still around Alf would look at life in the first phase of the twenty-first century with some disbelief – and then probably go stark raving mad. Most of all he would have hated the easy celebrity, the instant fame. Beckham's wages – and his deification – would have been a torment as he analysed his performance, measured it against those of Ball and Bobby Charlton and some of the others he had carried to the peaks of the game. He didn't believe in overnight success. For anything to be worthwhile it had to be worked for over a period of time. You didn't prove yourself in one match, or six matches, you did it on the long haul. You eradicated mistakes. You kept your eye, unwaveringly, on the ball.

He disliked excessive familiarity, indiscipline in any form, and, perhaps more than anything, losing to the Scots. That last fact worked very much in my favour. England lost twice to Scotland in Ramsey's first, difficult, year as manager which saw, traumatically enough, a 5–2 defeat by France in the European Championships – he wasn't crazy about the French, either – and after the second Scottish defeat in Glasgow, early in 1964, he was so depressed and angry he seemed at risk of opening a vein. But instead of that he dropped the reigning captain and right back, which was where I came in. Jimmy Armfield was a World Cup veteran of Chile, 1962, a quick, attacking full-back and one of the first in the English game to demonstrate the value of genuine pace accompanying a willingness to overlap, but he was also one whose defensive discipline, Ramsey formed the opinion, was a little suspect. This conviction burrowed deeply into Ramsey's psyche when, in the first of those defeats by Scotland, at Wembley, Armfield carelessly played a ball across the front of goal and into the path of the great Scottish hero Jimmy Baxter. The Rangers man, one of the most skilled players the game has ever seen, stroked home the opportunity.

For Armfield it was the equivalent of signing his own death warrant. In Ramsey's mind Armfield's long run as a fixture in the team was over. He stayed in the squad, and played a few more games when I was injured, and once when I was rested during a tour of Scandinavia on the build-up to the 1966 World Cup, but, after that pass, any time he spent on an international field was on borrowed time.

In football it is the oldest truth that one player's mishap is another's opportunity and my good fortune in the unravelling of Armfield's distinguished international career was compounded by another stroke of fate. It was the career-shattering injury of Chelsea's Ken Shellito. He was considered by many to be the heir apparent to Armfield, and for some very good reasons. He was strong and skilled and had a very good defensive technique. He played for England against Czechoslovakia in Bratislava a year before Ramsey brought me into the team.

That was his chance to make his mark – and to confirm the manager's doubts about Armfield's candidacy for another World Cup. Sadly for Shellito, the Bratislava launching pad fell apart. He was seriously injured and not only his international prospects but his professional career was over. Such are the random twists of football. One man falls, another slips back, and a race that seemed to be over is suddenly wide open. Being brilliant is good. Working hard is important. But without the breaks, you can disappear in one moment of bad luck. I was trailing Ken Shellito, but then suddenly his name was scratched out of the contest.

There are so many chance developments which can turn you one way or the other – towards your goal or oblivion. In my case I've never doubted that the most influential fact of my career, after I had established myself with Fulham, was the appointment of Ramsey to the England job. Though Ken Jones was absolutely right to kick me out of that mood of resignation when I lost my Under-23 place to John Angus of

Burnley, deep down there was no doubt in my mind that things had turned against me, and probably in a decisive way, when Ron Greenwood opted for the Burnley man.

Angus was a nice guy but as a professional decision I could never take it philosophically. I just didn't think it was right, and now I believe that if Ramsey hadn't come along I would have been very lucky to get involved in the World Cup. I had a run of eight straight appearances in the Under-23 team, but it all stopped when Greenwood was given the job. I wasn't entirely surprised. We hadn't exactly seen eye to eye when he played for Chelsea and when he arrived at Fulham he didn't extend the kind of help which often flows naturally from an older player. In fact I can't remember exchanging a word with him. He preferred Angus, which meant that with Armfield in residence and Shellito challenging, I was suddenly in limbo. Also available was the experienced and able Arsenal full-back, Don Howe. I played on, as hard as ever, hoping for the break which came when Ramsey got the nod from the FA. I understand he was not the first choice.

The FA's first thought was for Bill Slater, a fine wing-half shaped by Stan Cullis at Wolves and a man who had great bearing. Perhaps they also thought that the gentlemanly Slater would have been rather more in the mould of Walter Winterbottom, a little easier to handle than the more thrusting Ramsey. That, you have to remember, would have been a very big factor indeed. The people who ran the boardrooms, and the FA, operated from the basis of 'them' and 'us'. Players were fine if they knew their place, if they weren't too 'uppity'. Ramsey, who could never claim patience with fools among his great assets, would definitely have been placed in that latter category by some of the FA rulers.

Really, it was an absurd situation and no-one was more aware of it than the fiercely proud Ramsey. His new bosses may have thought of themselves as the colliery owners but it was spelled out to them quickly enough that in future they had better stay away from the coalface.

I was at practice with Fulham one autumn afternoon when I first got the call for England duty. Bedford Jezzard, the Fulham manager, came to me as we walked away from the field and said, 'I've had a call from the FA. You're in the England squad. Well done, son.' It would be another nine months before I played my first international game, against Uruguay in May 1964, but the first excitement of going along to the England team headquarters at Hendon Hall and mingling with Bobby Charlton, Bobby Moore and Jimmy Greaves was huge. I knew them all to varying degrees, but now I was joining their 'club'. Ramsey was in the hotel lobby when I arrived. 'Welcome, George,' he said in his formal, clipped way. 'I'm sure you know a lot of the players. Just settle in and enjoy the experience. I'm sure you will do well. Just keep working hard, as you have been doing for so long.'

That was the typically low key start to the most important professional relationship of my life, one that would give me my place in the game and take me to peaks of experience shared with just ten other footballers throughout the entire history of our national game.

The more I look back, the more clearly I see that when the FA chose Ramsey that were also doing me a vast favour.

Right from the start it was so easy to identify with his goals, and understand the way he thought. I suppose we just happened to have been brought up with the same values, and, of course, we were both right-backs, which maybe gave us a particular, if not peculiar, view of the world.

He didn't leave you in any doubt about why he had picked you. You had to be able to play to a certain level, of course. But you also had to bring something more to the table. He had to trust everything about your make-up. Not least he had to be sure that you wouldn't go missing when the blood and thunder came, which it inevitably would if you were going to get near to the greatest prize in the world of football. It wouldn't be all brilliant football. At times you would have to fight and scrap and put together some kind of result when really you were far from your best.

It is a remarkable fact that in the five years that I was a part of his team, one of his 'boys', we had just one sharp exchange. There was the odd frown, the piercing look, which told me that I hadn't completely delighted his soul with one of my performances, but those occasions were fleeting. For me there was just one major Ramseyesque eruption and in the circumstances I really couldn't be too aggrieved.

The incident came two years after my first call up and happened on a training field in Madrid, where Alf was honing his plans for the World Cup of the following year. We were playing five-a-side in our track-suit bottoms. It was one of those sharply cold winter mornings in the Spanish capital and there was a touch of frost in the ground. Alf always liked to join in the five-a-sides on an impromptu basis, but unfortunately for me on this occasion I was unaware of his intervention until the moment I turned into a tackle. I sent him straight up in the air and then watched, horror-stricken, as he fell to the ground and landed on his head. As I said, there was frost in the ground and I feared, as I heard the groans of the man who held my future in the palm of his hand, quite a bit of it had been transferred to Alf's heart. My whole professional career, and all the painstaking progress I had made, flew before my eyes. Waiting to hear Alf's reaction, or even more worryingly, to see if he was capable of one, was an agony that seemed to impinge on eternity. Eventually, he said, 'George, if I had another fucking full-back you wouldn't be playing tomorrow.'

Only once again would he get anywhere close to that level of impatience with me. It was in the lounge of White's Hotel in Lancaster Gate, round the corner from the FA headquarters and where the team usually gathered before foreign trips. A few of the players were at a table with Alf and the future Lady Vicky and when the tea was brought out, I volunteered to serve. The tea-pots at White's were notoriously unreliable in the pouring and I was making a bit of a mess of it. Alf couldn't stand to see my fumblings, and snapped, 'For heavens sake Vicky, pour the bloody tea before he scalds us all.' That was a rare slip in decorum because just as Alf worked hard to remove elements of his Dagenham accent, he also strived to acquire some of the niceties of polite society. You could never be quite sure how deeply his urge for refinement ran, but you were never in doubt that he had set himself standards and principles which he would never consciously compromise.

In that same White's Hotel three of the biggest names in English football would learn this quickly enough.

On the eve of a tour of Portugal, Ireland, the United States and South America in 1964 the players were told by Alf that they could go out for a drink but there would be a 10.30 curfew. Five of the players, including Bobby Moore, Jimmy Greaves, and, perhaps a little more surprisingly, Bobby Charlton, missed the curfew. Not to any shocking degree, not via some outrageous trawling through the early morning West End watering holes. They were just an hour late, but there was a shock waiting them when they arrived in their rooms. Their passports had been neatly placed on their pillows. They faced a fretful night's sleep and a tense team meeting.

Alf told us all that he had been deeply disappointed that five players had betrayed his trust. He said that if he could organise the right replacements to be at the airport in a few hours' time, the five miscreants would be off the plane. The truth was men like Moore and Charlton were, to Ramsey's mind, utterly irreplaceable. But whatever they might do for him on the field, he could not have the spirit of his team dissipated by indiscipline. He said he wouldn't be messed around.

The placing of the passports on this occasion was symbolic. But it was powerful symbolism and Ramsey's message went through football like bush fire. He was saying that though it had been some years since he played the game, he hadn't forgotten how some players thought and behaved. He knew how it was when players pushed the limits of

185

discipline and the manager didn't respond. He wasn't going to have any of that because it would make all his other work futile. He was an old pro, he wanted everybody to know, and he was not about to miss a trick. His basic attitude was that if players couldn't act like adults for the limited time they were with the team, there wasn't an awful lot of point in them being there. You couldn't really go on the piss and be sufficiently focused to represent your country.

He said he thought he knew players pretty well. He knew their hopes and their fears — and their weaknesses. He had done everything in the game, been part of a Double-winning team at Tottenham, played for England and created one of the greatest surprises in the history of football when he led Ipswich Town to the First Division title in 1962. He had also been through a war, which can be quite educative.

Ramsey told the players they could have it whichever way they wished. They could be treated as men but with clear demarcation lines on what they could do and what they couldn't. Or they could be belittled, told they were naughty little boys. Ultimately, it was their choice. A lot depended, of course, on the nature of the players. Maybe because of my upbringing, the administration of that slipper by Mel Roberts, the exhortations of those inflamed headmasters and something that was inside me, discipline was not so much of a burden, certainly not as it was, I always suspected, for Jimmy Greaves. Greavsie never seemed to grasp the principle of discipline, and the value of it, and that was always going to be a point of conflict with Alf. Greaves went out to play, spontaneously and often gloriously, and discipline was for other people. Football was a team game, no doubt, but for supreme individualists there was another, uncharted way.

That was how Greaves saw it. Ramsey's view was narrower, but as the days went by, and the sense of team grew stronger, there could be little doubting the sharpness – and the depth – of his focus. If a player was of value, if he could bring elements to England's play which would be otherwise lacking, he had a chance with Ramsey – but only on Ramsey's terms. It meant that as long as he was in charge many talented players would never pass through the doors of Hendon Hall.

Jack Charlton, who for much of his career had been one of the least disciplined of professionals and admitted that it was probably only the arrival of Don Revie at Leeds United in the early sixties that had made him take stock of himself and avoid an undistinguished exit from the game, understood very well what Ramsey was about. Early on, he said, 'I don't think Alf is any great coach but he has a genius for formulating a team. He understands how some players can work with each other – and others can't.' It was Jack, this big, bluff character who you could follow around by the trail of his fag-ends, who provoked from Alf one of his more famous philosophical statements. Charlton was getting a little emotional about his pleasure at being called to membership of the English football elite, and said, 'Alf, sometimes I just don't know why you called me up to the team.' Ramsey, as straight-faced as ever, said, 'Jack, you know I don't always pick the best players.' In fact, I believe Jack Charlton remains one of the most under-rated of players. He was acutely aware of his own limitations in skill when he played for England, but he brought a great rough authority to his work. He may have been in awe of the skill and the poise of Bobby Moore alongside him but he was never intimidated. Whatever his private fears, he had tremendous front and on one occasion, after an England work-out at Highbury, he declared, 'Alf, you're talking shit.' Ramsey's expression didn't change. He paused for a moment before saying, 'That's as may be Jack, but of course you will do as I say.'

Later Charlton traced the course of his relationship with the man who drew from him every ounce of his ability and his fighting character: 'At first I counted up the number of times Alf said no to me and the lads,' said Jack. 'Then I gave it up because I lost count. I would ask, "Alf, do you think a few of the lads could have a pint or two tonight? We've been training so hard and there are still four days to go before the match." He would wait between ten and fifteen seconds and then say, "No, Jack, I don't think so." You would go through the routine on every issue that cropped up. Maybe we would argue for a change of travel plans or a little shift in the training schedule. But there would be the usual pause and then the "no". Sometimes, like naughty schoolboys, we would slip one over on him, nip out for a quick half-pint. But we would be terrified while we did it. Soon enough Alf meant so much to all of us. He meant discipline and values and, more than anything, a bloody hard understanding that to do anything in football, and life, you had to sacrifice a bit – and work like hell.'

Ramsey told every new contender for a place in the team, 'I know what you can do for your club, and I like what you do because I wouldn't have picked you if I didn't. I will never ask you to do anything you haven't already shown you are capable of.' The fact was Alf wasn't just doing a job, he was defining it, setting a standard for everyone who would follow. But first he had to tear down all the nonsense that had gone before. He had to put the amateur FA councillors in their place. He had to tell the big name reporters that that they could write whatever they liked, whip up popular sentiment in whatever direction they wished, but they would not be picking his team. In one heated discussion with Eric Cooper, who was billed as the 'Voice of the North' and wrote for the millions of readers who then subscribed to the *Daily Express* in that part of the country, Alf got up from his seat, started to take off his jacket and invited his critic outside. Decorum would stretch only so far in disguising the fierce determination of a man who only accepted the job on the assurance that, unlike all his predecessors, he would have complete control of all team matters, starting with selection. That may sound a little bizarre today, but before Ramsey's arrival an England manager as knowledgeable and sophisticated as Winterbottom was obliged to weigh, and often act, on the recommendations of a selection committee composed entirely of men who had never played the game professionally. As Ramsey would say privately, 'I had to put the bloody thing right.' He did it with such passion because he could never wipe from his memory that day at Wembley in 1953 when the Hungarians arrived with an impact that could hardly have been greater if they had landed on the centre circle in a beam of extra-terrestrial light. The team of Puskas and Hidegkuti ravaged an England in which Ramsey had never felt more alone on a football field. He hated the humiliation of the 6–3 defeat at Wembley, which was soon followed by another massacre, this time 7–1, at the old Nep stadium in Budapest. He hated the fact he and his defensive team-mates were not so much beaten but cast out of a game with which they were not familiar. The Hungarians put a number nine shirt on Hidegkuti but withdrew him from the normal striking position. They had changed the tactical rules without telling England. One result was that England's veteran centre-half Harry Johnston, a traditionally hard-tackling, obdurate defender, spent an afternoon haunted by red-shirted ghosts. In the first, stunned aftermath the feeling was that what had happened was a fluke. The old truths of the game would be reasserted at the Nep Stadium. But the old truths, of course, received another mauling at the feet of the new realities of pace and movement and silky skill. England had to rearm against new and subtle forces and for Ramsey it would become a personal crusade.

In fact, if it was a catastrophe for English football, it was the making of Ramsey the manager. As the boss of Ipswich he gleaned the best players he could and made a team which in other hands would have been odds-on to go plunging back into the Second Division. But he gave his modest team a system of 4–4–2, and the means to win the title. He also gave me the kind of afternoon Ramsey himself had endured against the Hungarians.

On one Saturday Ipswich had looked no side at all at Craven Cottage, and we ran amuck, winning 10–1. But it was an utterly different story at their ground the following

Wednesday. I was marking Jimmy Leadbeater, a player I remembered from his days at Chelsea. He was a beanpole of a man and a useful player in his time, but Leadbeater was no longer a threat. The problem this day was that he was standing half way down in his own half. I said to Graham Leggett, our right-winger, 'Look, I'm not getting anywhere near him and we're 2–0 down. There's no point in me being right down there with attacks coming on the other side of the field.' They were pulling us all over the place and getting the ball up to their two strikers, Ted Phillips and Ray Crawford, who had been causing all kinds of mayhem throughout the season. At half time I said that I didn't understand what was going on, and Johnny Haynes said he was in the same position. Bedford Jezzard said we just had to go out there and mark man for man. We tried that but still lost 4–2.

There was some comfort for us in that Manchester United had also gone down by a similar score at Ipswich, and they had been warned by Ray Wilson. He told Bobby Charlton, 'You'll go there and dominate 89 minutes of the play and still lose.' Our runaway win at Craven Cottage was plainly something of an aberration. With scant resources, Ramsey had put in an extraordinary piece of football organisation – and motivation – and had a First Division title to prove it. His basic work, as is that of every winning manager, was to get solid defence and then make the most of what he had in the way of attacking resources.

Defenders are generally pretty basic people. They look at the odds and they figure things out. Ramsey's success at Ipswich was more than anything a practical achievement.

He had learned at Tottenham under Arthur Rowe the need for the quick transfer of defence into attack, and that was the basis of his approach to the World Cup. With England, of course, he had a nice foundation. He had Gordon Banks, Bobby Charlton, Bobby Moore, Ray Wilson and Jimmy Greaves. Most managers would fancy themselves to make a little progress with such resources. But Ramsey was determined to do rather better than that. He confided to us, 'Gentlemen, there is no question about it . . . we can win the World Cup.'

He knew what he had, and also what he needed. In my area of the field, fortunately, he needed speed. He needed speed because Moore and Jack Charlton, the heart of his defence, didn't have it. Moore had a cool, brilliant football brain. Charlton, who won his first cap when he was thirty, was an old pro who understood precisely what was needed. The speed had to come from elsewhere. Ray Wilson and I could give speed. So very quickly he had his back-four unit. We played together nineteen times before one of us got injured. We played thirty-seven matches together, and lost three.

So he had a back four which worked, and would do with more efficiency the more we played together – a simple reality which seems to be quite lost on the current England manager Sven Goran Eriksson when he makes his endless permutations in friendly games which, if they have any purpose, it is completely lost on me, as I'm sure it would have been on Ramsey.

Ramsey built patiently, block by block. Then he would

take a step back and make his periodic reviews. Bobby Charlton, having survived the passport episode, which, when you thought about it, was probably as much a threat to his career as a speeding ticket might be to Michael Schumacher's, was an obvious fixture. One dilemma concerned who played along with Charlton. Alan Mullery was playing extremely well for Tottenham, but the claim of Nobby Stiles ran a lot deeper in Ramsey's mind. Stiles read the game so well, he was fierce in the tackle and when he won the ball he basically had one thought in his head. It was, 'Where's Bobby?' When you have a player of the quality of Charlton, why not play somebody who can feed the maestro until he wants no more.

For a while there was a fashion to disparage Nobby. A lot of people looked at him and didn't see any more than a scrawny little guy who put himself about a bit and had a knack of getting right in the middle of any of the aggravation that from time to time spills over during a competitive football match. I remember reading comments along these lines from Martin O'Neill, one of today's most celebrated managers. O'Neill listed Stiles among the bad guys, suggested the little man's eminence was some kind of black mark against the game. When I read that I felt pretty much as I had when I saw the look on Alan Hansen's face when he put down my friend Jimmy Hill. I felt my hackles rising rather sharply.

Technically, Nobby was maybe not a great player. He didn't have the natural gifts which you normally associate with that assessment. But his contribution to a team was great and went far beyond his role as Ramsey's designated 'policeman'. On the field I always knew where he was and that if I had to leave a situation he would be providing the cover. A football game was for Nobby always an open book. He could read every nuance of it, and nobody needed to point this out to Ramsey.

In their different ways, Alan Ball and Martin Peters were also making claims that challenged orthodox thinking. If either of them made it into the team it would be at the expense of maybe the most cherished figure in the game, the winger, the trickster whose speed and cunning had for so long enlivened the domestic Saturday afternoon. Though Ramsey had been deeply impressed by the qualities of Ball and Peters, particularly the energy and brightness of the former, and the subtle movement and original thinking of the latter, he had his own agony of indecision.

As a full-back, no-one knew better than Ramsey the value of a good winger. He gave width and a constant point of danger. In his highest form as exemplified by a Matthews or a Finney or a Cliff Jones, he could transform a match by stretching and breaking a defence. But in the mid-sixties, with Matthews and Finney long retired and none of their successors quite separating themselves from their rivals, the big question had become the central dilemma of Ramsey's World Cup planning. Was the modern English winger really up to the job? He could bring balance to a team, he could go through the classic motions, but could he do enough damage? If any of Peter Thompson and Ian Callaghan of Liverpool, Terry Paine of Southampton and John Connelly of Manchester United was able to provide positive answers to these questions the boldest stroke of Alf Ramsey's career might well have been withheld. His liking for Ball and Peters would quite probably have been put on hold. He loved Ball's approach to the game, and the ghost-like quality of Peters, but Ball was a mere twenty-year-old and maybe the lean, economic style of Peters, which Ramsey had already announced was ten years ahead of its time, could be held back a little longer.

The front-running threat to both players was Thompson. On the trip to Brazil in 1964 for the 'Little World Cup' he had played brilliantly at the Maracana in Rio. He ran at the Brazilians with tremendous confidence and strength – and was quite the best English thing in a 5–1 defeat. If that sounds like a nightmare result, there was a good explanation. We had played games in Lisbon, Dublin, and New York before flying down to Rio with scarcely any breathing space. Within thirty-six hours of boarding the plane in New York we were running out on to the field in Rio. I was particularly badly affected. At half-time the team doctor Alan Bass said I shouldn't really play on. I was ill, but in those days before substitutes, the idea was that you more or less played until you dropped. I got through the game, somehow, and for most of the match we held out quite well. Then the legs of the whole team seemed to collapse, though Thompson's less so than anyone else. He was having the game of his life – and imperilling the chances of either Ball or Peters making it to the World Cup.

But it was a long, hard course and Thompson had injury problems. He couldn't shake away the competition. The truth was that despite Thompson's spectacular performance,

Ramsey returned from South America with just one solid conviction. It was that Brazil, the winners in Stockholm in 1958 and Santiago in 1962, could not possibly win their third straight World Cup. In Sao Paulo we saw Argentina beat Brazil in a ferocious match in which Pele was drawn into all kinds of violence, including a bout of head-butting. The temperature in the stadium got very hot indeed and there seemed to be a good chance that it would be burned down. Eventually, Ramsey stood up and said, 'Gentlemen, I'm ready.' As we marched into the night, he said that we could discount Brazil as a serious threat. Pele was a great player, of course, but he didn't really have anyone to play with. Garrincha was way past his best, pulled back by injury, and the Brazilian defence was extremely vulnerable. When Ramsey made an announcement such as this there was little inclination to debate the issue. He always spoke with great certainty, and, soon enough, we saw no reason to doubt him.

In December '65, he completed his battle to win our hearts and our minds. Our confidence in him hardened into belief. His breakthrough, and maybe his defining moment as a coach, came in Madrid the day after I had sent him crashing so painfully on to that frosty training field. We won 2–0. Without wingers. It was a brilliant performance, free and strong and very positive. Alan Ball made a huge claim with his clever, hard running and confidence on the ball. There was no shortage of width and some of it was supplied by Ray Wilson and me. Wilson was involved in the first goal, dashing down the left after being sent away by a swift free kick taken by George Eastham. For the second, I exchanged passes with Bobby Moore before the captain put in a cross converted by Roger Hunt. Spain were nonplussed and their coach Jose Villalonga could scarcely have been more flattering. 'England were just phenomenal tonight,' he declared. 'They were far superior to us in their experiment and their performance. They could have beaten any team tonight.'

Desmond Hackett, the famous sportswriter of the *Daily Express*, was positively rhapsodic. He wrote, under the headline 'Ramsey's Wreckers', 'England can win the World Cup next year. They have only to match the splendour of this unforgettable night and there is not a team on earth who could master them. This was England's first win in Spain. But it was more than a victory. It was a thrashing of painful humiliation for the Spanish. Gone were the shackles of rigid regimentation. The team moved freely and confidently and with such rare imagination that the numbers became mere identification marks on players who rose to noble heights. England's football was as smooth as the brush of a master – precise, balanced, and as lovely to watch as the ballet.'

Desmond, of the brown bowler and the purple prose, was very kind on this occasion – it wasn't always the case – and there is no doubt that what happened in Madrid fuelled the team with a new level of self-confidence. But his implication that we had turned ourselves into an Anglo-Saxon version of Brazil was not quite right. What was so good about our performance was the discipline and understanding of what we had to achieve while working from Ramsey's blueprint. We didn't have specialist wingers, but that didn't mean we couldn't have width and speed along the flanks. We had that aplenty as Ball and Charlton covered the ground quite relentlessly, and Stiles was careful to cover the forays of Wilson and my own. Hunt played with extraordinary commitment, putting his head into places which would have made brave men flinch. You could see clearly that night the extent of Moore's development as a captain and a master defender.

Sometimes people ask me about Moore the captain and it is not the easiest question. He wasn't really a captain in the usual sense. He didn't shout particularly. He didn't rage. He led mostly by movement, wonderfully assured movement that took him, it seemed entirely at his own pace, to the point of danger. He read everything, as though he had radar fitted beneath his blond hair.

Bob didn't have to read a book about leadership. He didn't have to learn too many lessons. He just found it in himself. I don't know if this really makes sense, but Bobby seemed to me such a good captain because he never announced that he knew that was his role. He never made demands. He was smart enough to realise that you couldn't play the traditional captain in the presence of, say, Ray Wilson. If Wilson made a mistake, which was the rarest thing, no-one was more aware of it than him. Bobby saw the whole picture from where he played. He looked around the dressing room and saw that he didn't need to play nursemaid. He was a guy whose sheer presence made him seem taller, bigger than he was. One of his greatest strengths was the depth of his response to the big occasion. The truth is he never played so well for West Ham as he did for England. He had a problem building himself up for an ordinary league game. But when a big international game came around you could see him growing before your eyes. In the thirty-seven matches we played together I never once heard him bawl or shout. But if he saw something he thought you might not have noticed, he would mention it, quietly. What we all discovered in Madrid under his guidance and the master plan of Ramsey, was a wonderful sense of team. Not quite all the parts were in place that night, not when measured against the stringent demands of our manager, who at the end of the game appeared to have made a remarkable recovery from his collision with the cold and flinty earth of Spain. But Gordon Banks was there, under-employed but watchful in goal. Wilson and I notched up another level of understanding. Stiles was ferociously attentive to every moment of menace. Moore, almost glacial beside the volcanic Jack Charlton, glided through the game. Ball hungrily grabbed his chance to impress the boss. Bobby Charlton, elegant as ever, ran like a gazelle. Hunt was Hunt, remorseless and as hard as nails. Seven months later all these players would line up for the World Cup final, as George Eastham and Joe Baker, who had recently returned from a stint in the Italian game, might also have reasonably expected to do after their work in Madrid.

Certainly it was no reflection on their efforts, or their skills, that they didn't complete the journey. They didn't make it all the way because – this seems a little amazing today when you consider the endless juggling of so many modern coaches, and not least Sven Goran Eriksson – Alf Ramsey had nine players already deeply installed in his plans so long before the start of the big tournament. But he had a few more things to try and a little more tinkering to do. There were also two other crucial matters for his attention. They were named Geoff Hurst and Martin Peters.

CHAPTER NINE

WINGING IT

It was a very good year, 1966, and in the spring there was a great confidence within the team that maybe it could indeed be the best of years. It is something you can't always put your finger on, but when you have it, you know it. One day it is not there. Then it is. Parts fall into place so perfectly that you wonder how there could ever have been any doubt.

Something changes, and you sense intuitively that some of the burdens you carry into the game, like fear for example, will never be quite as oppressive ever again. There was reason to believe that we had made a rite of passage. As winners.

We knew Alf Ramsey had made us something, and we had the results to prove it. The Madrid game was a watershed for both the manager and his players. It told him that he had options — good, solid options — and it told us that we had a boss who knew what he was doing, who had the nerve to absorb the odd setback without being blown off the course he had settled on right from the start, and had been so sure about even when the critical flames which came with that first bad defeat by France were licking around him. Some of our results before the break-out in Spain had not been awe-inspiring, it was true. We hadn't lit up the sky in a dull, goalless draw with Wales, and we struggled to beat Northern Ireland 2–1 with a late goal. Sandwiched between those rather drab performances was a 3–2 home defeat by lightweight Austria, a result which provoked one of Jimmy Hill's more caustic statements to the nation. 'England will not win the World Cup,' announced Hill, 'but don't blame Alf. No-one could win with this lot.' Ramsey brushed aside the doubts, however. 'Gentlemen we are building a team, a real team and what matters now is how we do in the World Cup,' he said. 'Rest assured, we will win the World Cup.' In Spain his belief in the building process, his insistence that a shape, a winning shape, was unfolding before his eyes, was confirmed. We swept through a build-up tour of Scandinavia and Poland, winning all four matches and as we approached the great tournament, and our opening game with Uruguay at Wembley, the mood of the team could scarcely have been better, or more businesslike.

Most of us were pretty sure of our places, but never completely so because Ramsey had always identified complacency as a major threat to any team. There was the famous occasion at Heathrow airport when the team party was breaking up after a foreign trip and Gordon Banks, who must have been as confident as anyone that his place was secure, said to Ramsey, 'See you next trip,' and Alf grimaced and said, 'If selected.' Ramsey hated the idea that some of his players might make easy assumptions about what they had achieved and where they stood in his regard. He was also vigilant that cliques, the slow death of team spirit, might form within the squad. Naturally, some players have more affinity with certain of their team-mates than others. Moore and Greaves tended to find themselves in each other's company, but it was never a rigid situation and Ramsey encouraged this by making sure that when players were required to room together it was done in a constantly changing pattern. The worst part of his job, he confessed to his trainer and confidant Harold Shepherdson, was cutting away fine players who didn't quite meet his particular specifications, men like Bryan Douglas of Blackburn, a wonderfully skilful little player, Johnny 'Budgie' Byrne, of West Ham, and Bobby Tambling of Chelsea. All of them had formidable claims but when they didn't quite establish themselves in Ramsey's grand design there was the ordeal of parting, the ending of dreams. Shepherdson once told me that I wouldn't believe how Ramsey agonised before he had to perform the chore of severance. He would do it as gently as he could, with no great show. He tried to lose players quietly but of course you could never really take away the pain. What he had to practise was a lethal injection on the highest hopes of some very talented players.

Les Cocker, who was Don Revie's trainer at Leeds, was the third member of Ramsey's Council of War but he was not as close to the boss as Shepherdson. Cocker was small and hyperactive and could be quite contentious when he felt the work on the training field wasn't being done properly. But it was Shepherdson, who was also trainer at Middlesbrough, who had Ramsey's ear. It's often the case that when two people work closely together, and under quite a bit of stress over a period of time, they can easily grow a little cynical, they get too close, where the warts tend to be more visible. But Harold never reached that point. His devotion to Ramsey remained absolute, in its way on a par with Lady Vicky's, and in the dressing room he was his boss's eyes and ears — and greatest protector.

Joe Baker and George Eastham were gone from the Madrid team when Alf announced the line-up for our opening game of the tournament, against Uruguay — a match which had received an extraordinary build-up as the nation became consumed with World Cup fever. Taking their places were Jimmy Greaves, restored after injury to his eminence as England's most deadly striker, and John Connelly, who got the Ramsey vote over the lean, impatient young Peters because the old full-back still couldn't find it in himself to turn his back on the deeply established idea that an attack without a specialist winger, despite all the possible compensations, had been dismembered.

We had played the Uruguayans two years earlier and we knew what we would be getting: a packed defence and tackling which would come at us relentlessly and land on various parts of our bodies quite indiscriminately. Alf didn't stress the potential violence, though. He was more concerned with their technical ability. Any mug defence could throw up a screen and crowd behind the ball, but the Uruguayans were far from mugs. They had twice won the World Cup, in 1930 and 1950, and no small-population football nation had ever fought so tenaciously to hang on to a great winning tradition.

All Uruguayan achievement had been built on formidable defence. It was in their blood.

'The Uruguayans,' said Alf in his team talk, 'are very good at getting men behind the ball but more important is what they do when they get there. They engage you, they just don't let you have the ball in front of them, they come for you and try to force you into mistakes. When they do get the ball they get goalside very quickly indeed, so Bobby and Jack must make sure we're never caught square.' It was a normal team-meeting. Alf was careful not to stoke up the emotional levels. He wanted committed footballers but it was vital that they were also clear-thinking.

One concern was our defensive wall for free kicks. It had been decided upon but there was a little twinge of doubt about one of its members. Ironically, this was Bobby Charlton, who probably put more power into his shot than any footballer on earth. His brother Jack explained the problem in his usual pithy fashion. He said, 'Our kid loves to whack the ball – but he's not so keen to have it whacked at him.' But then who was?

Defenders tend to accept the blows a little more philoso-phically, however, and it is generally true that forwards are not ideal components of a defensive wall. Their basic instinct is to not stand up when the free kick is struck. The other problem is that while defenders would be much happier to take their place in the firing line, they are obviously needed away from the wall to react to any critical situation that might develop. These were details, but Alf attended to them. All winning managers do. He announced the team on the eve of the game, having had a few words earlier with players he sensed might be least sure of their places. One player who always seemed particularly keen to know if he was playing was Southampton's Terry Paine, one of the clutch of wingers anxious about the possibility that they would be officially declared redundant. He showed plenty of confidence on the field and always gave the impression that he believed he should be playing, but perhaps Alf noted that this was something of an act.

On this occasion, though, he had to give Paine the hard word that he was out, before telling Connelly he had the job of outflanking the tank-trap defence of Uruguay. Connelly had not been given a favour, and nor had any of us. I was reminded of Ramsey's feel for detail as we went to the stadium. My first international had been the Uruguay game at Wembley two years earlier, and I recalled Ramsey taking me on one side before that game. He said I should go out on the field and walk around the far corner for a little while, because, perhaps as a consequence of the old speedway track, it tended to get a little soggy out there and quite a different consistency from the rest of the pitch. He was quite right and it was good information to have. It meant I wasn't going to be surprised by a suddenly changing surface when confronted by a quick winger going for an early kill.

Now on a hot, humid afternoon at the start of this World Cup, I had another problem and it rather took me by surprise. I felt nervous, more edgy, in fact that I had as a teenager going out to play Manchester United in an FA Cup semi-final. Driving to the stadium, seeing the crowds in the street, the flags, a feeling of numbness came. This was not like any football game I had ever played. It felt bigger, more important, more difficult to anticipate. I knew I was perfectly fit but I felt heavy. Looking back, I suppose it shouldn't have been so surprising, The team had been together for seven weeks, and in that time, as I said to him, even big Jack Charlton could begin to look attractive. It was a bit like coming out of a fortress. Suddenly you were out in the open and fighting for your life. I knew I had to get out of breath. When the pre-game formalities were over it was necessary to run hard and then you could relax a little, you could do your exercises and begin to take things in. You could feel the heaviness going out of your legs. It is then that the value of the people around you comes into play. I could hear the edge of aggression and confidence in Big Jack's rasping, drawling voice. Bobby Moore gave a small nod of encouragement. Nobby was chattering, not to anyone in particular but the general assembly, he always had to be doing or saying something at times like this, latching on to a point which he considered important. It was why he was such a good trouble-shooter or 'policeman'. He saw problems in the making.

The Uruguayans were as stubborn and difficult as the manager had imagined. We couldn't get round them or through them. Connelly ran into blind alleys, as did Wilson and I when we tried to steal a little ground on the overlap. Bobby Charlton was unable to get within firing range, Roger Hunt threw himself against a brick wall. In the end we were relying on Jimmy Greaves to thread his way through the thickets of blue-shirted resistance. The South American coach

Ondino Vieri made no pretence to any ambition beyond survival. He had a sweeper, the captain Horacio Troche, behind a back four and everyone else, including their most skilled and creative players, Pedro Rocha and Julio Cesar Cortes, in withdrawn positions. Body-checks and high tackles were commonplace and, ironically enough, Nobby received one of the worst. But he scarcely blinked and carried on. We ran relentlessly but only into an ever-deepening deadlock. It stayed 0–0 and was not quite the lift-off for which the nation had been primed by the flowing pen of Desmond Hackett. His great rhapsody of praise in Madrid was as distant as the sound of flamenco now and as we left the field, tired and frustrated, there was a smattering of boos, a sense from the terracing that a crusade had died before it had truly begun.

Alf was philosophical, however. He said we could have played better but then we could have played a lot worse. We were very solid in defence, and if ever a team, given their talent and their outlook, had a chance of shutting down a game it was surely Uruguay. We just had the small problem of failing to score a goal. The problem was resolved in our second game against Mexico by Bobby Charlton, though this is a mild way of saying it. Charlton's goal was worthy of the gods. It came after half an hour of battering against another packed defence. We knew we faced, yet again, a battle of attrition straight from the kick off when the Mexican player Isidora Diaz booted the ball downfield while his team-mates retreated into their defensive positions. I watched every stride of Charlton's goal. It was beautiful to see. The Mexicans defended hard, though not as skilfully or viciously as the Uruguayans, and they attacked you when they could. In their first game they had drawn I—I with our other group opponents, France, who Alf rated as quite useful, and overall they were not too bad a team. But they couldn't begin to deal with Bobby when he went on his majestic run.

Charlton gathered the ball inside our half and gradually picked up speed, changing his feet and his balance as though it was the most natural thing in the world. In those moments he reminded me very much of my brilliant adversary Cliff Jones. The Mexicans fell back and Bobby surged on, changing his feet again before hitting a tremendous shot across the goalkeeper and into the far corner. The range was from twenty-five yards and quite deadly.

By the time the ball hit the Mexican net it had turned egg-shaped. The goalkeeper, normally an acrobatic character named Ignacio Calderon, hardly moved. It was the classic Charlton goal. It was a sensation and brought our campaign to life quite magnificently. We scored another in the second half. It wasn't so spectacular, even though Charlton did some fine spadework, exchanging a series of passes before feeding Greaves, whose shot was blocked but not controlled by Calderon. Hunt pounced and the Mexicans were done.

We felt we had moved a notch up, that perhaps we were on our way. Ball and Connelly had paid for the Uruguayan impasse with their places in the team, Paine coming in on the right and Peters, to rather better effect, making his trade-marked stealthy runs. Ramsey was still hooked on the dilemma of whether or not to play a winger. Part of his problem was that none of the candidates had made his task easier with any kind of significant impact. Connelly had struggled in the first game and Paine, for all his ambition, had been just as marginal against the less formidable Mexicans – and at the sacrifice of the whirring energy of Ball. In the final group game against France, Ramsey would roll the last dice on behalf of the wingers' union, giving Liverpool's Ian Callaghan a run. But Peters had made his case and in the shadows you could hear the hard breathing of Alan Ball. No-one had ever been more fired with the desire for battle. Ramsey wasn't ecstatic over our latest performance but he said 'well done' to us all as we came into the dressing room, and you could see he was reasonably satisfied. We had shown a little more confidence in ourselves and no doubt he was privately grateful for the liberating effect of Charlton's stupendous goal. All the team appreciated Ramsey's calmness. He avoided extremes of reaction, which was a refreshing change as all his players could tell stories of managers losing their respect by ranting and raving in the dressing room. Such reactions never help anybody and sometimes it can destroy a player. Some players go out on the field scared, and they come back the same way, and quite often they have good reason to feel that way. But the manager doesn't help anyone by shouting and screaming. All he does, in fact, is diminish his own position. If a player has performed to the best of his ability or if, when he has not been in the greatest of form, he has played honestly, he shouldn't have any fear of the manager's reaction, at least not if he trusts the manager and knows that he is the kind of football man who understands the ebb and flow of form – and the difference between someone who has tried and another player who has cheated.

It is the saddest thing to see a manager losing control and destroying everything he has tried to build. Alf never did that. In fact the only times I saw him show real anger – apart from the time he responded to what he considered a series of Argentinian outrages – were in incidents off the pitch. Once he was being shown around a college building in Montreal, where the team had been assigned lodgings during the Expo football tournament in 1967, when he went into a shower area and discovered a Mexican washing his feet in a sink. He said, 'How bloody appalling.' His trauma didn't end there. When he inspected the pitch on which we were due to play he was stunned to see the remains of a circus, including mounds of elephant droppings. Whole areas of the field were scarred and these were being painted green. He hadn't been put in the best of moods by the behaviour of the celebrated football correspondent of *The Times*, Geoffrey Green. On the trans-Atlantic flight Geoffrey, a much-loved character and brilliant writer, had drunk rather a lot of Scotch before launching into a serenade of the team, which he accompanied with his beloved mandolin. This continued until we arrived at the big college building and Ramsey eyed him as though he might have been a visitor from another planet. He was similarly distressed when, after a match in Poland, a cleaning woman came into the dressing room carrying a long-handled broom, which was alarming in itself. We were all changing and Alf had just emerged from the shower and was quite naked. He turned to the faithful Harold Shepherdson and said, 'How absurd.'

Ian Callaghan contributed to the second of our goals in the 2–0 win over France, which gave us Group One and a place in the quarter-finals, but even that couldn't prevent Ramsey from finally turning his face away from wingers. Connelly and Paine, who had been judged failures in the first two matches, would never play for him again and Callaghan's next international appearance wouldn't be for another eleven years, by which time Ramsey had been replaced by Don Revie. We played well against France with Hunt scoring both goals. Their forward line, which our manager had considered potentially dangerous, failed to make any inroads into our back-four unit. But if Ramsey was 'reasonably pleased' he still believed we were some way from optimum performance and while he weighed up the tinkering which might bring vital improvement as we moved towards the more serious end of the tournament, he also had to deal with two major problems. First he had to fight off official moves to ease our 'policeman' Stiles out of the tournament, and as he did that he was obliged to consider how he would cover the other bleak possibility that Jimmy Greaves had suffered an injury which might mean the end of his World Cup. It was hard to know which would be the more damaging blow to both the physical and psychological health of the team. Stiles had become, apart from anything else, almost the mascot of the team. He was both our fun and optimism and our conscience as he tore about the field, making the tackles and delivering the ball to his master, Bobby Charlton, while at the same time making sure that any gaps which appeared in defence were properly filled. Greaves, although he had yet to hit his stride and was still looking for his first goal after three matches, was arguably the most natural-born striker in the game.

He had 43 goals from 51 internationals coming into this World Cup. If Hunt was the warrior charging the opposing defence, Greaves was the man with the stiletto. Stiles was in trouble with the authorities for a foul on the Frenchman Jacky Simon which, whatever its intent, looked horrible. Earlier Nobby was involved in a collision which left Simon's team-mate Roby Herbin limping. He was playing his usual game, committed and sharp, but when he lined up Simon for a tackle while the Frenchman waited to control a throw-in which seemed to just hang in the air as though shot in slow motion, you had this sudden apprehension that Nobby was coming in terribly late. Simon was a good, skilled player and he must have seen in the corner of his eye that Stiles was bearing down on him. A less confident player would have tried to lay off the ball more or less anywhere but Simon was more ambitious than that and he elected to sell Nobby a dummy. Unfortunately he didn't sell anything. He bought himself the tackle from hell, one that from the moment of its inception was destined to land somewhere between the Frenchman's thyroid gland and his crotch. I recalling grimacing and saying to myself, 'Jesus, that looked bad.' The Peruvian referee Arturo Yamasaki for some unaccountable reason took no action. A booking seemed an inevitable consequence, if not a sending off. There was huge relief in our team and no doubt on the bench. It was early in the game, there was no score and the French were playing it around rather well. By the end of the game, which had been secured by Hunt's second goal, Ramsey was much more concerned by the nasty injury to Greaves, who had decided to go for a 50–50 ball at precisely the same moment as a French defender. Greavsie lost, and the price was stitches to a deep gash in his shin and the fear that he had lost his place in a World Cup that had carried the promise of the supreme achievement of his career.

However, the Stiles business refused to go away. Apparently he had been booked for the tackle on Simon. Not by the referee, but by an official of the world governing body, Fifa, who had been sitting in the stand. The Fifa observer filed a damning report on Stiles's performance and the following day, when Ramsey should have been concentrating on what he considered the pivotal challenge of the tournament, the quarter-final game against Argentina, he was instead receiving a delegation from his employers, the Football Association. In the best of circumstances, Ramsey tended to bristle in the company of FA councillors – he had successfully moved that they travel separately from the team – and for him this was the least desirable of meetings, both in timing and content. The FA men wanted to know 'how necessary' Stiles was to Ramsey's campaign to win the World Cup. The point was that the FA men had been asked by Fifa to petition for Stiles's exclusion from the England team for the rest of the tournament. Ramsey was indignant, but he controlled his anger and said that he would speak to the player before making any decision. Ramsey asked Stiles about the tackle –

what was his view of it and what had been his intentions? Stiles, the most combative of footballers, was terribly upset. He said he knew how horrible it must have looked, but it was a question of timing. 'I got my timing wrong, Alf,' said Nobby. 'I hate the fact I've put you in this position and all I can say is that I made a mistake. I went to make the tackle and then I found I was late – terribly late. I'm sorry.'

Ramsey told Nobby that he accepted his explanation. He would not surrender him to the FA councillors and their Fifa friends. He told the FA, 'I have spoken to my player and I accept his version of events. If he is removed from the tournament I will remove myself.' There would be no argument, no negotiations. If Nobby went, so would Alf Ramsey. Nobby said that he would never, as long as he lived, forget the day that the manager of England had stood with him shoulder to shoulder. Nor would any of his team-mates. Ramsey had talked so many times about the value of loyalty to the team, and now he had shown us what he meant. There was still the worry of Jimmy Greaves, but at that moment no team in the history of football's greatest tournament had ever been so united behind the man who led them to the battle.

CHAPTER TEN

ANIMALS AND NOBBY'S BUSINESS

There was really nothing you could say to Jimmy Greaves. He was out on his own and however hard you looked for it, as you caught his eye in a hotel corridor or as he went to the treatment room, there was no middle ground. The more you thought about it the more clearly you saw that the World Cup, which now promised so much for the rest of us, had for him almost certainly come to an end. It did not help much that the French tackle that had so damaged his hopes was not malicious. Greaves and a Frenchman had gone for the ball and something happened quite by chance. So it goes – and so he didn't have anywhere to direct his anger; he had just the cold dawning that the greatest opportunity of his career had been taken away. Football, as everyone who plays it for any length of time knows, is like life itself in that it gives and takes away – and often with the most brutal timing.

It was, though, a more complicated situation than the public may have imagined as they read the headlines on Ramsey's agony of decision. Would he hang on and hope for a miracle recovery by his fabled striker? Or would he respond to another prompting that, some felt, had become increasingly insistent. It was the one that said England might benefit more from the thrusting drive of the young, strong Geoff Hurst alongside the warhorse Roger Hunt. Hurst, it was clear enough, would play against Argentina. The question was whether it would be a temporary solution or the start of a new order. My feeling is that when Hurst scored against Argentina, when he seized so hungrily, and so efficiently, on a beautiful cross by his West Ham team-mate Martin Peters, it was all over for Greaves. Ramsey had many splendid qualities, and he had fine feelings which were often disguised by a brusque manner, but in the matter of picking a football team mere sentiment would never figure highly.

When Ramsey saw what he had with the combination of Hunt and Hurst, when he measured the bite of the new man and the relentlessly applied strength of his more experienced partner, I believe he knew there was no going back. Greaves was one of the world's great scorers. He was a fantastic player. His timing and movement into the box were sublime. How could you willingly leave him out of the team? But the truth was that Greaves had lost a yard – maybe two. He had been ill with hepatitis, and, I suspected, he was still fighting off the after-effects. He had been able to score a flurry of goals in the build-up, but in the tournament he hadn't come truly on to his game. Ramsey knew how the nation – and the media – felt about Greaves. He was a legend, a demi-god – but could he deliver, here and now, in the fashion of, say, Geoff Hurst? Maybe because of his status in the game everyone, including Ramsey, whose natural inclination was to

Against Argentina in the quarter-finals. It may look like ballet but this was anything but a graceful game.

Alf prevents me from exchanging shirts with Gonzales after the game. Later he condemned the Argentineans as 'animals'.

Meeting the queen prior to the final. I was desperate to get underway.

Then and now, and still a close-knit team.

Back row, l-r: Harold Shepherdson, Stiles, Hunt, Banks, Jack Charlton, Me, Wilson, Sir Alf. Front row, l-r: Peters, Hurst, Moore, Ball, Bobby Charlton.

L-r: Nobby, Bobby, Ray, Geoff, Roger, Me, Jack, Martin, Alan.

'Legends' evening, l-r: Robson, Mullery, Marsh, Haynes, Me.

Fulham chairman Al-Fayed purchased my
World Cup medal for the club museum. It was
the winning of it that mattered. And how do
you leave one medal to two sons?

With the family after the investiture l-r: Andrew and wife Baldeep, Me and Daphne, Anthony and wife Helen.

The Forgotten Five, l-r: Ball, Hunt, Stiles, Me, Wilson. No top hat and tails in sight.

The last photo my life-long friend Dennie Mancini sent to me, before his death in 2004. He was described as the best 'cuts man' in Europe.

With my brothers Peter and Len, and son Andrew.

The grandkids, l-r: Charlotte, Christopher, Ben, Eleanor and Lewis.

Daphne and I on our Ruby wedding anniversary.

Over page: My nephew Ben and me. World Cup winners. A magical moment for me and I know how proud his father would have been.

be very forthright, and Greaves's friend and captain Bobby Moore, were tip-toeing around the problem. Ramsey was conscious that there was a lot of pain in Greaves and he said to Moore, 'How's your mate? He seems very quiet.' Bobby could only shrug and shake his head. There was not a lot he could do beyond being there if Greaves wanted to talk, which at the time he apparently didn't. Greaves was wounded – and living in the shadows, and for a footballer at that time it was a terrible place. He had everyone's sympathy and respect. You couldn't know precisely how he felt but it was the fairest bet that he was inconsolable. After recovering from illness, he had come to what he must have seen as the highpoint of his career – a World Cup in front of his own people. He had been on top of the game since his explosive arrival as a seventeen year-old at Chelsea. He had been lured to Italy and came back to blossom at Tottenham. His reputation was immense. No defender wanted to play against him.

In public Jimmy handled it well. You could see he was desperately upset but you could only speculate how he was when he retreated to his room. He kept his deepest feelings to himself. He was a pro and he was a man who had seen a few things and so he was obviously keen not to let himself down. Though the drama of his situation would be a great theme of the media throughout the tournament, when Hurst carried us beyond Argentina in one of the most controversial matches ever played, Jimmy Greaves could only bite his lip and know that as England's World Cup caravan rattled on there was, however many the acres of newsprint speculation, no longer a place for him. Football, in its arbitrary way, elected Geoff Hurst to be the man, but he must have known it would be no easy passage to the stars when he listened with his new first team-mates to the taut pre-match message of the manager. 'I don't think I have to tell you too much about what to expect against Argentina,' said Ramsey. 'I expect it to be a very difficult game in all respects and you will have to be on guard for ninety minutes.' Those of us who had seen Argentina overwhelm Brazil in Sao Paulo two years earlier knew precisely what he meant. If you could detach them from the hacking and the spitting and the constant harassment of the opposition – and often the officials – you could only admire the team dominated by its captain Antonio Rattin. There was no question in my mind that this game against Argentina had the potential to be a classic, but knowing their style, their extreme cynicism, you could only fear the worst, and especially now that the stakes had become so high with the brutal expulsion of Brazil by Portugal in Group Three. The man I had to mark, Oscar Mas, was difficult. He was quick, mobile and clever, and in the early going he administered a nasty shock. He gave me the slip as he went inside and I was perturbed to see that Jack Charlton didn't have him covered. Gordon Banks was required to make a save, fortunately not a difficult one because Mas mis-hit his shot. It didn't happen again but it was a sharp warning on the need for total vigilance. You couldn't break your concentration for a second because they were playing it slow, slow, slow, and then very quickly indeed.

They were niggling from the start. They made everything difficult, arguing with the officials, stalling over free kicks, and at the heart of all the mischief was Rattin, a tall, domineering figure who spat out his disgust – frequently literally – when things didn't go quite to his satisfaction. The first confrontation of the slight and, it seemed to me, timid German referee Rudolf Kreitlein and the swaggering Rattin warned of the problems to come. Rattin towered, threateningly, over the official, and increasingly he was voicing his complaints. Rattin was a natural bully, you could see that – along with his beautiful control of the ball and excellent positional sense. He was Argentina's centre-half but his influence spread into every corner of the team. Unfortunately there can rarely have been such a malign spirit seeking to control the course of an important football match.

The catalyst for a sporting disaster was a minor dispute over a free kick. Rattin spoke aggressively to the referee. He was stoking the fire. The game was running out of control when Rattin was sent off after thirty-six minutes. Later Bobby Moore said, 'We accepted in our guts it was going to be hard, maybe brutal – and it was. They did tug your hair, spit at you, poke you in the eyes and kick you when the ball was miles away and no-one was looking.' Hurst's evidence was equally damning of the Argentines. He said that he felt as though he had not been playing at Wembley but walking down a dark alley in a strange town. 'At any moment,' he said, 'and for no reason, you thought you might be attacked from behind.' Twice he was kicked on the ankle when he was nowhere near the ball. 'I swung round,' he reported, 'and there was a ring of blank faces.' Rattin refused to leave the field. It took him six or seven minutes to go and in the meantime another of the Argentines, the defender Rafael Albrecht, tried to march his team-mates off the field. We were obliged to talk among ourselves. One point of agreement was that if we had a vote on who should be sent off the Argentine skipper would have won it by a landslide. He was a hellishly awkward customer, but some of his play was simply heavenly. He was in the middle of the defence but he refused to accept any restrictions on his ability to influence every phase of the game, coming out of his line with great authority on the ball. You got the impression he could see everything on the field. It was part of Bobby Charlton's job to cover his breaks into midfield but Rattin was in the mood to take on our entire team. He was a master of the wind-up, and he had ten eager lieutenants in this department.

If you went anywhere near an Argentine there was every chance he would just fall down. It was a nightmare for the referee and — at that time — completely alien to us. Tackles were flying in — and so was the spittle. Our front men, Hunt and Hurst, were taking most of it. There were some amazing things going on up there, and even in defence we were getting hit late and dangerously. They were leaving their feet in the tackle as a matter of course, and tapping you on the shoulder and then pulling the short hairs on the back of your neck. Nothing particularly nasty happened between Mas and me. The truth was that when necessary I could do a bit of the naughty stuff myself. I never wanted to be that sort of pro but sometimes circumstances force you into behaviour you normally wouldn't even consider. In fact I did put the boot into one of the Argentines. It was Luis Artime, who had

been one of their more intimidating characters. I caught him
hard and he almost did a cartwheel – right in front of the
Royal Box. The hard-pressed ref took no action beyond
awarding a free kick, which they took very quickly. It was
rather amazing how swiftly they could change their football
personality. One minute they were spitting and hacking like
guttersnipes. The next they were playing quite beautifully.
There was no doubt in my mind, even in all that chaos and
anger, that whoever was going to win the World Cup first had
to beat Argentina. Someone later produced statistics which
showed that in fact we had committed the most fouls. My
first reaction was to quote the old line about their being lies,
damned lies and statistics, but of course in such a battle, with
the stakes and tension so high, there was always going to be a
large number of fouls. I would also say that there are fouls
and fouls, and if the Argentines didn't match us in numbers
there was no question about the level of their dubious intent.

Naturally we thought the goal, which came after seventy-
seven minutes, was a stroke of natural justice. Certainly it
marked the arrival of Hurst on the big international stage
after running a gauntlet of abuse and violence which would
make the football of Argentina notorious through the rest of
the sixties. Hurst took it brilliantly. Peters made it with all
the vision that prompted Ramsey's claim that the boy was
running so far ahead of his time – and ours. He was terribly
bright and, behind the boyish smile, quite a mean customer
on the field. He once admitted to me that he had a very good
memory for people who had taken liberties with him in the
past, and the implication was that he wasn't above delivering

a little retribution down the road. Now, at the most important of moments, he had delivered a killer ball, one that could only have been delivered by a front rank talent.

He got out wide and sent in the cross without really looking. It curved beautifully in its flight towards the near post and Hurst met it perfectly. It was a real West Ham goal because Hurst was expecting that ball and Peters knew he would be there to exploit it. I had my differences with their manager Ron Greenwood, but it was no hardship acknowledging the strength of his work at Upton Park. Ramsey had produced the blueprint for success but, unquestionably, some of the most vital parts had been designed and made in the East End. The Peters–Hurst move brought the gates of a World Cup triumph swinging open. It also defined what the combination of superior coaching and talent and hard work can produce in the way of excellent execution. Hurst arrived at the end of Peters' cross in the way of the very best players. As Peters raised his foot, Hurst was on his way – not a moment too soon, or too late. If he had been too soon he would have been covered by a blue-and-white shirt. Had he been too late the goalkeeper Antonio Roma would have comfortably gathered the ball.

There are so many memories of that vital day in the history of English football. Of course I could never forget the venom Ramsey put into his voice when, after seeing me about to exchange shirts with the Argentine player Alberto Gonzalez, he came rushing between us and told me, 'George, you are not changing shirts with that animal.' He would use the term 'animals' more publicly and it meant his second confrontation with the FA and Fifa in just a few days. Fifa said that he was guilty of unsportsmanlike behaviour, which was rather ironic in view of what we had seen on the Wembley pitch. The FA were told to reprimand Ramsey and demand an apology. Because he was so anxious to maintain England's momentum, and cut down distractions to a minimum, Ramsey made an apology – of sorts. There was never any question that he would get down on his knees. He was too proud for that and, anyway, in his stubborn way he believed he had been merely telling the truth. Certainly it was true that the anarchy brought by the Argentines provoked an official drive demanding basic standards of behaviour in international football, and especially in the matter of intimidating referees. It was also a fact that while Ramsey angrily responded to the events of a turbulent day he was also being something of a prophet. Football was repeatedly dragged into the gutter by Argentine club teams like Estudiantes and River Plate when they competed in the World Club championship with teams like Manchester United, Celtic and Ajax of Amsterdam, who found themselves caught up in terrible dogfights when they travelled to South America. Ramsey was the first to rage against this corruption of the game by a wonderfully talented football nation. He saw the terrible paradox of a team who could, when they put their minds to it, soar so far beyond the cheap skulduggery that so besmirched the image of both their own country and the whole game.

But then Ramsey had only a passing interest in the reform of international football. His preoccupation was with leading

England to an historic triumph, one which he believed would heal a thousand wounds inflicted on the national game of the country which had given football to the world. He had felt some of those wounds personally.

He had experienced the pain of the slaughter of England's reputation by Hungary and three years before that, in 1950, he had also been on the field when the national team suffered arguably its greatest shame – a 1–0 defeat by the United States in the mining town of Belo Horizonte. Ramsey was scratching about the organisation of England on the way to that disaster. England were deigning to play their first World Cup, in Brazil, but their performance was pitiful. England failed to play their way out of the group they shared with Spain, Chile and the American amateurs, and when Joe Gaetjens headed in the only goal, denying England a place in the final pool, Ramsey was particularly horrified. He claimed that the cross by Walter Bahr was really meant to be a shot and that the ball had entered the net via the ear of Gaetjens, who was alleged to have been ducking to avoid any contact. These were some of the demons Ramsey sought to dispatch on his way to the great prize and there was no doubt he felt that victory over Argentina had put him within touching distance. He was pleased with the way we handled ourselves under extraordinary pressure and if Hurst had put himself at risk with one reckless tackle born of anger, Ramsey accepted that both his front men had suffered outrageous provocation. 'Most certainly' he was happy that we had mostly kept our heads and at all stages tried to play good constructive football. He had hammered home the value of keeping possession against such skilled and potentially explosive opponents and clearly we had listened.

Ramsey said he knew we could play better but he was 'gratified' by several aspects of our effort. He particularly liked the willingness of Hurst and Hunt to keep returning to the trenches where their markers were behaving so atrociously, and he also recognised the difficulty we had faced in maintaining any decent tempo when the Argentinians so cynically stopped the play whenever we moved into anything like a dangerous position. His mood for several days after the game was more than anything a mixture of rage and bewilderment. Rage that players of the quality of Bobby Charlton had been placed at such risk by Argentina's methods, and bewilderment that the South Americans should so disfigure – and reduce – their own luminous talent.

That last mystery ran most deeply in my own mind – and it still does. When I think back to that incredible afternoon, when I recall Rattin's reluctant walk away from the Wembley pitch and his unforgettably wistful fingering of the corner flag before he went into the shadows with a storm of booing in his ears, one strange little incident always comes back. The memory is of Oscar Mas, the man who had given me that anxious moment at the start of the match, tapping me on the shoulder and pointing to the big scoreboard. It showed the score from the Portugal–North Korea quarter-final at Goodison Park, one that had brought a great gasp from the crowd: Portugal 0, North Korea 3.

Mas's expression said, 'Oh, oh . . . . It's a strange game, a strange life, isn't it?' It was indeed. Here was a potentially great Argentine team selling itself desperately short, and at Goodison Park, my favourite ground, a bunch of obscure North Koreans were running through one of Europe's most powerful football nations. If we got through this Wembley ordeal, would the North Koreans be waiting, without fear, to spring another ambush? Eusebio headed off the possibility with a storming fight back, and soon enough Ramsey was formulating another plan – one that gave the crucial role of stifling the destroyer of North Korea to Nobby Stiles, the man he had so recently protected so fiercely and who now, he believed, could help carry us on his scrawny legs to that football mountain top for which he had yearned so long.

In the meantime, however, he decided that we should all relax a little before the penultimate push to glory against Portugal. That meant Westerns, a visit to the Ken Dodd show – I was not the only one who muttered under his breath that all had been forgiven John Wayne and Alan Ladd – and a trip to Pinewood Studios, where they were making one of the James Bond films. Ken Dodd is a lovely man to meet but I've never been able to warm to his humour. Maybe it's a north-south thing. I say that because Nobby sat next to me during the show and he was crying with laughter.

There were merely a few sniggers when Alf made a speech of thanks after our tour of Pinewood. He couldn't disguise the fact that he was in awe of the movie-makers as he found the nerve to say, 'Thank you all for turning out to greet us and showing us around, and special thanks to Mr Sean Connery.' Unfortunately he pronounced Sean 'Scene'. Some might have said that that was the extent of Ramsey's education beyond the game, but if there were a few subdued chuckles from the movie people, they stayed out of his earshot. *We* could laugh with him, or at times at him, but as far as we were concerned no-one else was allowed.

We were members in a private club into which Alf did all the electing. That meant we were under his protection, with the result that he had our fierce loyalty. I noted that the well-known Scotsman Mr Connery kept a commendably straight face.

When Ramsey returned to the question of Portugal his authority inevitably came flooding back. He was concerned about the quality of Eusebio and instructed Nobby to take the great player out of the game, at which point Nobby came back with his famous response. There was no question about the size of the task being handed to the little man. He had to shadow one of the world's great players. There was no talk of shifting responsibilities, zonal coverage – Eusebio was Nobby's business. He had to man-mark him to oblivion – and stay out of the referee's book. As I never stop saying, Nobby produced a perfect performance. There was no violence – and this was surprising in that Portugal had been accused of kicking Pele and Brazil out of the tournament – just a performance of wonderful control and sheer football intelligence from Stiles.

I heard it said recently that if Stiles and Eusebio were playing in today's game only one of these key rivals would qualify as a star. The implication is that Stiles was somehow fortunate to be operating in such company. It is a nonsense. Stiles suffocated Eusebio by fair means. He moved quickly and thought quickly and the result was that we were free to play the more adventurous football. Bobby Charlton scored both the goals and his second was one of his more spectacular. Geoff Hurst raced on to a long ball I'd sent into the right corner, shook off a defender, and pulled it back for Charlton to drive home. That was in the 79th minute and though the Portuguese hit back with a penalty three minutes later after Jack Charlton had been forced to handle the ball, we knew we had the game won – and a place in the World Cup final against West Germany.

Many years later I had dinner with the fine Portuguese left-winger Antonio Simoes, and so quite naturally we re-played our semi-final. He said that they had been surprised by the quality of our football. They expected us to be strong and quite direct but they believed they had an edge in technical ability. They were a little taken aback by the ease with which we carried the game to them. This was an England team, said Simoes, which had more than beef and heart. Nobby's imprisonment of Eusebio was one key, he agreed, but there was also the formidable matter of England's defence. It was, one had to agree with all due modesty, true enough. When Gordon Banks chose to dive the wrong way for Eusebio's penalty it was the first goal against us in seven matches, which was a record.

Alf was delighted with the quality of our football against Portugal and he said that we were on a perfect ascent. He had always said we could win this tournament and perhaps now we also believed. There were times when he could convince us of anything. He had said we would be playing Portugal in the semis because Brazil in 1966 were a myth. Pele was surrounded by old men and young ones still in need of vital experience and there wasn't a decent full-back in sight. It was not insignificant in our minds that Alf had basically said all this more than two years before. He had taken another look at the Brazilians on a spying mission when Brazil played Sweden a few months earlier. He came back to say, 'Most certainly we can forget the Brazilians. They aren't going anywhere.' Unlike England, who were going all the way.

CHAPTER ELEVEN

IT'S COMING HOME

I was up early on the morning of July 30, 1966, the dawn of the World Cup final, and was a little surprised to encounter Nobby Stiles blinking his way into the dawn, too. He told me he was off to find a Catholic church in Golders Green, where he could make his confession and hear Mass. I said, 'Good luck.' And I warned him that he might not find his search very easy. A synagogue would be a rather different matter. There were, I pointed out, possibly as many synagogues in Golders Green as in the entire state of Israel. But Nobby was as indefatigable as ever. He marched off to make his peace with God — I've always wondered if he mentioned that tackle on Jacky Simon — and when I saw him a few hours later he said that his mission had gone well. Except that when they took the collection they didn't give change, but then what did he expect in Golders Green?

While Nobby attended to his faith, I had the breakfast I reserve for special occasions — peeled tomatoes and scrambled eggs. I had slept well enough despite reading a few pages of Dennis Wheatley, the master of the occult, before slipping off. But it would be wrong to say I felt particularly calm. While it is true we were all confident, at least on the surface, about our chances against the Germans – we had, after all, beaten them twice under Ramsey – the closer it got to kick-off the more difficult it was to forget the importance of the match. In those days before hype became an industry the build up to the World Cup had been less than hysterical. But as we progressed, with growing certainty after our struggle in the opening game against Uruguay, the expectations of the nation had risen steadily.

Now there were flags in the street and the front and back pages of the newspapers and the news broadcasts were dominated by one question: Could we beat the Germans and win our first World Cup? One sportswriter, Frank McGhee of the *Daily Mirror*, rather hedged his bets when he wrote, 'If on the morrow it should happen that we lose to Germany at our national game, let us not forget that twice this century we have beaten them at theirs,' but generally the mood was rather more upbeat. Forlornly, though, the media was still conducting a debate over the rival claims of Jimmy Greaves and Geoff Hurst. It was a good story, no doubt – the legend against the bright, brave new kid on the block, but because Hurst had done so well some commentators and writers had also brought Hunt into the equation. In reality the debate was dead, and you had only to look into Jimmy Greaves's eyes to know it. The issue had always been between Greaves and Hurst. Hunt was rock solid with Ramsey, who always knew what he would get from the Liverpool man – fearless, relentless work which nagged at an opposing defence like a toothache which couldn't be cured. Ramsey knew that if anyone was required to risk his head being knocked off it would be Hunt who would step forward. Ramsey had only to recall the number of times Hunt had gone in with the goalkeeper and knocked the ball down to a waiting colleague with a clear view of the net. He was a one-man workforce, which is perhaps not the most flattering of descriptions but it expresses the essence of him. How else, anyway, can you describe a fellow who is willing to run all day just to make the people around him look like decent players?

Over breakfast I recalled a meeting with Hunt on a beach in Majorca a few months earlier. I was running hard in pursuit of the fitness which had been threatened by a late season injury, a freak collision with the Stoke City left-winger Harry Burrows. Hunt was on an end-of-season trip with Liverpool and, naturally, Shankly had them playing football on the sand.

What else would a group of men be doing by the seaside while under the command of Bill Shankly? Hunt and I were football men between assignments and, maybe because of the weight of the pressure that was beginning to build around us, our collision on a holiday beach seemed a touch surreal. We advised each other to look after ourselves, which in my case was rather more than a formality. Because I knew what was coming that afternoon, nothing less, perhaps, than a definition of my career and those of the men who I had lived with so closely for several years now, I suppose I was a little more reflective than normal as I pecked at my eggs and tomatoes. I thought of all that football had brought me — the companionship of my team-mates down the years, how Roy Bentley had taken special care of me and the rather touching way Johnny Haynes had taken me on one side before I reported for the World Cup campaign.

He put a hand on my shoulder and said, 'Good luck son – I'll keep my fingers crossed.' Given all that I thought of Haynes, and all the joy and the pain we had experienced together out on the field, I suppose it was inevitable that a lump came to my throat. I thought of so many things. I thought of my father and how good it would have been for him to be at the stadium today, maybe wearing another white-and-black painted top hat, and I vowed that if I did reach the point of victory when the shadows came to Wembley a corner of my thoughts would be for him and all that he had done so uncomplainingly down the years to keep the food on our table and the shoes on our feet.

I thought of Mel Roberts and the training field in Wandsworth and the look of surprise on Ernie Shepherd's face when he couldn't burn me away. He said I should be a big fish in a small pond, and now I was swimming in the big football ocean. I thought of the exhilaration that football had given me – on and off the field, the doors it had opened and the experiences it had brought. I recalled the day I walked through the piazza of San Marco in Venice, a teenaged tourist with Fulham, and then bought the most expensive cup of coffee in the world without giving a damn because I had been taken so far from Eel Brook Common and the North End Road.

I had to chuckle a little at the memory of Tommy Trinder's

negotiating technique when I came back from that tour of Brazil with England, feeling that I'd finally busted into the big time and demanding that Fulham bring me up to the wage level my new status really demanded – £100 a week. Trinder had anticipated such a request and sent me a letter of congratulations and the offer of a £10-a-week rise. I told him it just wasn't good enough. He said, 'Georgie, I can't pay you a £100 a week, that's all I'm paying the best player in the world, Johnny Haynes.' I asked him if he would have expected anything less of a demand from somebody called Cohen. 'Ah,' said Trinder, 'but you're not a real Cohen, are you Georgie?' I asked him why he said that and he shot back, 'Because I've been in the showers and seen yours.' It was typical Trinder knock-about stuff, but he was a clever man and I had no doubt that in his way, and in his time, he tried to do the best he could for me.

The players drifted into the breakfast room in their different styles, young Bally buzzing, on fire, Jack Charlton full of bravado, his brother Bobby quieter, a little pensive – no-one ever had a more pensive face than Bobby, though it could break wonderfully into a smile of pleasure when things, after all, turned out all right – and of course Mooro, the young captain, was his usual island of calm. I could only thank God for my good fortune in being in this company on this morning – and in having the capacity to do all the hard work that had been required.

Some of the hardest, and initially most anxious, of that toil had come after the sickening accident which happened when I tried to get my foot across to block a shot from the

Stoke man Burrows. In his-follow through he sliced the bursar — which supplies the synovial fluid that lubricates the joints — in my right knee. It was a nasty feeling to sit, a few months before the World Cup, on a football field and look at your somewhat re-arranged knee covered in blood. I was carried from the field and after his inspection the club doctor sent me to hospital immediately. They had to apply a lot of internal stitches and for a little while it seemed possible that all my hopes had been swept away. But a specialist reassured me swiftly enough. He unwrapped the bandages, swung my knee around a little and said, 'Don't worry, I think you'll be fine. I'm not sending you out of hospital yet because I know you'll just start to work on it. You need a little rest — give it a few days and you will be okay.'

The Fulham manager Vic Buckingham came in to hospital to say that Ramsey had made a rather taut phone call but he had been able to reassure him. However, it did mean that my momentum had been broken. You don't lose your fitness in two weeks but you do shed a certain sharpness, and I knew I faced several months of heightened effort, both on my own and under the supervision of the hard-driving Cocker. On the Majorcan beach Hunt had said, with a faint twinkle in his eyes, that he was sure 'Shanks' would like it if I joined the Liverpool kick-around. I told him, quietly, to piss off.

I had missed the last two matches of the season with Fulham and it was clear that when I reported to England I would have to operate under a special regime. In fact I probably put in the hardest, most concentrated work of my career. Cocker and Shepherdson kept me back after team training, and Cocker was particularly demanding. He said he wasn't going to let me off anything. These were the biggest football stakes of our lives and nothing could be left undone. I worked so hard that I got the taste of lead in my mouth and everything turned black and white in my eyes. Someone told me that the same thing happened to Tour de France cyclists while they battled through the ordeals presented by the great climbs of the Pyrenees. They said the snow on the mountain tops turned black in their eyes.

But if it was hard it was also wonderful to feel the old sharpness coming back. Ten days without training work was the equivalent of ten days without sunshine. There was no uplift, no sense of bringing yourself to some regular peak of physical, and psychological, well-being. It wasn't in my nature to sit on my arse. Training had the other great benefit, for somebody who enjoyed his food. You could eat, more or less, what you wanted – and then burn it off.

In the weeks that had brought me to that morning in Hendon Hall there had also been much more than the fine tuning of fitness. Ramsey was terribly thorough. He drilled into us the details that in the end became almost a sixth sense. He told us who would line up in the defensive wall, who would take free kicks and throw-ins. In the World Cup final I wouldn't throw in anywhere in the last third of the field in enemy territory because of the risk of lost possession and the ensuing need to run as much as sixty yards like some hound of hell to cover suddenly unguarded space.

In 1998 Glenn Hoddle, one of Ramsey's successors brought down by the pressure of trying to reproduce the levels of concentration achieved in the campaign of '66, said that the England team he took to the World Cup in France was the best prepared in the nation's football history. It was a wild claim that was not exactly enhanced by the revelation that England had not practised the penalty shoot-out formula which did for them at the end of their tumultuous game with Argentina in St Etienne. No aspect of the game was too small for Ramsey, and it is just inconceivable that he would have neglected something that could so easily have been anticipated as a decisive factor.

After breakfast I walked around the hotel grounds. I phoned Daphne for the family team-talk before going in to hear Ramsey's final appraisal of the challenge that faced us in a few hours' time. In those days a player received just two tickets and throughout the tournament mine had rotated between my mother, Daphne, and her father. Today was Ladies' Day, and Daphne told me that she was sure it was going to be a joyful one. It was good to hear but a little more difficult to assume.

As always, Ramsey again avoided loading up the pressure – or bombarding us with his sure-fire master plan. His concern was always to make sure that individuals were in the best possible frame of mind, alert but not weighed down by their responsibilities. He said that he was sure I had the running of big Lothar Emmerich, who had come into the German team largely on the strength of his powerful left foot – which had produced a goal against Spain in a group game – but I should also keep a keen eye on Sigi Held, who would probably move out to the left to cover my breaks. The greatest challenge presented by Emmerich would probably come in the standing up to his fierce shots, which if not done properly could lead to some unpleasant surprises for Gordon Banks. Certainly the range of his game was some way short of the Argentine Mas and the Portuguese Simoes, who were much trickier and more mobile. 'I'm sure you know what you have to do, George,' said Ramsey.

Yes, I knew what I could do but on this ultimate football occasion, with the nation, not to mention Daphne and my mother watching, could I deliver? It was, I realised as I went into the secluded lunch room with the rest of the team for a slight taste of chicken, a question that had never before bitten into me quite so deeply. It tugged at me as I made a brief contribution to working through the great mounds of mail which each day had been delivered to the team room. It was one of the chores Alf expected of us, probably as much as anything else for its value in killing a little dead time — time which was beginning to weigh on me rather heavily.

The bus ride to Wembley broke some of the tension. There were plenty of people — and flags — in the streets and by the time we arrived at the stadium — about an hour and a half before kick-off — the place was crackling with anticipation. We went out on the pitch, tested the ground, gauged the atmosphere. It was hot and humid out on the field and my need for the action to begin was getting intense. The preparations were done and you didn't need telling that for the next hour or two you would be occupying a patch of terrain located squarely between heaven and hell. You bloody well knew that it was no time to unravel because, as never before, hell was just around the corner. And if you didn't know it before getting to the stadium, you knew it now.

When the Union flags were not being waved, they hung limp in the still, heavy air and it seemed as though you could hear the beating of your own heart. As a cocky, precocious kid I had breezed through that Villa Park semi-final with United, but the nerves that came to me at the start of the World Cup had returned with even greater force.

Lying around in some archive are newsreel shots of the England players in the dressing room an hour or so before the start of the game. I look haunted. You get the impression that you could have come up to my face and peeled it. The sound of the five-minute buzzer went through me. The one-minute sound had the same effect.

It would have been so much better if we had been able to go out on to the field, do our warm-ups, the running and exercises which meant that some sprinter wasn't going to come hurtling at you and catch you cold in the first minutes, and promptly play our game. But of course there were the ceremonials, the anthems and the presentations, to the Queen, Sir Stanley Rous, the president of Fifa, and several FA people Alf roundly dismissed as being unnecessary.

So the build-up was in such slow motion it seemed to stretch out interminably. I tried to do a little warming up in the dressing room, but the space was so restricted and if I was shedding nervous energy it was not in the right fashion. It was an eternity before we walked up the tunnel and into the light. In the tunnel the buzz of the stadium sounded like a bee-hive, but when you got out on the field the noise was unbelievable. It drove almost everything out of your mind, and what was left wasn't particularly helpful. Noise can be more of a factor in a football game than you might imagine. I remembered defending the Kop end at Anfield one night when Liverpool's Tommy Smith hit a drive to the far post at an angle of 45 degrees. I lost it in the lights and because of the noise coming from the Kop I didn't hear the usual ball-on-leather sound. I couldn't see the shape of the ball and I couldn't hear the sound of Smith's boot, couldn't tell the weight he had put on it because when a player chips the ball it makes a slightly different sound. So for that frozen second at Anfield, when I couldn't see or hear the ball, I could only tell myself not to panic. For different reasons, I was repeating the order as I walked towards the centre line to meet the Queen.

I felt like an infantryman going into the line and not knowing quite what to expect. There was no relaxation in me and when I looked round to see the faces of my team-mates I could see that I wasn't the only one feeling the strain. The great anxiety which I couldn't quite suppress was that I would do something to let everybody down. The effect, I speculated, would be like that of a pebble thrown into a pool, sending out little ripples which would stretch out and touch everyone I valued and lap out into every corner of the land I was so proud to represent. 'Don't bugger things up now, George — not now, when the job is so nearly done,' I said to myself.

I had to fight off a stream of negative thoughts. Maybe I would miss something, let someone get away from me and forget the fundamental need to keep everything covered.

Perhaps I would get distracted at a vital moment. Maybe I wouldn't be a hero but a goat. I just ached to be able to get into my warm-up, to wheel away from the ceremonials and start running off the fear. I would be okay when I did that. The heaviness would go from my legs and the Germans, even the lordly young Franz Beckenbauer, would suddenly be scaled down. They would no longer be monsters. They would be just another team to beat.

England generally had an advantage at Wembley because of the unique nature of the playing surface. It was about two yards slower than any pitch you had ever run on but unfortunately the ball went off the grass two yards faster, and though this was not exactly ideal for me, it must have been a terrible surprise for foreign players experiencing it for first time. The turf had so many tufts per square inch the effect was of running on several lush carpets. The density created the sensation of a cushion of air, which would have better suited my son Anthony, who has a lovely floating running action whereas his father, and his cousin Ben, the England rugby international, are power sprinters whose preferred going is good to firm.

The additional complication, especially for a defender, was if there was any dampness in the air – as there was on that muggy day against the Germans – the ball would skip off the surface at great speed. It meant that you had to be particularly careful in judging an interception.

You could sell yourself horribly short with the slightest of mistiming. Certainly this was a factor in the rather tentative opening exchanges. Both sides were desperate not to make a mistake. There were a few speculative shots from the Germans but Banks gathered them in easily. Our objective at this point was simply to be make things as difficult as we could, just discourage the hell out of them. What no-one could have anticipated was that Ray Wilson would make a mistake – in the thirteenth minute. I was jockeying Held. I couldn't go any deeper because he would have just come on to me, and so he hit the ball. It was a nothing ball and everyone could see that. But for some strange and absolutely uncharacteristic reason, Wilson got under the ball and his header dropped at the feet of Helmut Haller.

The German, who wasn't exactly a favourite among us because of his strutting demeanour and tendency to go for an Oscar every time he felt the breath of a tackle, didn't hit the ball perfectly but he got enough on it to squeeze his shot past Banks. Wilson had never made such an elementary mistake like that before – and he would never again. But there it was on the big scoreboard: England 0, West Germany 1. It wasn't quite what Ramsey had in mind.

But if it was a discouraging sight, it scarcely dented our spirit. Yes, there had been a gathering of tension before they took away the red carpet and the Queen had gone up to the Royal Box, but that was more a matter of individual concern that nothing you did would let down Ramsey or your team-mates. The conviction that we had the beating of the Germans was not lessened then, and nor was it when they were hugging Haller.

In fact I saw a scowl of impatience on the face of our captain Moore, and that was more than a mere gesture of defiance. In six minutes he had helped to bring us back level with the competitive edge and urgency which was always the mark of our best work. He moved purposefully down the left before being brought down by the superb competitor Wolfgang Overath. Bobby was up on his feet and taking the free kick before the Swiss referee Gottfried Dienst blew his whistle. He struck the ball beautifully with his right foot and Hurst burst perfectly into his path at the near post and glanced it inside the German keeper Hans Tilkowski, who hadn't moved a stride from his line. The entire German defence had been left stranded by a piece of brilliant opportunism – and technical ability. The ball had been driven just over head high at a static defence and Hurst's timing and power had made it just about impossible to defend. The thought that flashed through my mind represented the highest praise for young Hurst. It was a goal of which Denis Law, one of the deadliest, bravest strikers I ever saw, would have been most proud. It was also a goal which changed everything because it spoke of such power, and accomplishment, and though the score was 1–1 when we walked off at half-time we were still a little bit on fire. We felt we had them and Hurst's goal had opened up something of a divide. Alf was as calm as ever during the interval. He agreed with our consensus that we should be winning, but in football the better team didn't always come out on top. We couldn't build anything on the fact that Hursty had knocked in a superb goal and that we had achieved an edge in everything but the scoreline. He didn't spend much time with the defence and certainly didn't dwell on Ray Wilson's mistake. He knew all about Ray, his competitive instinct and superb consistency. Everyone makes a mistake sometimes, and nobody needed to tell Ramsey that the chances of Wilson making two in one match were probably millions to one.

Alf's main concern was the mood of excessive optimism that seemed to have gripped the forwards. No doubt if a long shot had gone in he would have been delighted, but he felt that we were giving the ball away too easily on such a sticky day. Retaining possession was one of his reigning principles. If you didn't do that, you were playing Russian roulette with your fate. He said that he felt we were taking over the game, but we still had to remember the basics of football – and that the Germans had in players like Overath, the veteran Uwe Seeler, Held and the always potentially brilliant Beckenbauer, the latent threat of sudden devastation.

Rearmed with Ramsey's quiet but firm statement of his most cherished values, we went into the second half with fresh determination and a strong reminder of the need for patience. It was plain that certain of our players were in the middle of the games of their lives. Nobby was again relentless in his willingness to cover all points of danger, Moore was bringing new definition to his quality as a player of big matches, and Ball seemed to be moving through a whole series of crescendos of effort, each new one more driven that the last. Where though, you might wonder, is the mention of two of the greatest footballers in history – Bobby Charlton and Franz Beckenbauer? The truth was they were largely being cancelled out by each other. Neither was having the kind of classic, dominating game which was their stock in trade. The

German manager Helmut Schoen later admitted that he made a mistake when he put Beckenbauer on Charlton. His respect for Bobby had been so huge that when he looked around his squad in the days before the final he decided he had only one player with the required skill and mental strength to shackle the great English player-maker and scorer of spectacular, utterly game-changing goals.

Schoen, a fine and generous football man, reflected that maybe he should have got someone else to shadow Charlton and released Beckenbauer, who would eventually emerge as the most decorated player in history, to weave his own sophisticated spells. It certainly seemed odd to note in the flow of intense action that the two most gifted players on the field had the priority of getting goalside of each other. Of course there is never a clear answer to such a dilemma. If a less able and intelligent German had been shepherding Charlton, might not the young demi-god of the English game, who had risen from the ashes of the Munich aircrash eight years earlier as a brilliant force of life, have erupted in some burst of irresistible action which would have wiped away all possibility of the extraordinary drama towards which we were building?

That would always be the agony of doubt for Schoen when he considered the other possibility that a Beckenbauer freed from his Charlton duty might have cut away at English confidence with the bite and subtlety of his passing, as he did four years later when Ramsey withdrew Charlton in the baking heat of Leon, Mexico, in the final phase of a World Cup quarter-final England appeared to have won quite comfortably. At Wembley the tactics dictated by the German manager meant that we saw only flashes of the class of Charlton and Beckenbauer as both teams worked feverishly towards the climax. We thought that had come in the 79th minute when Peters, the ever stealthy Peters, coolly attached himself to the ball that had flown into the air off a German defender after Hurst had mis-hit a speculative shot. Peters was accompanied into the box by Jack Charlton, who for one terrible moment thought that the ball was going to land at his feet rather than those of his young swordsman team-mate. But even as Jack was thinking, 'Oh shit, don't miss with this bugger,' Peters ghosted to his side and volleyed home.

For ten of the remaining eleven minutes we believed we were home, and had chances to put it beyond Germany, but suddenly, sickeningly, we unravelled when referee Dienst decided Jack Charlton had fouled Held, when in fact it looked as if the German had contrived the award by making a 'back', which is the football term for when a player fakes an attempt to head the ball while deliberately obstructing his opponent. The big problem was that we lined up too deeply to defend the free-kick, almost within our penalty area. We were pushed ten yards back and I looked along our line and I was filled with concern.

The big Emmerich may have seen this as his last chance to make some kind of impact and he drilled the kick hard. It shot off my body, took a deflection or two, and fell to the feet of Wolfgang Weber. Banks, who had been unable to get anywhere near the ball in the chaos of bodies, couldn't stop Weber's shot. Our glory had been taken away and if there was ever a time when we might have lost our belief, and allowed Ramsey's conviction that our destiny was to win the World Cup to fade, this was surely it. Perhaps we might have crumbled but for Alf. He was angry and magnificent in those spirit-dredging moments before extra time. He was animated in a way we had never seen him before.

Animated, urgent and emphatic. He spilled his frustration that we had missed chances with the game at our mercy quickly, and in a way that didn't demoralise us. It was as though his anger was directed mostly at the fact that we might be denied our just desserts. He said, 'Look at the Germans – their shirts are out, their socks are down. They're finished. You've won it once, now go and win it again.' As he spoke, you could see little Bally's eyes shining and Nobby's redoubled determination and you could see a whole team's shoulders lifting at this confirmation of what they felt in their bones to be true.

Ball, particularly, was in a mood of the most stunning determination. Over the ninety minutes he had run the fine full-back Schnellinger to the point of breakdown. Now in the last stretch he would find from somewhere another surge of energy. Along with Ramsey's latest call to arms, it brought a new charge of electricity to the team. My own situation was that I was feeling quite strong, but I wasn't going to do anything silly. My idea was to support. It was clear to me that 'The Kid' was having a great game. So the best thing I could do was back him up at every moment and make sure we didn't give the ball away.

That, more than ever before, was the priority, and maybe it is put into perspective when you remember that however hard I ran in this game, however many times I offered myself to receive the ball, the statistical reality was that it would never be in my possession for more than two minutes. Here, the most obvious fact was that Ball had Schnellinger on the hook, and my main job, as I saw it, was to do everything I could to help keep him there. I was about forty yards from the line when Hurst crashed in the 'goal' that broke the Germans, and of course from where I was standing it was the sweetest, most exquisite goal that had ever been scored. The debate has raged for almost forty years now and the entire German team will probably go their death beds mumbling, 'nein goal'. The relatively infant TV technology wasn't really conclusive, but when all the emotions had drained away, I had to concede that the most beautiful goal I had ever seen was also one of the most dubious.

Ball, inevitably, was involved. He chased down a ball from Stiles into the right corner and crossed it, first time. The German sweeper Willi Schulz made a desperate attempt to get to the ball, but he had run himself close to exhaustion and Hurst thrust him aside and shot against the underside of the bar. When the ball bounced down, Hunt threw up his arms. He realised that he wouldn't get to the rebound and so he celebrated, instinctively. The referee, who perhaps already knew that he had been plunged into a controversy which would never die, ran to the touchline and consulted the linesman, Tofik Bakhramov of Azerbaijan. At the time I thought this rather absurd. Mr Bakhramov was no closer to the line than I was, and I didn't have a clue. The linesman said the ball had crossed the line.

But then if the debate has rattled down the years it has never disturbed my conviction that we deserved to win, that in the end we were running harder, and biting more deeply, than a tremendously competitive German team. It is also true that if Hurst's second goal was questionable, his third was a magnificent statement of will that perfectly summed up both his and the team's performance. And, of course, it is also true the Germans scored only two goals, and we got four.

They were bending, critically, when the man from Azerbaijan ruled in our favour, and there was no doubt they were broken when Bobby Moore astounded Jack Charlton with his perfectly composed and beautifully accurate ball to Hurst with just a minute showing on the clock. Overath made a superbly game, gut-wrenching effort to catch Hurst but Schulz, the last line of German defence, was terribly compromised by Bally's last killing run of a game he had filled with passion and unbreakable stamina. Frankly, I thought Schulz's defensive instincts fell apart in those climactic moments. He retreated, made no effort to check Ball with the possibility of offside or force Hurst, on whom Overath was closing, into an earlier decision to shoot or pass.

But then if my first reaction was that I would have had difficulty in returning to the dressing room if I'd been part of the concession of a goal like that, time did soften the view. Schulz, like the rest of his team-mates, had run himself into that yielding turf and maybe, when he found himself isolated and Hurst bearing down on his goal, with Ball charging to his left, something cracked. For England, though, there was no analysis at that moment of triumph. That could come later when the mind cleared and the heart stopped beating quite so fast.

Some of that analysis would inevitably be tinged with bitterness, and it would go on down the years as Ramsey was shabbily discarded by the 'colliery owners' of the FA, who preferred to pay nearly a quarter of a million pounds' worth of corporation tax than pay the players anything more than a fraction of that which was handed to the Germans. It would be something to think of, perhaps, on a cold winter's night — not in the warmth of a high English summer when we had just beaten the world. Jack Charlton fell to his knees and held his head in his hands and shook with emotion. Tears rolled down the face of his brother Bobby. Bally found still more energy, ecstatically jumping all over everybody. Bobby Moore had a smile of pleasure, but in his eyes you could see something more intense, and it was to do with pride.

Nobby Stiles? Before performing his famous dance, he knocked me down in front of the Royal Box and gave me a big, bloody toothless kiss. I was later reported to have said, 'It looked liked copulation. I don't know what he was doing but I didn't enjoy it very much.' What I recall saying was, 'What the bloody hell do you think you're doing? It's like being kissed by a piece of liver.' We've joked about it down the years but the fact was that it was a rather long kiss and during the course of it his dental plate got caught in my teeth. Jimmy Armfield, whose place I had taken in the team, tried to drag Alf on to the field but he was adamant he would not go. It was a time, he said, for the players to celebrate. It was they who had won the World Cup. It was typical of the man. He hated shows of emotion. Whatever he felt, he kept it bottled up because that was how an Englishman behaved, was it not? I was told that when Hurst scored his third goal Ramsey had ordered the squad players around him to stop leaping about. For one thing they were interfering with his view.

My own feeling was that Alf Ramsey was mentally and emotionally done in. He was drained of everything he had because he had done what no-one in the country believed he could. He had taken on the FA, handpicked his own players and been absolutely unswerving in his convictions. That would have taken so much from any man. Everyone in the stadium was jumping about but he sat still, gazing into the middle distance. He had done, as one of his heroes John Wayne once said, what a man had to do. He had done the job more brilliantly than it had ever been done before and, quite possibly, would ever be done again.

CHAPTER TWELVE

GOODBYE, SIR ALF

Whatever else I might say about the long, lingering kiss Nobby gave me in front of the nation, there was no doubt that it was filled with sincerity and passion. These were qualities which certainly did not leap into my mind when I opened one item of post thirty-six hours after winning the World Cup.

The letter was from the secretary of the Football Association, Denis Follows, and I have to say I did not feel it was overflowing with the juice of life. It smacked a little, I thought, of the kind of note you might receive from the boss if you had been deemed worthy of receiving a gold watch for long service. It read:

Dear George,

On behalf of the Football Association I am writing to congratulate you on the part you played in winning the World Cup for England. The Football Association is proud of your achievement. We are conscious of the effort you have made directed towards the end of winning the Cup and we thank you for it. It is understood that the players forming the World Cup squad feel that every member of the squad should be treated in the same way and that the £22,000 allocated to the team as a bonus in the event of their winning the World Cup should be divided equally between them irrespective of the number of matches in which they played. The Football Association is only too happy to meet the wishes of the players in this matter and I have the greatest possible pleasure in enclosing herewith a cheque for £1,000.

With every good wish for your future success.

Yours sincerely,

Denis Follows.

So there it was, the big pay-off that would hardly have covered a few months' travelling expenses for a leading FA councillor. Things are very different now, of course, with the national team entering detailed negotiations before major tournaments to come to deals worth potentially millions.

Back in 1966, we would have been considered as impertinent as Oliver Twist if we had merely whispered that it would be nice to have a little chat about what might be on the table if we just happened to win the greatest prize in football. Marks and Spencer sold shirts which had our images on the front and in the shopping arcades across the country you could buy little towels emblazoned with the faces of the winning team. Of course we didn't have image rights and so we didn't receive a penny. Many years later, when some attempt was made to organise some of our earning potential, Marks and Spencer were asked to make some payment against past earnings. They said they had given to the Bobby Moore

Cancer Fund. That is a great cause, I know well enough, but the feeling was that we had better go away because, if not, we were going to be shown in a bad light. It was a dismissal of rights that are written into the contracts of today's footballers, and in the rejecting of our 'image' rights there was even a hint of moral blackmail. It is a very difficult area to discuss, and I avoid it whenever I can, but what can't be removed is a sense that the FA never took the slightest step to protect our interests. It seemed, more than anything, to be a matter of saying, 'Okay, you won the World Cup, now be good fellows, and just run away.' You look at that attitude and you have to compare it with the way, down the years, the Germans have treated the man they called 'The Emperor' – Franz Beckenbauer.

I have never seen confirmed the rumour that Beckenbauer received a bonus of £10,000, along with all his team-mates, for his work in the 1966 World Cup, but it is not so hard to believe when you look at the honour and the rewards that have been handed to Germany's outstanding footballer of his generation. Beckenbauer is always at the centre of the German game, moving from one important responsibility to another. He is both an icon and a statesman and when you see this it is hard not to cast your mind back to Bobby Moore, sick and badly diagnosed, working as a commentator for a radio station. You wonder what the FA might have done for him down the years – and what he might have done for English football.

Bobby, no doubt, was a different character to Beckenbauer. He was a self-effacing soldier rather than an emperor, but in his quiet, reflective way he had learned so much about the game. He had trailed after his hero Malcolm Allison at West Ham, eager to talk to the big man about his revolutionary ideas on how football should be run and carried to new levels. He was probably not a manager, or a public relations front man, but when FA coaches were teaching a new generation of kids to look for the 'Position of Maximum Opportunity' – meaning, in effect, to forget the craft of football and hump the ball down the field and hope that a striker won the resulting lottery – Bobby was being appointed manager of Southend. He may well have been glad of the job, but can we imagine for a moment Beckenbauer being shunted off into a football backwater where the odds against success were so huge. The FA should have taken care of Bobby, and given him a role that he would have enjoyed and which would have been of huge value to the English game. He could have told the coaches of schoolboys what was important, he could have cut through the technical jargon and made the game live for the kids whose heads were stuffed full of theories that had little relationship to the joy and the point of it. And this is not to mention the creation of good football. But of course that would have been to introduce professionalism of the highest quality into a world of schoolteachers and bureaucrats and personal empire-builders.

The Fulham manager Vic Buckingham once sent me down to the Bank of England training ground in Roehampton to run my eye over a young coach who was said to be something special. My team-mate Pancho Pearson came along. We watched the coach putting on his session, setting up his triangles and putting down his cones and there was no doubt he had a lot of ideas. But there didn't seem to be too much attention being paid to the basics of control and position, and as we left Pearson said, 'Now I know why I'll never be a great player or a great coach. I'm terrible at mathematics.'

The neglect of Bobby Moore was, when you think about, a national scandal in that it showed an absolute failure to appreciate and reward someone of great achievement and tremendous character. The problem for Bobby was that he was never able to make much noise. He never shouted the odds and that did make you sceptical about how he might prosper in the politics of the FA once he had served his function as a brilliant leader on the field.

A few years ago the *Daily Express* ran a piece about how people like Nobby and Roger and I worked on the after-dinner circuit and they mentioned the fees we were paid. They would probably have included Mooro, but he was never big on making speeches and, anyway, he had died. The *Express's* implication was that our memories belonged to the nation and that we were guilty of some kind of exploitation of something that didn't really belong to us. Geoff Hurst was listed as a £1,000-a-shot after-dinner speaker. They put £750 against my name. Bobby and Jack Charlton were the only names not on the list. I don't usually respond to such pinpricks, but on this occasion the *Express* hit a rather sore spot. I thought that profiteering from football invited some rather more compelling targets than the Boys of '66, and I asked the *Express* if they believed we didn't have the right to earn a living. I probably shouldn't have bothered but I suppose that sometimes you are forced to realise that some wounds run rather deeper than you may have imagined.

Those wounds are generally soothed, however, when you do get up in front of some gathering and do your little speech and perhaps answer a few questions. Recently I received a very warm reception at Fulham from an audience of 650. I did think, 'Well, George, if you don't get a good hearing at your old club you're really in trouble,' but in fact it wasn't untypical of the usual response given to any of the team on such occasions. My old team-mates confirm my view that the worst hazard is the occasional drunk, but then you can encounter one of those easily enough wherever you go, and generally the audience is split between those over fifty who know who you are and what you did, and the young ones who think, 'Well, he played in the England team that won the World Cup so he must have been a fair player.' The overall effect is pleasing. You feel you have provided a little entertainment, maybe the odd insight, and in return you receive a degree of respect – plus the fee that persuaded you to give up your free time in the first place.

The truth was that during the World Cup, money, strange as it may seem today, was almost the last thing on our minds. Eventually we were told that our bonus would be based on appearances in the tournament up to a maximum of £1,500. Bobby Moore gave us the details and said maybe it would be a good idea just to split it evenly through the squad irrespective of how many times each player appeared. There was no hesitation in saying yes. We all knew how arbitrary football could be, how it could toss out its favours one day and grab them all back the next, and this was surely a good way of saying that we had all been through something together and that the men who had spent most of their time sitting on the bench had also made a powerful contribution to the overall spirit of the squad. The first professional instinct was maybe to say, well, perhaps we should just all take our chances and get what comes to us. If Jimmy Greaves is injured, well, that's tough but does he have to have his share of an extra £500 that might otherwise come to me? Does Greavsie really need £500 of my money? But then we all quickly saw the point of difference between the professional thing and the right thing. We had all started this campaign on the same footing and we had been fashioned into a team in the truest sense. We should finish the job in that spirit.

If the FA thought it was right to pay us a bonus that represented less than ten per cent of the tax they paid the government (which was £242,000) on their profits in the greatest year of our national game, that was something they would have to live with down the years, and even if maybe some of the FA councillors who waded into the junkets and the lavish entertainment that was so much part of their lives on the international circuit without ever reflecting for a moment on how they had treated their winning team, again, that was something we could not really afford to dwell upon. We knew what we had done, and how we felt about each other and I think, deep down, we all realised that we had to avoid the trap of bitterness. Still, it was exasperating to think that not only were the FA happy to pay tax which would have been reduced by a little more generosity to the players, they in fact paid far more than was due. Some terrible bungling had gone on in the Lancaster Gate office. The FA had made contributions to the cost of ground improvements at club stadiums across the country which were staging World Cup games, and of course this money was tax deductible. However, no claims were made and of course the FA tax bill was all the greater for this oversight. Meanness was one thing. Incompetence was another, but no easier to tolerate.

It was also hard to suppress a flash of anger on the night of the World Cup victory. The banquet was for the winning and losing teams and for officials and unspecified hangers-on. There was no place for wives or mothers, though in the latter category Cissie Charlton, maybe on the strength of the fact that she had delivered two team members, escaped the prohibition. Cissie was a high-profile World Cup mother. The others just didn't make it to the official celebrations. While the players were shepherded into the banqueting suite of the Royal Garden Hotel in Kensington, our wives were taken to the Bulldog Bar, where they sat and talked amongst themselves and from time to time said how nice it would have been to have shared some of the most precious, happy hours of their husbands' professional lives. There was no place at the table for Vicky Ramsey, but I imagined she was more philosophical than the younger generation of footballers' wives. She had had that much longer to come to terms with the ways and the thinking of the colliery owners. The wives watched so many 'hangers-on' streaming into the Royal Garden Hotel, while my brothers Len and Peter took my mother home for a family celebration. Looking back it seems a little odd that we didn't say, 'To hell with this,' and go our own ways with our own people into a night that was described as one of the most joyful in London and the country since the celebration of VE Day. But of course we didn't. Whatever his private feelings, Alf would not have approved. He hated so many of the attitudes of the FA, but he knew that rebellion could only be taken so far. He had a strong sense of duty, however onerous this particular one happened to be. His position, which he expressed in a personal letter to each of his players, was that we had all worked hard on behalf of the country and ourselves and that we could all take pride in what had been achieved. We had stuck together and never given less than all we had. He was proud of the way we played — and also the way we behaved. You could almost imagine him writing the letters while draped in the Union flag. It was certainly better to dwell on Alf's simply expressed, but deeply felt, sentiments than the irritations provoked from within the FA offices. A note I received from the FA a few days after the final said that I should go in to collect a case of Bollinger champagne and two others containing red and white wine. I remember driving into the car park at the FA and thinking, 'My God, where is all this booze going?' You could have fitted the players' allocation into a couple of car spaces but here were all these other cars waiting to pick up their freebies. That was the kind of thing that came along regularly to put you on edge. Players played and took what they were given, and the FA rode a gravy train which on this occasion had taken on a massive supply of champagne and the finest burgundy. I suppose, all in all, it was quite nice of the FA to remember us at all.

However, in all of this there was the greatest of compensations. You got to work under an outstanding manager while playing for your country at a time when it had been established beyond all doubt, with the most concrete evidence, that you could compete with anyone in the world. That prospect stretched into the foreseeable future. I would be just thirty when the next World Cup was scheduled to be played in Mexico. I would, I vowed, be as fit as ever and I would also have four more years of experience under the guidance of Alf Ramsey. I wasn't to know that my football career would be history by the time of Mexico and that the manager who had carried England to the top of the game would be beginning his own bitter descent from the status of a national hero knighted so soon after his greatest victory, to someone baited in the press and earmarked by the FA for exile at the first opportunity.

However, for a little time there was a honeymoon unsullied even by the controversy surrounding the 'goal'. Alf's achievement was generally accepted as stunning. He had moved English football into a new age in just three years and even Helmut Schoen, the German manager, acknowledged that we had been deserving winners. Schoen had always been candid about the fact that he thought it would be a 'hell of a match'. The difficulty for him, he said, was the character of the English player, which was very strong and determined, and that the match was at Wembley. When it was over, he said he thought England had been a goal better. That was his only glancing reference to the row over the linesman's decision. In fact the Germans handled their defeat very impressively indeed.

Their attitude was that even though they thought it wasn't a goal, we were good winners. My view was that they were magnanimous – and right. I will always believe that if the game had gone on another ten minutes we might have scored two more goals. I feel this because while they looked absolutely finished in those last few minutes, some of our players found extraordinary reserves of energy and competitive character. I consider the goal that settled everything. I see the lung-tearing run of Hurst and the crucial support of Alan Ball and Bobby Moore's ability, when the pressure was at its highest, to play a ball that terrified Jack Charlton (he would rather have seen it hoofed into row 89) almost as much as it thrilled him. And when I do that the other frustrations just dwindle away.

Some people questioned the quality of the football played that day. It has been said to me, 'Well, you could have won better.' And I say, 'Of course, but then we could have lost worse.' In fact I believe that both teams played some excellent football and apart from the technical ability on display there was an absolutely ferocious commitment to winning the game. Reviewing the England performances, I cannot even begin to doubt the contribution or the effectiveness of any one individual, and that I think is a remarkable thing to be able to say.

Beyond everything, however, is the belief that without Ramsey we would still be looking for our first World Cup victory. I'm sure Walter Winterbottom was doing the best he could before Ramsey took over. But his circumstances were just impossible. Winterbottom had some great ideas about how the game should be played, but as long as he operated within the restrictions laid down by the amateurs of the FA Council he had no real chance. Ramsey knew this when the offer from the FA came in and he said, yes, he would do it, but in the only way the job could be done properly. The old relationship between the Councillors and the team had to be swept away. There would be no more of the old mentality, which had the FA bigwigs in the front of the plane – and the players at the back.

He would have been shattered to know that one day the FA would decide that there was no Englishman fit to lead the national team, and whatever he thought of the qualities and the experience of Sven Goran Eriksson I'm sure he would have said something like, 'Yes, most certainly, he is an experienced football man but what does he really know of an Englishman?' Whether that is so relevant today in the cosmopolitan world of football I'm not so sure, but perhaps there should be something beyond the normal demands of a good coach–player relationship. Maybe it is important to have a sense of your country, and the real meaning of it when you go out to represent it on some great stage.

Ramsey's assumption was always that the players he had picked out would grow when they got into an England shirt and that was almost certainly what was underlying his remark to Jack Charlton that he didn't always select the best players. In just one way I'm glad that injury took me away from the

England squad before Ramsey entered that downward spiral which led to his dismissal after the team's failure to qualify for the 1974 World Cup finals in Germany. It was hard enough watching the process from a distance, but my memories of the aftermath of '66 with England are filled with some happy and rather revealing times. Revealing mostly, that is, of some of Alf Ramsey's undoubted quirks of nature.

As I mentioned earlier, the trip to Canada for Expo 67 in Montreal was a terrible trial for Alf, but some of the results were both hilarious and touching in that they showed the players quite how much he had come to think of them. He hated the big college building that was to be our living quarters, and I remember him snapping to Harold Shepherdson, 'This just isn't good enough. We're going home.' We were not, but Alf did what he could to improve our circumstances. The Canadian officials were rather shocked by Alf's fierce reaction to their arrangements. It didn't help that they referred to him as Sir Ramsey. He said, 'Do you not realise you have the world champions here – does that not mean anything to you?' Alf won a small victory in convincing the officials that we should have our own rooms – and that our daily expense allowance should be raised from £2 a day to £10. One of the players had gone out for a haircut and came back with the bill for around £10. He said, 'We can't really survive on £2 a day Alf,' and Alf replied, 'Most certainly, you are right.' Mike Summerbee, who was part of Alf's plans for his second assault on the World Cup in 1970, and Budgie Byrne both had good senses of humour and they organised a kind of regimental pay-parade. This was one of my last tastes of life on the road with Ramsey's England and I suppose it is why I remember those humid days in Montreal with particular warmth. There was a tremendous sense of being part of something which had become solid because of fine leadership and great achievement. The last great drama of my time with Alf and England was defeat by Scotland at Wembley. The Scots went berserk with their victory, naturally, and even though we had finished the 3–2 defeat down to nine fit men, with Jack Charlton at centre-forward (from where he scored our first goal) and Ray Wilson with a badly damaged knee that would signal the beginning of the end of his career, our conquerors believed that they had taken over the mantle of word champions. You can imagine that this left Alf in something less than wonderful humour. It didn't help that the Scots had produced some tremendous football, notably from the superb Jimmy Baxter, who always took a specially intense delight in tormenting the English at Wembley.

But perhaps what incensed Ramsey most was an incident at the evening banquet at Wembley, which was attended by both teams and had all the natural warmth of a convention of Mafia chieftains. The Scots sat on their table and we sat on ours and between them there was not supposed to be a hint of inter-action, at least within the eyesight of the smouldering Sir Alf Ramsey. As I was saying before, he never took defeat so hard as when it was administered by the Scots. Once a cheery Scottish sportswriter said, 'Welcome to Scotland, Alf', when we arrived for a game in Glasgow, and Alf responded, famously, 'You must be fucking joking.' On a south-bound train following defeat at Hampden Park, a Scottish ticket inspector had poked his head into the carriage and said, 'Not such a good day for you, Sir Alf.' He meant it amiably enough but it didn't prevent Alf pursuing him down the corridor with a few carefully selected expletives.

On the night of his banquet of barbed wire at Wembley his beloved Nobby Stiles was to bring even greater bleakness to his mood. Suddenly, Alf boomed, 'George,' and for a moment I thought my table manners had slipped. 'Where's Nobby?' he demanded to know. Nobby, who without his contact lenses was probably never quite sure where he was, was sitting with the Scots, chatting and joking in his inimitable way. 'Go and get him for God's sake,' Alf said. He was beside himself. It was bad enough losing to the Scots – now one of his favourites players was breaking bread and drinking wine with the enemy. It was a little too much for Alf. On less fraught occasions, however, he imposed his authority with a touch of humour. Often he would invite us to vote on the preferred evening entertainment. On one occasion the majority picked out a war film showing in the West End. 'Right,' he said, 'it's decided. We'll go and watch *Wild Bill Hickok*.' We all groaned and then trooped along behind him.

Soon enough, Alf's caravan would be rolling along without me and I could only chart his progress from a distance and, for a while at least, glory in his continued success. Keith Newton, a good quick full-back of Blackburn Rovers who would move on to Everton, was my successor at the next World Cup, which until a hot, fateful afternoon in Leon, Mexico, gave the promise of another Ramsey triumph. Mexico, where some felt Alf had produced an even better, more talented team than the one which had won at Wembley, was ironically the breaking of Ramsey. Right up until the moment he replaced Bobby Charlton with Manchester City's Colin Bell – a brilliant player who was wonderfully athletic – he was a man in charge of a finely honed, powerful and gifted team. Then, suddenly, he was in the minds of some hostile sections of the press, and perhaps a groundswell of opinion within sections of the FA who resented his take-over of power and prestige, a bungler who had lost his touch. It was, by the standards of any courtroom, a harsh judgement.

The case for the prosecution was that Ramsey had committed the cardinal football sin of tinkering with a brilliant performance which didn't need fixing. Bobby Charlton was shaping the game, creating so much pressure on the German defence that the great Beckenbauer was obliged to think of containment rather than play-making of his own. England, leading 2–0 with twenty minutes to go, were looking a lot like potential winners of the tournament. They had fought a magnificent group match with Brazil in Guadalajara, when Gordon Banks made his miracle save and Pele and Mooro swapped shirts and embraced as warriors who knew they had been involved in an epic battle, and here in Leon they were coasting to a comfortable win. But then suddenly Charlton was gone and with him England's confidence and cohesion. Beckenbaur leapt into the void, the prosecution would say, and inspired the 3–2 German victory.

Ramsey's defenders paint a rather different picture. They

say that in the draining heat of Leon, Ramsey was right to protect his most important creative player, and that when he replaced Charlton with Bell he was giving the team another high-class performer. The problem, they say, was not the arrival of Bell. It didn't prevent Francis Lee and Geoff Hurst continuing to threaten the German goal. The trouble was not Bell but Bonetti, the Chelsea goalkeeper who was brought in when Banks went down with stomach problems just before the game. Bonetti, an extremely talented goalkeeper, fell apart under the pressure. Ramsey, his apologists say, couldn't be blamed for the sickness of Banks or the fallibility of Bonetti. He had the new luxury of substitutes and on this occasion he had used them intelligently.

That was the debate in which the defence had good arguments, but it was one in which over the next few years Ramsey steadily lost ground. In some ways he couldn't help himself. He didn't court allies, didn't seek out friends in the media. He wanted to be judged on his work alone and he refused to change his style at the first sign of rough weather. He was not embraced by football, in or out of the FA. I remember having dinner with Alf and my friend Sidney Brickman, a wealthy property developer who had connections at Arsenal, at a time when Bertie Mee was slipping out of favour after his success in guiding the Highbury club to the Double of First Division champions and the FA Cup of 1971. Brickman said there was a feeling that Alf would make a very good manager of Arsenal, but he was promptly discouraged by Ramsey. Alf was emphatic that he was not interested in such speculation because Arsenal had a successful manager and as long as that was the case he was not interested in the discussion.

Alf would always be his own man, independent as far as he could be as a working professional in a game in which amateurs often had the final word, and so there would be no comfortable dotage when his glory as England manager was over. He did a brief stint at Birmingham City, which was not a great success, and then he retired to his unpretentious little fortress in Ipswich. From there I would occasionally get a carefully handwritten letter, commiserating with me when my playing career came to an end and responding to news of my fight against cancer. In February 1976 he wrote:

Dear George,

Sidney has just phoned me in connection with Alan Mullery's testimonial, and also informed me that you were in hospital recovering from an operation. Writing letters is not one of my strong points but I felt I would like to sit down at once and put a few lines on paper. Vic and I were very sorry to hear the news and send you our best wishes for a successful and speedy recovery with all the sincere feelings we have for you. Good luck, George, and kindest regards to your wife, not forgetting the family.

Sincerely,

Alf Ramsey.

Another note, the following year, came at a new critical point in my illness. He wished me well, on behalf of Lady Vicky and 'all the lads' before I went in for another operation, and concluded with the words 'God Bless'. Writing letters, he said, was not his strong point, but a strength of feeling and loyalty to the people he cared about certainly was. He would have been more devastated by the untimely death of his young captain Bobby Moore if his hold on daily reality had not been slackened by the onset of Alzheimer's disease which progressed through the nineties, gently at first but, as is its way, ultimately disabling and disorienting.

I saw him for the last time at a garden party at Buckingham Palace thrown for the nation's leading sportsmen and women. He was being led by the arm by Lady Vicky, and for a little while all seemed well enough when he chatted with his old players. But one by one we noticed there was something wrong. We noted how carefully he was prompted by Lady Vicky. 'Oh look Alf,' she would say, 'here is Alan and Lesley,' and, 'Look Alf, it's George and Daphne.' He was able to take his cues well enough, and talk about football, particularly, with his usual bite, but as the afternoon wore on you could see things were not quite right. Later, I told Daphne of my concerns and she was a little surprised, even though her own mother had suffered from the disease. She didn't know Alf so well, had not been exposed so long to the precision of his speech, which at times could be almost painful. At one point he said something to one of the players which was completely wrong. That was the forlorn clincher. We were seeing, beside the lake in the garden of the Palace, the passing of our chief.

When the nation paid tribute to Bobby at a memorial service at Westminster Abbey, the place on the pew allocated to Alf was left empty. But like all my old team-mates, I felt

Alf's presence strongly on that sad, proud, sunny day of an English summer. When, on a similar day in the spring of 1999, we all travelled to Ipswich for Alf's own memorial service in his local, ancient parish church, I carried a tribute which I had worked on with my journalist friend Ken Jones. It was a hard speech to deliver partly because, like most of the congregation, I knew how uncomfortable Alf had always been with easy sentiment.

Recently, I found the speech among some old papers and as I read it over again I felt the rush of those old feelings. From the pulpit I declared, 'Alf's achievements in football will be recalled for as long as the game continues. But few of the many rich tributes recently paid him have got even close to the sort of man he really was. He was a very private man. A loyal man. A man passionate about his football. A proud patriot who put only Lady Vicky before his country. Anyone who ever played for Alf quickly came to the conclusion that correctness in all things on and off the field was the cornerstone of his philosophy.

'He established a strong bond with his players that stood before every other consideration, and out of it came the spirit that was evident in the teams he put out for Ipswich and England. He could also be terribly amusing, though not always intentionally. I still chuckle over his response to a suggestion, put to him on our behalf by Bobby Charlton – it was usually Bobby who got lumbered with the chore of putting our requests to him – that we be allowed to make a long journey in casual wear instead of the official uniform. Alf told Bobby that he would give it some thought and walked a few yards before turning and saying, "Bobby, I think we will wear the suits."

'Who of us in that squad can forget his loyalty, almost to the point of resignation when he defended our friend Nobby from over zealous officialdom – after Nobby accidentally floored the French player Simon with a tackle so late even Virgin Connex South East would have been embarrassed. There was no way of course that he was going to lose his little midfield policeman. I know I speak for the entire 1966 World Cup squad when I say Alf's influence changed our lives. Not just for what we achieved under him but for the enrichment of our lives for having known and played for him.

'Lives of players like the young Martin Peters, who is now an MBE. The young Geoffrey now Sir Geoffrey, and the young Alan who speaks of Alf with the same affection as he speaks of his own late father. These are lives that are now less for his passing. Many of us here have personal memories of things Alf said and did.

'His eye for detail. His strength and purpose that made it so easy to believe in him. Sad as it is to know that Alf is no longer with us, I feel we are here to celebrate not only the life of a great football manager but a great Englishman. One who should he now be looking down at this particular time is probably thinking – "Yes, George, I think we've had enough of that."'

I wouldn't change any of that, but perhaps I might add something. I might say that it is not until someone is gone that you quite realise how much they represented in your life, and how their value can be so quickly forgotten.

We walked out into the East Anglian sunshine mostly locked in our thoughts. The old footballers knew, more surely than any had ever known anything, they would never again see a man of their business quite like Sir Alf Ramsey. No, most certainly not.

CHAPTER THIRTEEN

BUILDING THE FUTURE

It was December 2, 1967 and I was marking Peter Thompson of Liverpool when I got the injury which I knew was serious. Unfortunately, the sharpness of my concern was not shared by those whose job it was to provide diagnosis and treatment, and so when I look back at the premature end of my playing career it is not always so easy merely to shrug my shoulders. The ball came from the Liverpool goalkeeper and was loaded with top-spin. I tried to get my body over the ball to smother it. But it dived more steeply than I expected and came four or five feet off the ground. My idea was to play it wide on the outside of my foot and as I did so I apparently, according to the medical jargon, 'externally rotated' my knee. I felt the cartilage go and the pain was immediate and intense. I hit the deck screaming and watched the knee swell up at a speed which seemed unbelievable. I received a cold sponge — we didn't have sprays in those days — and stayed on the field for another five minutes. It was futile and stupid. I told the trainer, 'I heard it go.' He said I should see how it went over the next few minutes. Maybe it hadn't gone. I knew something was wrong, but I couldn't be sure what it was. One thing I was certain of: it wasn't good. The other certainty which came later was that I shouldn't have lost a career over it. I was told that because there was blood in the joints the problem couldn't be cartilage, a cartilage being a piece of gristle without its own blood supply. I was sent to a senior consultant, a brilliant surgeon, it was said, who announced that they would bandage the knee tightly and perhaps later put on plaster because it was still swelling. I had several 'aspirations' which sent raspberry-coloured fluid spurting from the knee. An aspiration is not one of the more pleasant procedures of life. They insert a needle and draw off the fluid. Eventually it was decided that I should go into a private hospital and have the external part of the cartilage taken out. In the meantime, however, I had been fighting to get fit despite considerable pain, especially when the knee suddenly locked. The first cartilage was removed six weeks after the accident but as hard as I tried, and disastrously so it would emerge – there was no real progress. After a year, by which time my return to football looked as elusive as ever, the second cartilage went. I was sent to Harley Street, where a consultant told me that because of all the training I had done my knee was basically beaten up beyond repair.

By this time I had played a couple of games after being told that the problem was probably ligaments and I would able to work my way through it. I was very angry when I was told that was it all over for me. When the consultant said that I would never play again I protested that it couldn't possibly be true. Playing was my life. 'I'm sorry,' he said. 'The joints are wrecked . . . they look like sago pudding.' Really, he wasn't telling me anything I didn't know. I had run on with the hope that suddenly everything would be fine, as it had always been, but this time there would no reprieve, none of that exhilaration which comes when you have confidence in your body and you feel you are ready to go again – and maybe beat the world. As the consultant handed down the grim news, I kept thinking to myself, 'This shouldn't have happened . . . it need not have happened.' I was particularly angry because I felt that I was certainly moving to my prime as a footballer. The World Cup had given me great confidence and so many of the old anxieties had melted away. I was at the top of my business.

With modern procedures the bad result just wouldn't have happened – and today I'm sure the consequence of such a situation would be legal action. But back then you tended to take what was given to you. The most frustrating thing was that I had known what the problem was right from the start, but whenever I said, 'Listen, I heard the snap,' my words were discounted. Looking back I should, of course, have made a stand, and said, 'This is my body, my career, for Christ's sake, listen to me.' But I didn't. Soon after my visit to Harley Street, Daphne and I were invited to dinner at the home of the new Fulham chairman, Sir Eric Miller.

Miller, a property developer around whose extravagant lifestyle there was always much controversy and who was eventually under investigation by the Department of Trade before he shot himself in rather mysterious circumstances – two bullets were used, which is not usual in a suicide, of course – had taken over from Trinder and had some big ideas about where he might take the club. He was famous for his generosity at the hotel he owned in the West End, The Churchill, and at his beautiful home in Chelsea. He was known as Mr Champagne for his love of Dom Perignon. He had always treated me well and he was particularly attentive this night. While Daphne talked with his wife Myra, Miller took me down to his luxurious den and said straight away: 'George, will you ever be able to play first class football again?' I told him of the hard word from Harley Street, which no doubt he had already heard, and confirmed that while I could still run forwards as hard as ever, turning was impossible. He said we had to discuss financial arrangements, and the offer he made was certainly fair by the standards of the day. The club had insured me for £100,000 and out of this I would receive £18,000. I would also have a testimonial game. He said he would go to the Tax Council and try to make the payment tax-free because I could no longer carry on with my profession. Because of the terms of the insurance payment I would have to stay at Fulham for a little just to prove it really was all over for me in terms of playing. The pay-off would be something of a cushion against the uncertainties of a new life, but the reality was the one that comes to so many footballers who can be easily lulled into the idea that the days of playing will never end. Of course inevitably they will, but football was like a cocoon for as long as you could run on to the field. In some ways it was an extension of childhood. Now for me all such illusion had been stripped away by the visit to Harley Street. The idea that you could spend thirteen or fourteen of the best years of your life running around various fields and helping to fill great stadiums sometimes twice a week and then find yourself finished in the only trade you know – and with a fraction of the insurance your employers would collect on the breakdown of your body – was not exactly comforting.

Of course it would have been wise to have taken out my own insurance but my highest weekly wage at Fulham, after tax, was £80 a week and that didn't leave so much to invest in savings or insurance. My testimonial match brought £8,000, which was gratefully received but did not, obviously, set me up for life. Johnny Haynes did no better. His testimonial yielded £7,000. Of course you always appreciated the support of the fans, but you also had to question a system that required them to help provide the pay-off for players they had paid to see down all the years.

None of this, of course, touched the emotion I felt on the night of the testimonial. That emotion would have been more intense if I had been able to take one last run out on to the field, at least for a short spell, but I had recently suffered a bout of pleurisy and pneumonia and I was advised by the club doctor that I shouldn't risk it. Of course I had already been through the wrench of hanging up the old boots, but something about the night brought it home with some finality that a huge part of my life was over.

The Boys of '66 came down to Craven Cottage and they were led by Sir Alf. He made a presentation to me and paid tribute to my career. As he spoke I had the inevitable flashbacks that come at such occasions – I heard all the shouts of the crowd, including the one that told me to give it to the Rabbi, and all the training days and times you just had to stand back in admiration of the passing skill of Johnny Haynes. All that was over and nobody needed to tell me that I had to lock it away for good.

For my enforced year-long stay at the club, they put me in charge of the youth team. I enjoyed working with the kids but it was frustrating to see the best of them whisked into the reserve team – and all the risks that that implied – without really getting a proper grooming. It wasn't an entirely wasted time, however. I did bring a few good lads through and it was wonderfully satisfying to see them make careers in the game, and watch them grow up. John Fraser and Les Strong were players who did well at Fulham and in their different ways they made strong impressions on me. John was a very sound defender, and he grew up to be a good footballer and a good family man who came through the game un- scathed. It's strange how quickly a kid changes from dreaming about football to dealing with the realities of life. Les Strong is a buccaneer of a fellow who travels around North America and is always telling me about some new project that he has in the works. My third 'discovery' was big John Lacy, who I saw when coaching at the London School of Economics. Mickey Stewart, the former cricket captain of Surrey and coach of England who played some professional football, had been doing the job but he had been called back to cricket and asked me if I would cover for him for a few months. You don't expect to find big centre halves at the London School of Economics but John was a delight to the eye of an old defender. He had long, gangling legs and anything that came to him he knocked away immediately. I told him, as my father had told me, that he should not neglect his studies, but like I was at his age, he was desperate to have a go at professional football. So I took him down to Craven Cottage and in no time at all he had moved through the reserves and into the first team. Tottenham were impressed by his strength and his natural instincts as a defender and they paid Fulham £100,000 to move him to White Hart Lane. Some things, I noted, never changed.

Football had been my life, of course, but I realised I wasn't going to provide a great living for Daphne and the boys as the youth coach of Fulham. I'd seen so many old players just hanging on, hoping that something turned up, and I told myself that I wouldn't do that. The thinking behind hanging on was easy enough to analyse. Maybe things are changing a little bit now, with new pressure on the finances of even the top clubs, but there are still easy enough livings to make within the game. A football man can get himself a coaching job and find himself earning something in the region of £2,000 a week. Now you have to get yourself a damned good job in civvy street to be earning that kind of money. In that sort of comfort zone it's going to take a lot to persuade you to set up a window replacement business or learn a new trade. For one thing, most footballers don't know anything much beyond the game. The margins of their lives have been governed by the touchlines of the field. It is also true that one of the tricks of hanging on in football is to do it well enough so that when the guys above you get the sack – as they always do – you could just land yourself a top job. A lot of 'best mates' of football managers and coaches have walked into big jobs on that basis. Where that left the friendships is of course an entirely different matter. I remember seeing a quote from David Pleat once, talking about the 'brotherhood of football managers'. I thought that was a rather interesting concept. However else the 'brotherhood' works it unfortunately doesn't remove the necessity to watch for a knife in your back. It all meant for me that while I enjoyed working with the young footballers, it was a life without security – and part of the uncertainty was the fact that not many of the new generation of players seemed to have much idea of discipline. Not too many of them showed much evidence of receiving the Tanfield treatment or the Mel Roberts slipper. They didn't seem to think the word of the manager mattered too much, and I definitely wouldn't have wanted the future well-being of my family placed in their hands. Among my own contemporaries there was a much stronger awareness that a successful manager–player relationship had to be based on trust. Certainly I always knew that whatever you thought of a manager the only way he was going to earn a living was if his players were good enough and willing enough on the field. So you did your best and hoped it was noticed.

No, a future in football wouldn't be for me, even though it was all I knew but for a brief time in the spring and summer of 1962 before I was married when I worked for the Cecil Gee tailoring company. My Fulham team-mate Roy Bentley arranged for my extra earnings after the club had refused me permission to take part in a tour of the Far East which was being led by Tom Finney. It would have been a great experience but Fulham had negotiated their own close-season tour of Zimbabwe, then known as Southern Rhodesia, and they insisted they needed all their senior players. Politics intervened and the Fulham trip was scrapped, which left me with time on my hands and the need to supplement my football wages on the run-in to marriage. Bentley was a great friend of the brothers Cyril and John Benjamin, who were high up in the management of Cecil Gee as well as being fervent Chelsea fans.

I enjoyed the work of a clothes salesman and was, to my great surprise, quite good at it. One of my best sales was to Sir Richard Attenborough, who bought a set of jackets for a theatre company. Attenborough was quite a fierce Chelsea fan and he knew his football. He was surprised to see me, and demanded to know what I was doing in a clothes shop. I said I was just earning a living. It was an enjoyable time when I got to know quite lot of people in the trade, including a wonderful character named Frederick Freed. He made ballet shoes for Margot Fonteyn. Cyril Benjamin thought I had a future in the trade and offered me a full-time job, but I declined with thanks. I said I had other plans and they included playing football for England. This did not deter the Benjamins from providing me with my wedding suit. Footballers can be quite lumpy with all the training that develops certain muscles but the suit was carefully built up around me and though perhaps it is immodest to say so, I thought I looked rather grand when I walked down the aisle. The custom built suit was of self-striped mohair. As I said at the time, Daphne didn't look too bad either.

Now that the football was over I had to make another move. I wanted something secure, something on which I could map out my future with some certainty. So instead of football I chose the property business. Maybe I had headed away too many crosses.

Sidney Brickman opened the doors to my new and rather tumultuous life. He was a friend of Jimmy Greaves and I first met him before one of my early games for England in Lisbon. It was an open stadium and it was raining and Sidney didn't have a raincoat. I lent him mine, which had been bought at Marks and Spencers – with no rebate for image rights against future earnings. I didn't see Sidney again on that trip but when I returned home there was a knock on my door and someone handed me a package from Liberty's. Inside was a Burberry raincoat and a note from Sidney, which said, 'George, I'm sorry I ruined your coat. Please accept this as a replacement.' Realising that a Burberry cost roughly ten times more than its Marks and Spencers rival, I called him to say that he shouldn't have been so generous. He just brushed that aside and said, 'George I would like you to come to my end-of-the-season dinner at The Savoy.' Sidney was devoted to Tottenham and he wined and dined the players at the end of each season, however their results had gone. It was a fine evening and certainly not diminished by the fact that while Daphne and I ate haute cuisine and drank fine burgundy in the company of Tottenham stars like Greaves and Cliff Jones, my Fulham chairman Tommy Trinder was hard at work as the cabaret.

Trinder was in his costume, which included tights, when

he spotted me among the diners. He shouted, 'Stop the music, stop the bloody music. Ladies and gentlemen, I have to introduce you to one of my players, George Cohen. Apparently he can afford to eat here.' As it happened, I was also laying down the foundations of my future beyond football. At the Savoy I met Henry Osborne, who owned a firm of architects in Camden Town which did a lot of work for Brickman Properties. Osborne, who is a friend of the actor Robert Powell, was most charming and it was the start of a great friendship. When I finally made the break with Fulham to join Brickman Properties, Sidney sent me to Harry's office to learn the business. Fortunately my education at Fulham Central had been technical so I could make sense of the drawing and do some of my own. I also had to learn about planning law, which meant that a lot of my time was spent reading the works of Sir Desmond Heap. He was the foremost authority on the subject and had to be read, if not particularly enjoyed. He was a man of great knowledge. But he wasn't Dennis Wheatley.

Much later, when I fell ill, Harry was very loyal. He would regularly call to see how I was, and how the family was holding up. Though I don't remember much about it, Harry spent a day with me at the Royal Marsden hospital during the worst of times, when I was receiving heavy radiation treatment. Apparently he pushed my wheelchair from one hospital department to another. With Sidney and Harry's help, I trained hard to be a land buyer and I realised quickly enough that if the adrenaline supplied by football had dried up, my new business came with its own supply. I had a tremendous surge of excitement when I was told to work on my first deal. The objective was a lovely old house in a beautiful park in Tunbridge Wells. My job was to persuade the owner, another property man, that I was an ex-footballer who wanted to get into the nursing home business. I knocked on his door and said, 'My name's George Cohen and I'm wondering if you want to sell this building.' It was a mansion with three acres of land and its own lake. In 1973 you could get that sort of thing for around £35,000. I pulled off the deal and it turned out to be a genuine coup. We had a right of access and planning permission to develop a number of luxury units. Sidney was delighted. He sold on the property and I received a bonus of more than £1,000, which I worked out quickly was the equivalent of about three months' wages for a First Division footballer. It was, briefly, a time when it seemed our future was made. We were comfortably off and I suppose the rabbit hutches of Walham Green had never seemed further away.

The end of my football career had been sudden and quite traumatic, but any apprehension I had had about my ability to properly provide for Daphne and my sons had begun to fade. In 1967, the year of the big injury, we had moved from Chessington to a fine, 2000 square feet detached house in Worcester Park in the Surrey stockbroker belt, and now, with the pay-off from Fulham and my new career in the property market, we could think of moving further up the ladder. I had good prospects and a generous friend in Sidney Brickman. It started with a borrowed raincoat and it ended with my becoming the son he never had. With his backing, I worked quite boldly and with good success. Of course from time to time things could go wrong – there are many slips and snags between the conceiving and the executing of a property deal and for every success there was plenty of frustration.

But by the time Sidney fell sick, and died quickly, in the early seventies I had reason to believe that I had won his confidence. In his will there was a final act of generosity. He left me a 25 per cent share of 25 Devonshire Place, a building he owned opposite the London Clinic in Harley Street. This was not a straightforward legacy, however. Sidney's ex-wife disputed the will and claimed that she was without any resources. I felt this not to be true and paid out thousands of pounds trying to protect my inheritance. In the end, with my legal bills up to around £17,000, we settled for 12.5 per cent and my share was bought by Sidney's sister Barbara, who owned the Wallace Dress Shop group. The battle took twelve years to resolve and by the time it was over the great security that Sidney had intended to bequeath me was not much more than a point of light in the enveloping financial darkness.

For several years after Sidney's death I ran the business before forming my own company, George R. Cohen Properties. We had some good success. I was very pleased with one little deal I pulled off for a 26-space car park next to the Pantiles, the historic old centre of Tunbridge Wells. There were some profitable stable conversions. I felt we were building to a point where the life of my family was rock solid, at least from the point of view of a good standard of living and freedom from any material worry. And I continued to enjoy the cut and thrust of the work. I particularly enjoyed the telephone conversation I had with a guy who provided protection against woodworm. I called him after getting hold of five cottages on the edge of Tunbridge Wells, a quite beautiful location. I told him what I needed and asked for his price. He said the cost was £500 a unit for the proper service and £250 for the 'Jewish crash job'. I said I was curious about the 'crash job'. He explained, 'Oh, you know the Jew Boys just want you to tear up a couple of floorboards, squirt in a bit of chemical and bung them a certificate.' I thanked him and said I might call him back. I remember the rest of the conversation quite vividly. He said, 'Could you give me your name for future reference?' I said, 'Certainly, it is Cohen.' He said, 'I suppose that means we're not going to do business.' I said it wasn't necessarily so. We talked a little longer and then I made an order. I wanted the proper job, and of course I got my price: £250.

By now we lived in a split-level house on Culverden Down outside Tunbridge Wells. It was surrounded by flowers and woodland and each morning you could see several generations of foxes and badgers. It was an idyll, and it seemed to me that we were on the point of getting ourselves set for life. All it needed was one big, sweet deal and, with three partners, I was moving in for the kill which would tie up the rest of a comfortable life. The plan was to buy a large plot of land next to an old school in Tunbridge Wells which was about to be demolished. It was a fine location and the intention was to build residential units for retired people. We had budgeted £2 million each. We believed our land was about to be re-designated for development and we also believed we had an option on the school land. We had been very thorough, doing our homework on the fine details. This was naturally so because this was a heavy investment, certainly the biggest I would ever make. When planning permission was refused by Kent County Council the explanation was that we didn't have a strong enough 'Section 52'. This is a planning ordinance that governs the designation of desirable units, and it is entirely in the hands of the council.

We were conforming to all their demands, and the fact that our proposed units were for retired people effectively countered the possible objection to increased traffic into the nearest road. We received a solicitor's letter congratulating us on our proposal and saying that all we needed to do was put in another application. In the meantime, a senior planner who had dealt with the case originally passed the file on to a junior colleague. Only one Labour councillor supported us, objecting to the way our case had been dealt with by the county council. We were devastated. We had put so much time and money and now the purchase of the school and grounds without planning permission was a waste of our money.

The Ombudsman said that we had a very strong case for maladministration but it would cost us another £250,000 to take the case to the House of Lords. We were beaten. There was no rescuing a project into which I had invested all my capital. The only way I could stay in any kind of business was by selling the house that sat amid the flowers and the wildlife. So we sold the house and rented, with the idea of reinvesting the money at the right time, which was not then in 1990 with interest rates at 17 per cent, making the putting of one brick on another a near impossibility. I'll never really know why the project crumbled like that but it is certainly irksome that part of our planning application was for the nearby school, for which we were the preferred purchasers from Kent County Council at a price of £250,000. Eventually the school land was sold to Barclay Homes for £1,250,000. There, you can buy one of the houses for between £500,000 and £750,000.

There is no point in dwelling on such a disaster. You have to take the blow, absorb it and get on with your life. If you don't it will just eat your insides out. It is the same when you look at the wages of today's footballers. You have to remember you're looking at a different world with different rules. My own rule is that if you can't change it, don't let it destroy your life.

We've made a recovery, though not a full one. My company now owns property worth around £1.6 million. I don't own all of it. I have partners because when your base is destroyed you need ideas and energy around you. We will make a profit and eventually we will come back. I'm working on some schemes now which I believe will do very nicely. Had the big scheme worked, I wouldn't be talking like this now. I never hankered for the big money, I never saw the pursuit of it as a goal in itself. So if we had got our plans through, I would have cashed in gratefully. I would have taken Daphne to all the places I'd half seen as a footballer. We would linger in Venice and explore the difference between Buda and Pest and maybe take a look at Rio without the need to risk one's skin in the great Maracana stadium. And when we tired of the travelling we would have gone back to the house on Culverden Down where on the weekend, when your mind had gone, completely closed down, you would wake up on a Sunday morning and walk into the garden where nothing was happening and not hear a damned thing. Then you would hear one bird, and then another. I used to do that regularly. Just walk into the garden. And stand there.

We were very upset when we had to walk away from that. Daphne handled it brilliantly. As I've said many times, the women are stronger than the men. My wife is a very calm person. Occasionally she hits the roof but living with me can't be easy. She was upset by what happened but she is the kind of person who says, 'Well, look, what are we doing about it? You've got to have an answer. You can't say I'm not doing anything about it because I can't. You can always do something.' So we sold the house and waited for the economy to change. At the lowest moments she said, 'George, you have your life. Things could be rather worse.'

CHAPTER FOURTEEN

BITTER PILLS

The poet was right, if a little optimistic, when he wrote that into every life a little rain must fall. In my own life there have been two great downpours. I don't imagine I'll ever get them completely out of my bones.

My mother and my younger brother, the father of England's international rugby wing Ben, died deaths of terribly sudden, random violence — nearly twenty years apart — my mother in 1971, my brother in 2000, and in the intervening years much of my time was spent in a battle against cancer. Twice I assumed victory, and then the shadow came yet again when my doctor said, 'George, I'm afraid it has come back. You have some more fighting to do.'

Of course you do it because what is more precious than life? But sometimes there is a terrible weariness. You cannot imagine yourself dead, especially if you have Jewish blood in your veins and not so long ago helped to win a World Cup, but you are bound to speculate a little about its possibility, and at the same time realise that something that happened on a football field cannot really be related to the dawning possibility that tomorrow – literally tomorrow – you might not exist. There is a particular edge to such a likelihood before the drugs have properly worked and it is four o'clock in the morning and the pain is digging so deep.

In the end you make a compromise, you take what you can, and are grateful for what you get. And, most of all, you thank God for a family you want to be around for as long as you can be, who make the business of fighting not a chore onerous almost to the point of impossibility, but the deepest instinct you have, and one you know they will always support with all their means and all their love. Daphne twice was told that she had better make sure I had my affairs in order – and twice she shook her head. When the financial roof had collapsed, when we had to leave our beautiful home, she had said that matters could have been worse, and when it seemed that they could hardly be more desperate, she simply said that the facts had to be engaged – and fought with every resource of spirit we had.

When my brother Peter was killed – the Crown Court verdict in Birmingham was that the blows and kicks, and bites, of a group of men of violent background who attacked him in the foyer of the nightclub he owned in Northampton amounted to no more than 'unlawful violence' – I was back in that other horror which had swept over me nineteen years earlier. Peter was killed by a gang of thugs. My mother was run down by a juggernaut. One moment she was walking briskly down North End Road, a vigorous woman of sixty-two, acknowledging an old friend of mine who was cleaning windows and had waved down to her as she paused for the traffic lights at Lillie Road on her way to work as the manager of a Marley Tiles store, and then she was gone – crushed by the rear coupling of the huge wagon. She had thought the great vehicle had passed, but it was turning on its vast axis.

My window-cleaning friend turned back to his work and then heard the terrible commotion. I have never been able to reconcile the casual savagery of that fate which ended a good and loving life. When it happened I was spending the day working at the clothing shop of my friend Cyril Benjamin. He called me to the back of the shop to take a call from Daphne, who gave me the news in the only way that is possible in these circumstances: straight and unvarnished. There is no way to soften such a blow. She came to pick me up because I couldn't trust myself to drive. I had to identify my mother. My brothers couldn't face the task and, anyway, I was nearest to the hospital, St Stephen's, which has gone now. It was where my father died, I remembered as I walked into the hospital. She had very few bruises and cuts but, of course, you could see the force of the impact. You could see the indentations. You never really get over a shock like that. You push into the furthest corner of your mind but you know it will always be there. Peter, the youngest, the darling, was inconsolable. He lived with my mother and he thought she would always be there. Unlike my brother Len and I, he had the privilege of addressing her as Kate and my father as Harry. It was a family joke. Peter could do no wrong and I suppose it was inevitable that when I was told Peter had died in hospital after a series of a strokes, a month after he had been attacked, my first thought was of my mother and how

broken she would have been. She loved all her sons passionately, none of us ever doubted that – but nor did we question
Peter's role as the apple of her eye. She fought for both Len
and I; for my football career and literally when Len told her
his marriage plans and she said he was too young and hit him
over the head with a broom-handle.

Just as I couldn't accept the shocking manner of my
mother's death, nor could I that of Peter. When my mother
died I was appalled by the freakish way she had gone. No-
one was to blame. It was a conspiracy of horrific, casually
assembled circumstances. You just had to ask why?

It was different with Peter. You knew why it happened –
there was no shortage of specific evidence. Unfortunately a
lot of this passed by the jury without appearing to register.
For several months I was in a state of permanent rage after
Colin Kerr, his brother Gavin, and a friend, Robert Evans,
were cleared of manslaughter – three others had been
involved but not charged – and given sentences ranging
from three and a half years to two and a half. I couldn't
bear to spend more than a day in court because I didn't have
any confidence that my brother would have justice, and
when the verdict came in my lack of surprise did nothing to
reduce my anger.

These people were known troublemakers and they had
been out on the town before arriving at my brother's club.
When they appeared they were noisy and aggressive and the
manager called Peter to the foyer. The defence alleged that
Peter attacked six people. When I heard that I just recoiled in
disbelief. Peter would always stand up to be counted; anyone

who knew him properly would not presume too much of his essentially passive nature. You couldn't kick the dust in his eyes and assume there would be no response.

But he was not an idiot. He had responsibilities, and a family he was proud of and loved deeply. What happened was somebody jumped him from behind and he got knocked down and hit his head on a machine, which, medical evidence said, was the cause of his death because it triggered a series of strokes. He was even bitten on the face. When he came round the doctors could see that he was paralysed down one side. He couldn't talk. I was on a cruise with the World Cup squad when it happened and I was flown back from Madeira. My son Andrew picked me up at the airport and drove me straight to Nottingham, where Peter had been taken to a special unit which treated head injuries. I returned several times to the hospital and received daily reports. He died when they got him up to wash him down and he suffered a massive heart attack. There had been deep-vein thrombosis from bruises on his legs. They did all they could to revive him, but they couldn't stop him slipping away.

The witnesses for the prosecution were emphatic but when I looked over at the jury on the day I was there I was not impressed by how closely they appeared to be following the case. To me, some of them did not give the impression they quite understood what was going on. One of the witnesses was told by the defence that he had a criminal record. He denied it. The only thing on his record was a parking ticket. They got his name wrong. It was a detail in all the sweep of what was going on but it left me peculiarly angry. I thought, 'For God's sake, you would think these people would at least get their facts right. Didn't they realise my brother had died? A life had gone. Why? And while you're asking, for heavens sake, get your facts right.' The dominating fact, in my mind, was that this was a downright miscarriage of justice and the people who killed my brother should have gone to prison for a long time. They had been in trouble before on several occasions, even assaulting a policeman. When previous convictions were announced it was a long list. When the case was over I made an appointment with my local MP in Kent. I called the police. I raged. My brother, the one I had shared a bed with when we were boys, the one I protected so fiercely at Fulham Central, had been snuffed out and nobody was beginning to pay any kind of price.

I never liked the nightclub business and I often said how I regretted he was involved in it. But he made a living out of it and he enjoyed it and sometimes I would go along to hand out a few prizes at one of his presentation evenings. He was a powerful man, two or three inches shorter than me but very thick-set. He would always stand up for himself, as the youngest boy, but he could never be called aggressive – except on a football field, where he could be a total embarrassment – because he had to be sorely provoked to get involved in any trouble. The jobs he chose before entering the nightclub business were never particularly forward-looking. He drove lorries and then he rented car parks. That's what took him up to Northampton. You always got the impression he had more talent than he was ever prepared to bring out. Basically, he liked to be around people while making a living, and I suppose that's what drew him into the nightclubs.

At one point he ran one of the biggest clubs in the Midlands, but when a recession hits, nightclubs are among the most vulnerable of businesses. He tried to hang on, tried to keep his people employed, but eventually he had to declare bankruptcy. Like so many people at the turn of the nineties, however, he bathed his wounds and fought again to make a living.

It was Peter's sons Justin, a policeman, and Ben, the rugby star, who finally got through to me that my anger was spilling, and would keep on spilling, to no real effect. I called Justin and said, 'Look, I know Peter was my brother but he was your father so what do you really want me to do?' Justin said, 'Uncle George, you have to put it down. We cannot get Dad back. The law, whatever you think of it, has taken its course. We have to get on with our lives.'

He was right, of course, but when you accept the logic of that you cannot always subdue the emotions which rise up in you suddenly. Both Peter's sons behaved very well. Justin, the eldest boy, took charge of the family and Ben, who was completely shattered, had to wrestle with a decision about playing in England's next international, against Australia at Twickenham, which was a few days after Peter's death. Ben asked me what I thought. I advised him not to play. 'What will happen to you,' I suggested, 'is that you will go out there for about fifteen minutes and then it will all fall apart. But it is your decision, Ben. You have to work it out for yourself.'

My feeling was that in Ben's emotional state he might be

lured into the belief that his father would have wanted him to play, but at that level of international sport you just cannot think like that. His father would have wanted always for him to go out to play to the very limits of his ability, and I just thought that for Ben it would be asking too much of himself. The last thing Peter would have wanted was for Ben to foul up. Ben just didn't know how much emotional energy he was using just dealing with the situation. He might think he could go out and put in his usual eighty minutes but rugby is a very physical game and you have to think your way through it. You are taking tackles, making tackles – expending energy all the time, and in the end you just might not have it up there.

Ben didn't play and he was right. His coach Clive Woodward was very good. He didn't crowd him. He said that it was his decision and he would respect whichever way he went. But he had to be very sure that he could get through it – he owed that to his team and himself and maybe even his father. What he didn't have to doubt was the degree of pride he brought to his father. I sat in the crowd with Peter at Twickenham when Ben scored two tries, and it was wonderful to be there to see the pleasure that came to my brother's face when his son went over the line.

On each occasion I leaped from my seat with tears in my eyes. Daphne restrained me, saying, 'George don't do that, you never get out of your seat.' It was true, but this was different, this was blood. It is curious that at such times you think of the strangest things. I thought of how Ben would come to our house in Tunbridge Wells with Peter, who used to dress up as Father Christmas and knock on our front door and my boys would rush to open it and when they saw him shout, 'Oh, hello, Uncle Peter.' He would be quite deflated. Ben was a determined and quite deliberate boy. On one drive to our house he had developed the need to go to the toilet. While the rest of us walked into the kitchen, he stopped to make use of a large ashtray, a presentation from Feyenoord Football Club, which sat on a coffee table in the lounge. God knows the mechanics of the operation, he was just a toddler and the coffee table was for him quite high, but he managed to fill the ashtray to the brim. Then he carried it carefully into the kitchen and presented it, quite formally, to his Aunt Daphne. They filled the streets of Northampton for my brother when he was buried. They stopped the traffic lights in the town centre and the cathedral was jammed. Two senior police officers spoke highly of his work for local youth, of his training of young rugby players – an interest he developed with the rise of Ben's career – and how he kept his club clear of drugs and violence. That was ironic in a rather forlorn way. The defence alleged that there were traces of the drug Ecstasy in my brother's blood, but that was disputed and I have never accepted it. He hated the culture of drugs.

When the tragedy came he was winning. But then I suppose it is true that in this life we can never be utterly sure of what truly is the score. You may think you're ahead, going very nicely, thank you very much, and then suddenly someone has stuck a couple of goals in the back of your net and you look at the big clock and you realise it is very late indeed.

For Peter the game ended long before any need for extra

time. In the choked traffic of Northampton – the trial had been moved to Birmingham because of the feeling that Peter was so popular in the town there would no possibility of a fair trial for the accused – which later struck me as another irony – our life together as boys played back in my mind.

Because he was so completely Mummy's boy – and Daddy's for that matter – Len and I could be a little wicked with him at times. Sometimes we played hide-and-seek – I cannot recall quite how we managed it in a three-room flat – and Peter's favourite hiding place was behind the fire which had a water-tank attached at the back. So we used to trap him in there by pushing up an armchair. We would let him out only when we heard our mother or father putting the key in the door on their return from work. Peter would come out of there quite berserk, but of course we denied all involvement. While our parents weren't looking we would knock his food on the floor – a near capital offence in our household. On occasion we might ape our father and give Peter a crafty flick on his ear. When my father did this to Len or I, we would protest and ask him why he had done it. And he always gave the same answer. 'So you don't start.' But in the car going to Peter's funeral there was an overwhelming memory of happiness and fun all those years ago in Walham Green.

Peter was just a little kid when Len came in from work one night to find our father pounding away at a piece of meat. Len demanded to know what type of meat it was as Peter and I watched, fascinated, the tenderising process. 'Is it best fillet?' asked Len. 'No,' he was told. 'Is it rump?' 'No.' 'Is it from a cow?' Len persisted. 'No,' he was told again. 'What is it then?' My father said, finally, 'It's bleeding horsemeat.' And Len said, 'Will it be tastier than that piece of whale we had the other night?' Our father led the laughter.

Some might have thought Len, who is a brilliant individual who might in a different age have been a star in industry or business rather than a gas fitter like his father, took the deaths of our parents and Peter less intensely than me; that he just got on with his life. But I always knew differently. Len grew up in an age when men didn't cry, however badly they felt. The nature of the deaths of both his mother and his brother shocked him deeply. But Len had a front – and he boxed things up. The only time I saw him lose that front was when he was diagnosed with the same kind of cancer I had been fighting for seven years.

He was shattered and he gave me the impression that he wasn't really up to the fight. His wife Raymonde confirmed this when she made a very anguished telephone call to me. She said, 'George we're at our wits' end – Len is giving up, he seems to think he is going die and there's not much point in fighting. Do you think you could do something to help?' It was the great role reversal of our lives. Len who had led me into life, who always had an aura around him as far as I was concerned, looked as though he might be inclined to stay on his stool when the bell rang for the big fight of his life.

So now had come the time when I was no longer little Georgie who had to be taught how to use a knife and fork, a status which my achievements on the football field had done little to dissipate down the years. I drove to the hospital in Basingstoke, where Len was wired up to several machines and drips. I stood beside his bed and gave him a very hard word indeed. I said I wasn't going to see him wallow in self-pity. Christ knew, I had faced the temptations of that myself over the last seven years and had a gut feeling, in the most literal sense, that I might have it return. But I had a family and a life and I was damned if I was going to let it just fade away.

Len owed the same obligation to his own family, to me and anyone who loved him – and, most of all, to himself. It was, you can imagine, an emotional scene. We were both in tears, and that was unfamiliar country indeed for Len. We were a tactile, emotional family and we didn't hesitate to express our emotions physically. But this wasn't a kissing time. This was a time when everything that needed to be said was said, and as I said it I noticed Len's family and Daphne huddled together in a corridor. Len didn't want to see anybody. He just wanted to lie there and die and, frankly, it rather pissed me off.

Len lives happily in retirement now, surrounded by his family, and enjoying himself in his dry, laconic way. We haven't gone over that old ground – it is still not Len's style, and I suppose you have to bear in mind that not only did he grow up in a time when strong men didn't show emotion, but they did not even utter the word cancer because back then it was something you just couldn't fight. It was a killer. It didn't take prisoners and when you were told you had it there was nothing your friends could say or do except take a collection for your family. Raymonde later said that our confrontation had helped to bring Len out of his isolation – and it is certainly true that his doctors in Basingstoke consulted with mine at the Royal Marsden to see what they might learn from the handling of my case.

Cancer had claimed my father when it was still the scourge that consumed lives and hope. My mother walked unwittingly into the confusing path of a juggernaut. Our beloved kid brother would fall victim of a bunch of lightly punished thugs. But Len and I would fight. We would, he finally agreed with a slightly sheepish grin, carry on like a couple of old wandering Jews.

CHAPTER FIFTEEN

RIDING THE STORM

When the cancer eventually came into my pelvis, all in a rush, it seemed, in the small hours of the morning I tried biting a pillow but it was no good. I couldn't trust myself not to scream and alarm the boys. So I went downstairs and stretched out in the hallway, covered in sweat as Daphne called for help.

Fog was covering the Kent countryside and the locum doctor told her that he didn't want to risk it down the country lanes. Fortunately, our neighbour Margy Harley was a nurse. She went on the phone and listed her qualifications and the doctor said, yes, she could inject me with the morphine we had in the house. How do you describe the pain with any degree of precision? It is not so easy. The best I can do is say it is like somebody constantly boiling water on a certain part of your body, in this case my pelvis.

People in Daphne's position have a different kind of pain. They can't stop it, but the most devoted of them all, in whose number I unhesitatingly include my wife, take it on themselves. They suffer every deep stab of it along with you. They tell you that which cold logic says is untellable. They convince you that you are not alone. They make the fight worth fighting. They take away the longing to swallow a whole bottle of tablets and be done with it.

It started in 1976, when I was thirty-six. I had been in business for some time and it was going rather well. We were, by most people's standards, in an enviable position. I was taking my usual five-mile run between the Kent villages of Bidborough and Penshurst. It was a run I could normally eat, but on this day I didn't feel right. I felt bloody tired and it was a tiredness I didn't recognise. My stomach was very tight. It felt awful. I went home with diarrhoea, which was very severe and I thought I might have something like a touch of colitis. It went on through the night and I realised this wasn't just another stomach bug. On the following morning I went down to see my GP, Denzil Law. When I walked into his office he got up from his chair and said, 'Good Lord, George.' I knew I looked ill. I told him what had been up with me and he gave me an internal examination. He was very matter of fact. He said, 'It doesn't seem right in there – I'm going to send you to see a surgeon, a friend of mine, Gordon Larvey.' I liked Gordon instantly. He was a former missionary to China. He had a lot of presence. He gave me another internal examination and took a biopsy. We would get the results in forty-eight hours, but he said that it felt like a growth. When I came out of his office I was breathless. I got into my car but didn't drive away. I just sat there and I thought, 'This can't be happening to me – I'm George Cohen, England footballer, athlete, indestructible. I can't tell anyone. I can't tell my wife.' Well, of course, that was my first irrational reaction. I told

Daphne I had a blockage and they weren't sure what it was. Denzil Law got back to me after a couple of days and asked me to go in to see him. He told me I had cancer.

He had already booked me into hospital, and when I arrived there a few days later I had the most degrading experience of my life. I had to get washed out — the medical term is colonic irrigation — and the job was performed by two wonderful ancillary nurses. They put the water under pressure and then release it when they wash you out. It is odourless but nevertheless quite awful. These two splendid girls did this job for me twice. They did it as though it was the least of things — and they took away my inhibitions about my condition. They brought me back onside. Before he operated, Larvey talked at some length to Daphne and me. He said he was going to cut away as much from the bowel as he could. He didn't really know what the reaction would be. It was a case of cutting and waiting to see. The operation went well, and for a little over eighteen months it seemed that I might just be in the clear. Then the original symptoms came back. I saw Gordon Larvey again. Daphne was with me. He confirmed that the cancer was back and outlined three possibilities. If the condition was more severe than he hoped I might have to have an illiostomy, which is performed higher on the body and which I quickly decided might be a little too much for me to take. A colostomy was the second possibility. The third option wasn't really worth thinking about. It was doing nothing. It was at this point in the discussion that Larvey repeated to Daphne what he said eighteen months earlier. It would be a good idea if I got my affairs in order.

Her response was again, 'George isn't going anywhere.' I admired and very much appreciated her consistency. I also thought it was a great act of faith – and how difficult it is to imagine yourself dead. Gordon had provoked that last thought when he said, 'The worry is that we may not have caught this soon enough.'

They had – but the margin had been very fine indeed. I could be saved. The price was the colostomy. The idea of body waste passing into a bag attached to your body is not attractive, but I suppose a lot depends on your perspective. One man's revulsion is another's salvation, and that was the way I was obliged to see it. It was not so easy. My first thought was: what would she make of it, how would she deal with it? We were in the prime of our lives and when the marriage deal is struck the phrase 'in sickness and in health' might not necessarily cover the shock to your system, and sensitivities, which comes with a colostomy.

I took it hard but I also knew that the alternative was even bleaker. I had to come to terms with it, and the sooner the better because unlike my brother Len, who was informed that his need for a colostomy was possibly reversible – as it proved – I was told that I had to accept that this was a permanent part of my life. It was especially shocking, I suppose, to someone who had always prided himself on his fitness. I had worked hard for that fitness, but I also believed that it was mine by right of both effort and birth. I had been given certain natural assets and I had been determined not to squander them. It had become a matter of macho pride and now I was being taken by a young girl to the hospital 'colostomy bath'. I lay back in the water and thought, 'Jesus Christ, I'm the only professional footballer I know who can have a bath and watch himself take a crap at the same time.' I burst out laughing and the girl wondered why. I tried to explain that it was silly things like that which kept you going.

But mostly it was Daphne who did that. Soon after my operation I had a visit from a lady who described herself as a 'colostomy counsellor'. She said her name was Mrs Diamond and soon enough I thought it was appropriate. I told her my fears about Daphne's reaction. I wondered about life in the bedroom. She told me that it was the preoccupation of almost every man who had the operation. I had to step beyond my fears.

She said it would be good for me if Daphne, as soon as possible, saw the stoma, the wound at the point of exit of what was left of my bowel. When Daphne came to my bedside the surgeon told her that the operation had gone well and asked if she would like to see what had happened, though he pointed out that at the moment it was still a bit of a wound. She said, quite matter of factly, 'Yes of course,' and when they uncovered me, she said, 'Is that all it is.'

It must have shocked her. It would have shocked anybody. She looked at this stomach which just a few hours earlier had been cut open so that bodily functions could take this new route for the rest of my life and she didn't blink an eye. I don't suppose I'll ever quite know how appalled Daphne truly was when she saw what had happened to me. I don't really think it is possible not to be shocked, and at least initially, repulsed by such a sight.

Fortunately the stoma was not active the first time Daphne saw it. I marvelled at her strength and it was an admiration which spread beyond her support and love of me and, down the years, only increased my conviction that she just happened to belong to the stronger sex. It was a view strengthened some time later when I addressed two sessions of a 'Health Awareness' conference organised by the Hong Kong and Shanghai Bank in Sheffield. The room was filled with women, which was a rather daunting prospect, especially when I considered what was at the core of my speech. But I didn't try to apply any cosmetics to the situation. I gave it to the ladies straight. I asked them how they might feel if they had to go through life with a bag attached to their bodies. Would they perhaps wonder occasionally what their husbands might think? Certainly for a professional athlete with a bloody big ego it was a rather horrendous thing to happen. I told them the biggest question in my mind was always the same: What will my wife think?

The women crowded around me, asking questions and saying that they appreciated my candour. They said that in future they would look at this problem in a new light. It would have more of a human face, they would think of the emotions as well as the practicalities. In a way the experience was also good for me. It was, when I thought about it later, a kind of unburdening in a very public place. I had talked about how it was, and the terrors it had created in my mind, and these women who I had never met before seemed to understand all of it so clearly and with such uncoiling sentiment that I felt much of my own horror and resentment dwindling away.

The trouble was that living with the colostomy was only part of the problem. I had also to deal with the possibility that the cancer could come back at any time. You push it into the back of your mind, you try to get on with the business of making a living, but you have to do everything in the short term. You live by the day, putting a new value on that, and you do not make deals that might stretch out for more than six months. When the cancer came back so strongly four years after my colostomy operation and attacked my pelvis so strongly I did have a fear that this time it would overwhelm me. But then when it moved into my pelvis I did have one great stroke of luck – and one that was denied my World Cup captain Bobby Moore. It did not also reach out to my liver. Once that happens you have basically run out of options.

I experienced an extremity of pain lying in that hallway, and though I came down from the worst of it, it was a long and draining job. Eventually they reduced the cancer in my pelvis to the point where it no longer pressed on my sciatic nerve and the blood could flow through my veins there. Around this time I was at my lowest ebb. My morale was at zero, I was on my back and deep down I wondered if I was truly ready to be counted out.

But my wife kept pulling me off the canvas. She wouldn't let me be soft on myself. You could easily slip into that state of mind because the drugs do knock you down. Daphne's performance was particularly brilliant because she was also dealing with the business, my sons and her beloved, sick father. I was having morphine injections in the morning and the afternoon and in the evening my wife would give me extra painkillers – all listed drugs. I was having radiotherapy to reduce the growth in my pelvis and then I was switching to chemotherapy. The world was beginning to look like a bloody balloon. I was beginning to look forward to the shots of morphine – and that lovely warm feeling of slipping into sleep and away from the pain. I was a stretcher case taken from Tunbridge Wells to the division of the Royal Marsden in Sutton, Surrey. It was there that I met the surgeon Q.M. Mathias. He was a much more extrovert, and optimistic, character than Gordon Larvey, but the debt I now owe to both men is indivisible. Mathias arranged my drugs and treatment, and he was aware of the desolation that had come to a sportsman who had always prided himself on being in good shape. He also loved sport and he said he was going to rescue me. 'Don't worry about this George, old boy' he said, 'We're going to burn this out of you.' They couldn't operate at that point but Mathias just shrugged and said how he was going to bombard me with drugs.

Of course it wasn't exactly a joyride but, as he pointed out, it simply had to be done. Mathias was moved back to the Fulham branch of the Royal Marsden, and I followed him there on my stretcher. It was a little chilling to go back to the place which in my youth was capable of creating such fear and despair in the hearts of all those who were summoned within its walls. I don't think it could have quite happened like that in today's overstretched National Health Service. I certainly didn't have the means to pay for my own care, my medical insurance with Fulham having run out some years previously. By the time I reached the Royal Marsden in Fulham my file was probably nine inches thick. I asked Mathias to estimate the overall cost of my treatment and he said there was no point in telling me because I couldn't have begun to pay for it.

I was finally discharged in 1990 – sixteen years after my run between Bidborough and Penshurst had turned into such an ordeal. There have been a few false alarms down the years and of course I have regular tests – as do my sons. The genetics of my family insist on this, my father having died of cancer and Len and I having fought battles against almost identical forms of the disease. Naturally it was one of the most exhilarating moments of my life when one of Mathias's assistants, a woman doctor, said, 'Yes, we are talking cure here.' It was a tremendous credit to my doctors and the jaunty way Mathias, along with Daphne, had kicked me into resistance. 'I want you to be a success, my boy,' said Mathias, who had also told me to live my life with a little optimism and not to forget that no-one was really sure what lay around the corner. Daphne had a wide, lovely smile when we got the news and she hugged me. Of course I was rather emotional. Sixteen years is a hell of a long time, especially when quite a bit of it had as its highpoints the shots of morphine that came at 10 o'clock in the morning and 10 o'clock at night. It was tough getting off the drugs. They answered all the immediate problems and they gave you this warm, fear-reducing glow. It takes a little time to kick-in but then you get this almost unbelievable sense of well-being. It's a bit like coming out of the freezing cold and stepping into a warm bath. It is all-enveloping. It is probably easier for me than most people to understand how it is that you get hooked on drugs, but that knowledge has never lessened my anger when I hear how common is the indulging in 'recreational drugs'. I've learned not be judgmental in life and I accept that most people who abuse drugs don't want to kill themselves. They have become trapped, most often because of their own weakness, but there must also be many cases of people whose lives are so horrendous they find them almost impossible to deal with. A lot of people just don't take their lives seriously enough, and that's when they slip into trouble.

But then of course there are the other cases when they are ambushed by circumstances. An overwhelming number of people just wanted to do away with themselves during the Holocaust, for instance. In my own case I needed those drugs to survive and afterwards there was no doubt I had big problems. I became very fidgety, and I found myself blinking a lot. There was no way I would have taken anything I didn't need, but the problem was that my need was so great. I definitely didn't become a junkie but the illness dragged on for so long and I was probably on the way.

I can certainly understand the problems of people fighting something like multiple sclerosis. I have a friend in that situation and he battles brilliantly and works so hard. I've never asked him if he resorts to cannabis. If he did I would understand easily enough – anyone who has lived with pain for long periods would. There are times when you just don't want to live with it – it is just too excruciating. I never reached the point of wishing I was dead, or wanting to make it happen – I suppose I was lucky enough to have just too much to live for – but there were times when I wanted to be away from the house and in hospital because I was very concerned that the boys shouldn't become too anxious and they should continue with the daily rhythm of their school life without too much interruption. It was quite late in the game before they began to understand quite what was happening to me, and they will probably never quite understand how much they helped to persuade me that it was really very important for me to hang around. So I rode out the storms – and the false alarms. The latter were caused by the shadows left by all the incisions and the tissue damage caused by the radiotherapy. The heaviest weather came when I had tremendous stomach-aches and cramps – and when I vomited every time there was a convulsion when my gut twisted.

I made it out into the light. Bobby Moore didn't. I was lucky with my doctors – perhaps Mooro wasn't. It is something that comes into my mind quite often. I wasn't close to Bobby, he liked to operate within a close circle, but I liked him a lot. He was marvellously understated and we shared the London habit of calling everyone 'son'. I spent quite a bit of time with him in Dubai in 1990, when the United Arab Emirates made it to the World Cup finals for the first time. The place was agog with football and Bobby had landed some work there. He had a spare ticket because his second wife Stephanie, with whom he was plainly deeply in love, wasn't making the trip. I hadn't been aware that he had suffered a bout of testicular cancer when he was still playing. Now I was hearing rumours that it had come back into his bowels and he was at the beginning of the fight that would not go well.

In Dubai Bob had to spend a lot of time working, but suddenly he was questioning me quite intensely about my medical experiences over the years. Typically, he didn't rush into the subject. I was sitting on the beach when he came by and said, 'Fancy a swim, son?' We went into the sea, swam for a while without any conversation, and then came back, naturally, for a couple of lagers. I remember the time quite vividly. He looked well enough and he had a good tan and I have a wonderful picture of a toddler coming up and prodding him. When the baby was taken away, he asked me how I was feeling – and how I had handled all those years of fighting cancer. I was as positive as I could be without skimming over too many things, and he listened intently. The following day we played a round of golf on a beautiful course with the Liverpool winger Ian Callaghan, who had briefly been a World Cup colleague in 1966. Bobby didn't say much but that was normal.

He loved to be in the company of professional footballers. It relaxed him. It was something of a comfort zone. When we flew back to London Stephanie met Bobby at Heathrow airport. They embraced quite passionately, which is something you normally wouldn't look at or comment upon. It was a moment of private intimacy in a public place, but with Bobby involved it was hard to take your eyes away because this was the laid-back captain of England, the man who Jack Charlton believed twenty-four years earlier, when that sculpted pass went winging to Geoff Hurst, had ice in his veins. But of course off the field Bobby was a man like any man, and here he was with the beautiful love of his life, happier it seemed than he had ever been but worried that his time might be running out.

Two years later – and a year before he died – I saw him at the National Gallery where the Boys of '66 assembled for the unveiling of a portrait of Bobby Charlton. Mooro looked ghastly. I asked him how he was feeling and he said, 'Not good, George.' I didn't really know whether I should question him any more – I knew well enough how such probing can get you on edge when things are not going so well – so I just said, 'What's happening?' He said that he was receiving treatment but it wasn't having that much effect. It looked to me that he was pretty much worn down and, by the sound of the medical report, he had been left with not much more than the love of Stephanie – and his own great dignity.

Bobby Moore was dying and when I left the gallery and went into the traffic I wondered why I had made it and the likelihood was that he wouldn't. It occurred to me that it doesn't really matter who you are. If something wants to strike you, it will, and there is not a whole lot you can do about it except fight it the best way you can. Bobby died very quickly. It was just like turning off a tap. He knew he had so much left in his life, something that couldn't be measured by wealth and celebrity. But the break he needed, and the one I had received, didn't come.

When we went to the Abbey to remember him there was

much pomp, which if he had been around might have made him a little uncomfortable. He might have said, 'I don't really need this, son.' But we needed it. Our captain, the hero of our best days, had gone first and a certain spell had been broken. We needed the ceremony to get us through the passing of a great and humble man.

CHAPTER SIXTEEN

THE KENNEDYS
OF TUNBRIDGE
WELLS

When I sold my World Cup medal some people, no doubt well meaning in their way, shuffled their feet and mumbled their sympathy. You would have thought I had parted with something of myself, something utterly integral to who and what I was. I just couldn't see it like that. I didn't need to look at a medal to know I had helped to win the World Cup.

In perfect circumstances I would have been happy to put the medal in a glass case and keep it for the pleasure and pride of my descendants. But which ones? I have two sons, Andrew and Anthony, and I was damned if I was going to choose between them. The medal was valued at between £75,000 and £100,000. I could put that money to good use, invest in a pension plan which, after the turbulent years of business, would be something in the way of security. I talked it over with Daphne and the boys and there was no dissent. The sale made sense. It was a practical thing. When it was announced the medal was going up for auction, Kevin Keegan, then manager of Fulham, called me to ask if I would sell it to my old club. The chairman of the club and proprietor of

Harrods, Mohammad Al Fayed, who employs me for home matches as the host of the George Cohen international lounge, wrote me the cheque and said that the medal would always be available to me. He asked me not to disclose the amount he was paying, but I can say it was a generous price and when the deal was completed I didn't think I would have felt any different if I had just sold an antique or a piece of art which had been hanging on my wall. I had realised an asset. I hadn't sold my soul.

With kinder fate my elder son Andrew might have won some medals of his own. He was a wiry little boy, but as he grew up it became increasingly obvious that he was a natural with a ball. His eye-to-ball co-ordination was fantastic. He was extremely quick and when I looked at his movement and control of the ball I shook my head and said to myself, 'Is he going to be a footballer or what?'

I was never more excited by him than when he sprinted along the driveway at the house in Bidborough. It stretched a hundred yards and it was uphill. Andrew flew along. He had a wonderful natural action and when he reached twelve, I taught him how to move his arms. He was able to get his steps in with a tremendously high knee action. He was, I could see with great pleasure, someone who could float over the ground, and then when I put the clock on him over sixty yards his times were quite phenomenal. I made a conscious decision not to push him, but he seemed to work naturally and everybody could see that without him the school didn't really have a football team.

It meant that I was completely unprepared for the reaction

of Fulham when I took the boy down to Craven Cottage. They measured his feet and his hands and announced that he wasn't going to grow. I was surprised and angry.

I told Fulham that when I first met Jimmy Greaves he was 5ft 5ins and something like nine stone. Then there was that little weakling Denis Law. Johnny Haynes wasn't exactly Superman when I first saw him. I asked if I needed to go on, but it didn't do any good. Today, in his mid-thirties, Andrew stands 5ft 10 ins and weighs around twelve and a half stones.

When he was fourteen, I was utterly convinced he was going to be an outstanding player. He played wide right and had it all: speed, natural strength and that really impressive eye–ball co-ordination. I was also stunned when I saw him take his first swing at a golf ball. It wasn't exactly classical, but the ball flew like a rocket. There was no doubt in my mind that Andrew had far more talent than I had ever displayed. I was a good athlete but I was obliged to work very hard on my football. Andrew was genuinely gifted.

Naturally, I wasn't going to let his rejection by Fulham wreck his potential for an excellent professional career. We went down to Charlton. I liked the approach at Charlton. They didn't seem to be stuffing their kids with information. They were also avoiding the trap of teaching children to compete before they had begun to properly develop their skills through technique. Charlton liked the look of Andrew, noted his skill, his easy technique and also the fact that apart from speed he had stamina.

I felt sure Andrew would prosper in this atmosphere. The stress was on development of skill rather than the hoarding of youth trophies. All the work at Charlton was centred on the ball, and it was a reminder to me of a lesson I had learned earlier in my fleeting time as a coach at Craven Cottage. Sir Eric Miller asked me to take a team to Dusseldorf for a youth tournament. We won the competition, which was quite an important one, rather easily, but I was not deceived. We had some physically mature young players who were just a step away from the first team, but there was no doubt about the basis of our triumph. It was to do with the fact that we were stronger rather than better. In fact, our European opponents had infinitely more developed skill – and in a year or so's time they would also be physically strong. We would be left with just our strength.

There is no doubt in my mind that if English football is to truly return to the first rank we have to develop a new culture of the game. We have to see that there must be something fundamentally wrong if a big country with a good standard of living, and the oldest tradition in the wide world of football, needs to import 60 per cent of its top professional players.

At Charlton I felt I might have seen a little gleam of a better future, as I did from time to time when Jean Tigana, who as a player was a superb example of the growing strength and sophistication of the French game, produced a performance of poise from Fulham. As soon as Tigana arrived at Craven Cottage, I liked what I saw. My old club were beating teams by playing football, pure and simple. He also seemed to be operating a no-blame policy. Players were being encouraged to play a positive game, one free of fear. Of course, that all ended in tears. Today, under the youthful, but in some ways very impressive, leadership of Chris Coleman, Premiership survival is the understandable priority. Tigana's attempt to become involved in the new age of English football didn't work out, and unfortunately, my son Andrew, my bright protégé, would also miss out. One morning he went off to play Sunday League football with his pals and wrecked his knee. It was a terrible disappointment, but Andrew wasn't inclined to mope over his setback.

He got on with his life and today he runs a successful bricklaying company. One day I got a call from him and was a little surprised when he said, 'Dad, can I come to see you?' I asked him whenever did he need an invitation to come home. He replied, 'Well, I've got a surprise for you and I need to tell you about it in person.' When he arrived he suggested we went into the garden and I said, 'Andrew, what on earth is the matter?' He said he was getting married, which was something of a shock because Daphne and I didn't know he had a regular girlfriend. The second surprise was that he was planning to marry a Sikh.

I said, 'Well, that is interesting – a Cohen and a Sikh, that's a combination I don't think you would find in any cocktail bar in London.' They had met at a football match and apparently there was some trouble with her family. Her brother was indignant that she might marry a non-Sikh, and her father met Andrew for the first time on the wedding day. But since then we have become good friends. The Cohens, perhaps not surprisingly given our experience down the years – not to mention the centuries – rather took things in our stride. It was not so difficult. Baldeep is beautiful and it was not a mystery to Daphne and I that Andrew should have fallen in love with her. They have two sons, Lewis and Ben. They are little tearaways but the women, particularly, love them. They have eyelashes that the ladies would die for – and penetrating eyes.

Anthony was born a year after the World Cup – you could say he was part of the on-going euphoria. He enjoyed sport but he was never going to be a pro. He was a bright boy who wanted to join the navy as an officer but he was told his mathematics weren't good enough. Now he deals with tens of millions of pounds every year as a contracts manager in the telecom business. At one point in his brilliant career he commandeered part of our house and set up a communications system which I sometimes suspected was part of NATO.

He tried to educate me in the intricacies of his rather amazing world but the best I could do most of the time was to offer to make a cup of tea. He, too, has a great marriage to Helen, who runs marathons. They have three children: Charlotte, Christopher and Eleanor. They live next door. We knocked down the fence and of course the kids just come running across whenever they feel like. They are lovely and they make me feel young. The Kennedys had their family compound in Hyannis Port. The Cohens have their version in Tunbridge Wells.

It is wonderful to see all these kids growing up and to have a family that stayed together through the toughest of times. Maybe you have to go to the very edge to put a true value on these things. In the end you know that they run deeper than anything that might happen on a football field, even the one on which England won the World Cup. It was the day of our sporting lives and it would colour everything that followed.

But it didn't help Bobby Moore when his life so swiftly ran away. Or me when I cried for the morphine on that foggy morning in Kent. When the civil servant called to offer the MBE and I told Daphne she smiled and said, 'Are you kidding?' The prize, such as it was, had come to us down through all the years that separated us from the gilded day at Wembley when our lives stood still. The phone call had come from Downing Street but as we embraced we didn't need to say that really it might have been from another world.

A YOUNG
AND THRILLING
VINTAGE

The world Daphne and I made for ourselves after the terrible blows in business and health has for me always been wonderful and precious, always a gift, but then I have never lost sight of the fact, even in the happiest moments of my family's life, that it is also fragile.

However grim the medical procedures I had to go through, I told myself it was so much superior to the alternative of being dead. So what do you do when the bad days come back? You take whatever is given to you and are grateful.

I tried to remember that on the journey home from Ben's World Cup triumph in Australia. I could see that my son Anthony was worried about my condition; whenever I awoke from some fitful sleep, he was there, looking at me intently, asking me how I was. It was becoming the pattern of my life now: anxious looks from family and friends, a loss of weight confirmed on the scales at 14 or 15 pounds. And all the time you feel that little bit more vulnerable. Also, in a strange way, you have the idea you are becoming invisible.

There was a heightened sense of that when we arrived at

Heathrow airport filled with excitement. Our plane had touched down within a few minutes of the one carrying the rugby heroes, and of course they were swept through the airport to the accompaniment of great waves of cheers. They deserved every moment of that acclaim, and the extraordinary amount of it that came when they were paraded through the streets of London a few days later. But for someone like me, who had known a little of that attention but felt utterly detached from it now, and from much else that was going on around me, it was indeed a little as though I was disappearing.

At such times the strangest thoughts come into your head, and I was reminded of something said to me many years earlier. Somebody was speculating on how a beautiful woman must feel when her youth is gone and she is no longer conscious of anyone looking at her. Of course, I could never know that. But maybe in this odd way I had a better idea, a little deeper sense, of how it is when one's life is just running away, a feeling that perhaps came to Bobby Moore that day we had a couple of beers on the beach in Dubai. Maybe as my young nephew was enjoying his great moment, one so similar to that which I had once enjoyed, I was encountering for the first time that dawning sense of my own invisibility which sooner or later we all to have face.

None of this, though, was anything I was about to place on Anthony's shoulders as he found our baggage and helped me out of the airport. I simply said, with some feeling, 'Get me home, son.'

It was some months later when Professor John Northover, a leading expert in bowel cancer at the Northwick hospital in

Harrow on the Hill, explained to me what had been going on inside my body. It is not the prettiest of subjects but I'm afraid it's quite central to my life, at least most of the last half of it. The 'drain' which the surgeons create when you have a colostomy is supposed to heal through 'granulation', a process quite like the setting of concrete, which dries from inside and produces heat. I had assumed that this arrangement would be fixed for as long as I lived, and if it meant that it became distinctly uncomfortable a few times a year, well, I was very happy to pay that price.

Professor Northover had some news that rather shattered this agreement I had made with my body. The 'drain', put in 27 years earlier, when I had my last operation, had finally got round to deciding it wasn't going to heal. The body's decision was that the tissue being supplied by blood vessels had become alien with the effects of radiation. Suddenly, said the doctor, a part of my body didn't belong to me anymore.

The good news was that the cancer hadn't come back; indeed, after studying a series of tests he had concluded that I probably hadn't had cancer at the time of my last operation. It almost certainly had been cleared away by the surgery and the radiation. But I had scar tissue which had become infected; scar tissue from the blasting effects of radiation, not the cancer which I knew had returned so viciously when I lay in the hallway of my house in Kent more than ten years previously and prayed for the moment when the morphine would come to do its work.

But if that dreaded word cancer had been, retrospectively, removed from my life it didn't mean that all serious hazards had also gone away. The survival deal I had made with myself, the resolve to take the best that my life still offered and live with the rest, was beset by serious complications . . . the life-threatening, permanent risks of septicaemia and peritonitis. I said to the professor, as lightly as I could, 'So these are dangerous players?' He nodded his head and said, 'Yes, extremely so.'

By the time I got to see Professor Northover my condition had worsened considerably since I had struggled along the streets of Sydney. He explained to me that the chief cause of my weight loss was my high dosage of antibiotics. You look at these tablets and study the list of possible side-effects and imagine that you are suffering from all of them. My strong suspicion was that in fact I was. Most seriously, I had terrible, immobilising depression.

Often I lost my balance and suffered nausea. The professor said he would do some more tests, but in the meantime I had to come off the antibiotics. Good sleep, good food, which he thought I would have an appetite for again, might provide some natural resistance to the infection, but if the problem, and the risk, deepened perhaps there would have to be major surgery.

A desperate, almost forgotten weariness came to me when I heard those words, but as I tell you this, and cross my fingers, I can also report the worst effects of the infections have not reappeared. However, I have been told that if they do, I have to respond with great urgency. I have to get myself to the nearest hospital and to underline the point the specialist gave me his home number. 'Call at any time, day or night, George — it may be necessary to save your life,' he said.

The big problems come with a sudden rise of toxins, something which I have been reminded of regularly down the years. At times, in the early years, the situation was so bad that I couldn't get by without a jab of diamorphine. Now when the risk of septicaemia comes I have to have an immediate pethidine injection.

It is called a 'rigour' and it triggers the most urgent action. It almost sounds like some technique you might try out on a training field under the gaze of Jose Mourinho, but I cannot tell you how much I would give for it to be so. It comes at the most unexpected time and, quite frankly, the effects are terrifying.

The first serious attack came a few months after the visit to Sydney, when I was shaving before going out to a Sunday lunch invitation I had willed myself to accept. Suddenly I began to shiver and then felt all of my strength draining out of me. The shivering was replaced by great shudders that ran through my body. It was a little like standing in the middle of an earthquake. As I had so often in the past, I could only thank God for the presence of Daphne. She kept very calm although I imagined that beneath the surface she was alarmed. She is a very practical lady, quite business-like under pressure, and as I tried desperately to relax myself — with no success — she got me into bed within minutes and called a doctor.

The lady doctor gave me an injection to calm me down and handed Daphne some very powerful antibiotics. It was then that I could see fear in my wife's eyes. She had carried me through so much, and for so long it seemed that with her help I had beaten off the worst of my problems, but these last few weeks had been among the toughest we had known . . . when you think you have something licked, and then it comes back at you with a new force, well, you have to fight all the harder not to be demoralised.

The worst of it was that terribly dark depression, something I couldn't shake off for weeks on end. I was doing some corporate work, tied in to the coming European Championships in Portugal, but it became increasingly difficult. I was coming home absolutely drained, just collapsing in a heap. The worst aspect was the loss of control. As a footballer you can break a leg or ankle and you can deal with it, know that the problem will pass as you get treatment and rebuild your fitness. But now I was in the vicious circle of needing the tablets to fight off life-threatening infections while all the time knowing what they were doing to my head. Occasionally I would look at a picture of myself in my playing days, charging across a field. I would note the muscle definition, the sharpness of my expression and all the energy it conveyed, and then I would look in the mirror. It wasn't a good thing to do.

Then came maybe in some ways the most shattering episode of all. It happened at one of those golf gatherings which the Boys of '66 and their wives enjoy so much. This time we travelled to a health spa, and all the boys were there, including Alan Ball, who we had wondered about because we all knew that his wife Lesley was fighting a brave but losing battle against a cancer that had come from nowhere with stealth and, finally, devastating speed. Lesley, so full of life, so feisty and bright, like all our wives knew the meaning of these gatherings, how they represented for all of us the most thrilling days of our lives. Bally said that Lesley had insisted he came along. He told us he had good days and bad, days when life suddenly seemed impossible, days when Lesley succeeded in making the point that whatever happened to her, Alan's life must go on. He had responsibilities to himself and to the family they had made. From my perspective I could only admire the courage of this couple we all loved so much.

On the first day of that gathering I played golf, but very poorly, with that deep weariness which had become a part of my life, and in the evening it was rather like my experience in that night club in the Rocks in Sydney when the England rugby players and all their friends and family were filled with such joy and satisfaction while I had a desperate sense that my life was unravelling. As the night wore on my situation became much more serious. When Daphne and I returned to our bedroom I was suddenly gripped by terrible stomach pains, and then it became clear I was in the middle of another rigour.

The hotel told Daphne that their on-call doctor didn't want to come out. My wife was very concerned, and angry, and eventually an ambulance came to take me to the hospital, which was about 10 miles away. I was very stressed when we were told at the hospital that the doctors there would have to investigate to see what was wrong with me. Daphne said that we knew well enough.

In the end I passed out with pain, at which point I was given an injection. I had gone to the hospital in pyjamas and a gown, and when I came around, and the pain had ebbed, someone asked Daphne, 'How are you going to get home?' Daphne said she had assumed it would be by ambulance. The hospital official said that this was not possible. I was no longer an emergency case. We had better call a taxi. When we arrived back at the hotel it was light and Gordon Banks was coming out into the dawn. 'George,' he said, 'what on earth have you been up to?' I told him that I'd had quite an eventful night.

Though these events created something of a sour taste, it would be wrong and ungrateful in a very deep way if I did not acknowledge the great work of the National Health Service and say that for all its problems, it is indeed something we should be fighting to protect and support with all our means. At the most critical moments of my life, it was the NHS which came to my rescue, not just with basic treatment but brilliant work by some of the best doctors in the land. Because of the downturn in my business life, I could never have afforded such care in the private system. The NHS was my lifeline and it proved strong and consistently effective.

That was true from my first crisis back in the seventies, when the news that I had cancer so soon after my success on the football field landed like a hammer blow, to the days of my return from Australia. My consultant, namesake of the great journalist Alistair Cooke, said when he arranged for me to see Professor Northover, 'If I had to choose someone to work on my guts, he would be the man.' It is impossible to overstate the confidence created by such a remark when you feel that your back is against the wall as never before.

As it turned out, Professor Northover would not – at least in the immediate future – be working on my guts. For several months I lived under the prospect of major, and quite dangerous surgery, but in the end the professor decided that it would indeed be risk-laden and invasive and that the best policy would be new medication – and great vigilance.

So where did that leave Daphne and me? It was where, I suppose, we had been ever since that first day when the certainties of our life together had been disturbed by the diagnosis of cancer. We would continue to hoard every day we had together, we would be lifted by the pleasure of our family, and the little incidents involving our grandchildren which bring a splash of sunlight to the greyest day. Our youngest grandchild, Eleanor, told Daphne when she was picked up for the first time from her 'grown up' school, 'You know grandma, I've been here all day.' And then my grandson Ben asked me if I would like to see the balance of his bank account, a massive £138.00, and when I said yes he showed me the book, but with his hand covering all but the bottom line. 'I'm sorry, granddad,' he said, 'but I can't show you all the details of my business.'

Who knows, maybe he will make the millions that so often I thought were just within touching distance. For myself, I still have my dreams of that life of comfort that comes from the big, winning deal, and this is despite the fact that from time to time my luck hasn't always been of the highest.

When this book was first published in hardback two years

ago the original publisher promptly went bust, with substantial monies unpaid. When set against the sweep of my business life it was not the most significant of reverses, but it made me shake my head a little as my friend and associate David Davies, who had helped me in the sale of my World Cup medal at another critical time, worked so hard to revive the project. I travelled many miles, spent many hours, selling my book, selling my life, but any feeling of bitterness, I can swear, is swamped by all that I have received since I had the privilege, one denied wonderful players like my friends Johnny Haynes and Jimmy Greaves, of playing for my country on the greatest day of its football history.

Now I'm working with three of my colleagues from that day, Geoff Hurst, Martin Peters and Alan Ball, on a project called 6606. You might say we are gathering in the last of that summer's wine as we recall the day that touched the nation. But from my perspective, at least, you would be wrong. It is a vintage that for me will always be young and thrilling despite whatever comes in the night.

WHAT THE TEAM AND THE MANAGER SAID

I was told that when George came back from an under 23s tour in 1960 he said: 'That's me, finished.' He knew that by the time the next match came along he would be over age and the conclusion was he felt he was not considered good enough for the senior team.

How wrong he was.

He had all the qualities required of an international player, particularly in defence. When he went forward his finishing was perhaps not all that could be desired. However this was not how he should be judged. He was a serious-minded young man, dedicated to his task. Playing against him must have been a very frustrating experience. I was grateful to him for the job he did. His injury cost the game an outstanding player while he was still at his peak.

Sir Alf Ramsey

If all players were like George there would be no problems for captains. England's World Cup players were a reliable bunch, but nobody was more willing or dedicated than him. Any job he was given to do he did without complication or complaint. He was the same off the field, too.

We were all upset and disappointed when we heard of the injury which ended his career. On behalf of everybody, I would like to wish him well.

Bobby Moore

I will always be grateful to George for the way he helped me when I first came in to the England side. He was an established player and though he was far from being big-headed he was so obviously sure of himself and of his ability. How different I felt. It was a great honour to be picked but there was a lot of doubt in my mind about whether I was really good enough. George welcomed me into the squad and did me worlds of good with just a casual word here and there. So much of this game is confidence. You need somebody to tell you that you are doing the right thing and to spare a word of praise when you have done it especially well.

Martin Peters

George and I always got on well. We had a system of working together that dovetailed beautifully. The basic reason it worked so well was because I knew nobody could run him on the outside. If they came inside he might be in trouble and it would be up to me to help out. If they went the other way George could give anybody two or three yards start and still beat them to the goalline. He was so fast it was barely believable at times. He and Nobby Stiles and I formed a triangle on the right hand side of the field and there's a story concerning the three of us I will always remember. Nobby is a notorious shouter on the field and I'm not exactly the silent type myself. We often used to have a go at each other while George would seldom say anything more than 'yes' or 'no' or 'OK'. One day against Germany over there, I shouted to Nobby about him not picking up somebody – as usual he didn't like being told.

Nobby, as you know, took his front teeth out when he played and he came over to me swearing and growling and showing his fangs. I pretended to be frightened and put my hands to my throat and said 'No, Nobby, no'.

George watched all this which was taking place while the match was still going on and he was as silent as ever. But when Nobby turned away he came close to me and said, 'He looks just like an animal, doesn't he.'

A few months later everybody else in the world was amused as Nobby, still without his teeth, did his little jig of joy while holding up the World Cup he had helped to win.

Jack Charlton

Three things stick in my mind about George. The first was on the eve of my first international against Scotland at Wembley. It was all a bit of a trial and I was glad when we were taken to see Ken Dodd at the Palladium. How that fellow tickles me. I have this funny laugh to start with and

Doddy had me rolling round the floor in hysterics.

Then I wiped the laughter tears away and looked at George sitting next to me. He had not moved a muscle. If there was an expression on his face at all it was a sneer, or maybe bewilderment. It was embarrassing. I thought I must be making a right fool of myself, but other people were laughing so in the end I began to wonder what sort of bloke this George Cohen was.

The next thing I recall about George is the way he used to play in five-a-side games. I always used to try to get picked on his side. If I did we won, if I didn't, we lost. George was a great colleague, I could not have wished for better.

Nobby Stiles

The great thing about George was how difficult he was to shift off the ball. I was never keen to play against him and when I did so I always seemed to get chinned by his elbows. You may not have noticed his elbows from off the field but you soon found out if you had to play outside-left against him.

Apart from his strength, he had a tremendous heart for the game. They reckon I'm quiet off the field but George was just the same. On the field too he talked very little. He just got on with the job like the really fine professional player he was.

Bobby Charlton

George was the easiest fellow in the world to get on with and I have never met anybody more dedicated. He was a fitness fanatic. All the times we were together I never saw him smoke or drink.

That includes the time I met him in Majorca after the end of the season and before we played together in the World Cup. He was supposed to be on holiday but he had been injured and I saw him training on the beach every day, running and exercising. He hardly stopped.

The injury that put him out of the game happened when my club were playing at Fulham. It was obvious straight away that he was in bad trouble. Peter Thompson was near him at the time but there was no tackle at all. George just twisted and dropped down in obvious pain. We all guessed it was cartilage trouble. That's how it happens. It is always serious but we didn't realise then that he would never really recover.

Roger Hunt

George and I used to be the ones who would overlap down the right and we worked up a good understanding. There was one match in particular when we kept overlapping. The only trouble was that when he got up there he kept crossing the ball behind. We were in front so the pressure was off and it was all really a bit of a giggle. Then came the point when he trotted back looking really shattered. The ball came back to me and I hadn't the heart to push it in front of him again. Then I was in trouble and all I could do was give it to him. I felt guilty about it but away he went again like a good 'un.

I could hardly believe it. He was very quiet on and off the field but he was the first to thank you for coming back and giving a hand. He'd say, 'Well done young man' and give you a bit of a grin and you felt he really meant it. He was also the first to reach you when you were in trouble. Even in training he gave everything. Nobody liked playing against him in five-a-sides!

Alan Ball

Of all the '66 World Cup team we all thought for sure that George would be there in Mexico to defend the trophy. He made me look lazy, he had so much stamina. While I was a floater when I was running, George would really drive along with a high knee action. He was so fast off the mark. He would go into a sliding tackle and seemed to be getting up almost as he was going down.

I never met anyone who did not take to him but he had his own way of doing things. While we were in Canada George just disappeared for four days. It became a bit of a joke — we'd say George must have gone home without telling anybody. In fact he was in his room reading, keeping out of the sun.

Ray Wilson

I thought I was a keen trainer but George left us all cold. He was a fanatic for fitness. He was a great defender, very quick and fearless and I think it was his condition that gave him the confidence to play the way he did.

You could not ask for a better team-mate. Off the field you never saw George without a book in his hand. On coaches, trains and planes, wherever we went George would have his head buried in a paperback. Most of the lads would play cards but George was the big reader. Well, anything that turns you on. It certainly worked for George because his concentration on the field was terrific.

Geoff Hurst

STATISTICS

George Cohen, born Kensington, 22 October 1939.

Career: Henry Compton School, Hammersmith; West London Boys, London Boys, Middlesex Youth.
Fulham amateur 1955, professional October 1956. First League game v Liverpool March 1957. Division 2 runners-up 1958-59. Coach to Fulham juniors 1969.

Honours: 37 full England caps; 8 Under-23; 4 Football League Representative XI. World Cup Winners Medal 1966.

Season	League		FA Cup		League Cup	
	Apps	Goals	Apps	Goals	Apps	Goals
FULHAM						
1956–57	1	–	–	–	–	–
1957–58	26	–	7	–	–	–
1958–59	41	1	4	–	–	–
1959–60	42	–	2	–	–	–
1960–61	41	–	1	–	1	–
1961–62	41	1	8	–	2	–
1962–63	38	–	2	–	1	–
1963–64	41	1	2	–	1	–
1964–65	40	2	2	–	2	–
1965–66	39	–	1	–	3	–

1966–67	35	I	3	–	3	–
1967–68	17	–	–	–	5	–
1968–69	6	–	I	–	–	–
Totals	408	6	33	–	18	–

England Internationals
1964 Uruguay, Portugal, Republic of Ireland, USA, Brazil, Northern Ireland, Belgium, Wales, Holland.
1965 Scotland, Hungary, Yugoslavia, West Germany, Sweden, Wales, Austria, Northern Ireland, Spain.
1966 Poland, West Germany, Scotland, Norway, Denmark, Poland, Uruguay, Mexico, France, Argentina, Portugal, West Germany, Northern Ireland, Czechoslovakia, Wales.
1967 Scotland, Spain, Wales, Northern Ireland.

Under-23
1959 Hungary, France.
1960 Scotland, Holland.
1961 Scotland, West Germany.
1963 Yugoslavia, Romania.

Football League
1964 Scottish League, Italian League.
1965 League of Ireland.
1966 Irish League.

INDEX

Abramovich, Roman 44
AC Milan 122
A'Court, Alan 91–2
Albrecht, Rafael 222
Al Fayed, Mohammad 156–61, 323–4
Ali, Muhammad 52–3, 78–81
Allen, Chesney 140
Allison, Malcolm 68, 129, 258
Alzheimer's disease 273
Angus, John 97, 180–1
Argentinian national football team 220–8
Armfield, Jimmy 114, 179–81, 253
Arsenal FC 41–2, 169–71, 271–2
Artime, Luis 222–3
aspiration (medical procedure) 278
Attenborough, Richard 285
Attlee, Clement 56
Austin, Les 101

Bacuzzi, Joe 88–9
Baker, Joe 199, 204
Bakhranov, Tofik 251–2, 265

Ball, Alan 10, 17, 21, 29, 35, 116, 178, 194–9, 209–10, 237, 247, 250–3, 265, 275, 336–7, 340, 345–6
Ball, Lesley 336–7
Banks, Gordon 21, 192, 199, 202, 220, 230, 241, 245, 249, 270, 338
Banks, Tommy 121
Bass, Alan 169, 195
Baxter, Jimmy 179, 268
Beckenbauer, Franz 244, 247–9, 257–8, 270
Beckham, David 25–32, 37, 178
Bell, Colin 270–1
Benjamin, Cyril 285, 297
Benjamin, John 285
Bentley, Roy 66, 95–101, 104, 113, 165, 236, 284–5
Berbick, Trevor 52
Bergkamp, Dennis 89
Best, George 39, 129, 167, 172–5
Blackman, Honor 94
Blanchflower, Danny 122
Bobby Moore Cancer Fund 257
Bogart, Humphrey 94

Bonetti, Peter 271
Booth, Tony 94
Boothby, Robert 140
Bowles, Stan 129
boxing 73–80
Brazilian national football
    team 26, 30, 195–6
Bremner, Billy 33, 130, 132
Brentford FC 153
Brice, Gordon 91, 128
Brickman, Sidney 271, 286–9
Buckingham, Vic 39, 59–60,
    112–13, 124–34, 167,
    171–2, 238, 258
bullying 71, 79, 221
Burrows, Harry 235–8
Busby, Matt 41, 103
Byrne, Budgie 203, 267
Byrne, Roger 102–3

Cafu 34
Calderon, Ignacio 209
Callaghan, Ian 194, 210, 212,
    320
Campbell, Sol 28, 35, 122
captaincy 113, 118, 198
Catterick, Harry 168, 171
Cecil Gee (company) 284–5
Chamberlain, Tosh 105, 113,
    120–3
Charlton, Bobby 1, 6, 10, 21,
    34, 103, 107–8, 116,
    133–4, 172, 175, 178, 182,
    185, 191–3, 199, 205–12,

222, 227, 230, 237, 247–9,
    253, 259, 270–1, 274, 321,
    344
Charlton, Cissie 262
Charlton, Jack 6, 159, 187–8,
    192, 199, 205, 207, 220,
    237, 249, 252–3, 259,
    265–8, 320–1, 342–3
Charlton Athletic FC 68, 325–6
cheating in football 92, 211
Chelsea FC 44, 66, 68
Christie, Linford 67
Clarke, Allan 59, 113, 130–1,
    135–6
Clay, Cassius see Ali, Muhammad
Clay, Ernie 151
Clifton Suspension Bridge
    100–1, 109
Cockell, Don 79
Cocker, Les 203, 238–9
Cohen, Abraham Benjamin
    ('Jewey Cooke')
    (GC's great uncle) 51–5, 70
Cohen, Andrew (GC's son)
    18, 64, 93, 143–6, 299, 303,
    316–19, 323–8
Cohen, Anthony (GC's son)
    5–8, 18, 64, 93, 144, 136,
    244, 303, 316–19, 323, 328,
    331–2
Cohen, Baldeep (GC's daughter-
    in-law) 327–8
Cohen, Ben (GC's grandson)
    328, 339

INDEX

Cohen, Ben (GC's nephew)
1–14, 50, 244, 301–3,
331–2

Cohen, Catherine (GC's mother)
18, 22, 49–50, 57, 62–4,
75, 93, 146–7, 173, 241,
295–8, 304–7

Cohen, Charlotte (GC's grand-
daughter) 328

Cohen, Christopher (GC's grandson) 328

Cohen, Henry Louis (GC's
father) 22, 48–50, 57, 61–4,
68, 72–5, 80–1, 108, 146–7,
236, 283, 304–7, 317

Cohen, Daphne (GC's wife)
3, 18, 22, 60, 64, 76–7, 88,
139–46, 154, 161, 163, 168,
240–1, 273, 279–88, 292–3,
296–7, 302–3, 306, 309–17,
323, 327–9, 331, 335–9

Cohen, Eleanor (GC's grand-
daughter) 328, 339

Cohen George
birth 57
at school 67, 72
first game for Fulham 87–8,
91–2
in first team at Fulham 95,
106, 149
in England Under-23
team 97, 149, 180–1
as Fulham captain 113
first game for England 182
injuries 66, 235–8, 266–7,
277–9, 341–2, 345
end of football career 280–2
wedding 142, 285
family life 143–6, 296, 328,
331, 339
work in tailoring 284–5
work in the property business
286–92
health problems 6–8, 12–13,
18–22, 142, 272, 287,
295, 306, 309–19, 332–9

Cohen, Helen (GC's daughter-
in-law) 328

Cohen, Jack 48

Cohen Jacob Solomon (GC's
grandfather) 48, 56

Cohen, Justin (GC's nephew) 301

Cohen, Len (GC's brother) 22,
49–50, 55, 58, 64, 140, 263,
297–8, 304–7, 312, 317

Cohen, Len (GC's uncle) 22, 61

Cohen, Lewis (GC's grandson)
328

Cohen, Peter, (GC's brother)
2–18, 22, 57, 71–2, 263,
295–307

Cohen, Raymonde, GC's sister-
in-law) 22, 305–6

Cole, Ashley 43, 90

Coleman, Chris 159, 327

colostomy 311–15, 333

Culverden Down 290–3

Connelly, John 194, 204, 207–12

Connery, Sean 228–9
Cook, Maurice 112
Cooke, Alistair 338
Cooper, Eric 189
Cortes, Julio Cesar 208
Coventry City FC 156
Craggs, Angela 139
Craggs, Ken 139–40
Craven Cottage ground 157, 160
Crawford, Roy 191
Crazy Gang 140
Crowther, Stanley 103
Crozier, Alan 25
Cullis, Stan 171, 181
culture of football 326

Daily Mail 259–60
Dallaglio, Lawrence 6
Danish national football team 36
Davies, David 340
Dawson, Alex 107
Dean, Dixie 166
depression 334–6
Devonshire Place, No. 25 289
di Stefano, Alfredo 114
Mrs Diamond 313
Diaz, Isidora 208
Dienst, Gottfried 246, 249
discipline
    in football 40–1, 44, 86, 98,
        124, 179, 185–8, 284
    in school 67–72
Dodd, Ken 228, 343–4
Dodgin, Bill 112–13, 133, 135

Douglas, Bryan 203
Downs, Terry 77
drugs, use of 317–18
Dwight, Roy 104–7

earnings of footballers 81,
    93, 95, 99, 122, 144,
    148–52, 161, 163–5, 237,
    259–62, 281, 292
Eastham, George 77–8, 149,
    151, 163, 169, 196, 199, 204
Edwards, Duncan 103
Emmerich, Lothar 240–1, 249
English national soccer team
    23–7, 32–6, 39, 171, 197,
    266–8
Eriksson, Sven Goran 25–8, 32,
    38, 40, 46, 192, 199, 266
European Cup (1960) 114
European Football Championship
    (2004) 25–8, 31–2, 36–7,
    45–6, 336
Eusebio 20, 228–30
Evans, Robert 298
Everton FC 166–71
Eyles, Walter 52

FA Cup 85, 102–3
Ferdinand, Rio 42
Ferguson, Alex 38–43
FIFA 214–15, 225, 242
Finney, Tom 118–19, 164, 194,
    284–5
fitness 29, 94, 238–9, 346

INDEX

Flanagan, Bud 140

Follows, Denis 255–6

Football Association 24, 40, 181–2, 189, 214–15, 253–66, 270–1; *see also* FA Cup

Football League 147, 151

Foreman, George 53, 79

Fraser, John 282

Frazier, Joe 53

Freed, Frederick 285

French national football team 27, 36–7, 209

friendly games 192

Frisk, Anders 44

Fulham Central School 22, 67, 69, 287, 300

Fulham FC 47–8, 60, 65–8, 71–2, 76, 81–7, 94–108, 111–12, 115, 120–36, 139, 151, 155–61, 168–71, 181–2, 236–8, 260, 280–5, 323–7

full-back position 87–91, 121

Gaetjens, Joe 226

Gans, Joe 52

Garrincha 196

Gascoigne, Paul 38

Gerrard, Steven 33

Giles, John 33, 117–18, 130

Gillies, Matt 130

Goldberg, Ada 64

Goma, Alain 159

Gonzalez, Alberto 224

Grace, W.G. 53

granulation 333

Greaves, Jimmy 5–6, 11, 33, 122, 137, 169–73, 182, 185–7, 192, 203–19, 234, 261, 286, 325, 340

Greek national football team 36

Green, Geoffrey 211

Greenberg, Ada 56

Greenwood, Ron 68, 97–100, 181, 224

Gregg, Harry 107

Guinness, Alec 94

Hackett, Desmond 197, 208

Haller, Helmut 245

hanging on
in football 283–4
to life 319

Hansen, Alan 147, 152, 161, 193

Hardaker, Alan 147–51

Harley, Margy 309

Haynes, Johnny 31–3, 47, 76, 79, 81, 89, 96, 100, 102, 105–7, 112–27, 131–9, 148, 155, 169–70, 191, 236–7, 281–2, 325, 340

Heap, Sir Desmond 287

Held, Sigi 240, 245, 247, 249

Henry, Thierry 42

Herbin, Roby 213

Heskey, Emile 28

Hidegkuti, Nándor 189–90
Hill, Gloria 152, 154
Hill, Jimmy 47–8, 68, 99, 107,
    112–13, 119, 122, 147–56,
    161, 163, 169, 193, 202
Hoddle, Glenn 33, 239–40
Holocaust, the 318
honours awarded to footballers
    14, 17–23, 45, 329
Howe, Don 169, 181
Hungarian national football
    team 189–90
Hunt, Roger 17, 21, 197–9,
    207, 212–14, 218, 222,
    227, 234, 238, 251
Hurst, Geoff 10, 21, 23, 97,
    200, 218–30, 234, 246,
    249–54, 259, 265, 271, 275,
    320–1, 340, 346–7

'image' rights 256–7
Ipswich FC 190
Italian national football team 36

Jancker, Carsten 35
Jewishness 49
Jezzard, Bedford 104, 112–13,
    132–3, 182, 191
John, Elton 104–5
Johnson, Martin 6
Johnston, Harry 190
Jones, Cliff 122, 170–5, 194,
    209, 286
Jones, Ken 97, 167, 180, 274

Jones, Mick 131
Jones, Wendy 74

Keane, Roy 43
Keegan, Kevin 158, 323
Keetch, Bobby 104, 113, 123–5,
    170
Kendall, Howard 166
Kerr, Colin and Gavin 298
Kleberson, Jose 30
Knocke, Charley 53
Kreitlein, Rudolf 221

Lacy, John 282–3
Langley, Jim 104, 107, 126
Larvy, Gordon 310–12, 316
Law, Denis 128, 246, 325
Law, Denzil 310–11
Lawler, Robin 86, 91, 104
Lawton, Tommy 164, 166
Leadbeater, Jimmy 191
Lee, Francis 271
Leeds United FC 130–1, 167
Leggat, Graham 96, 112–13,
    191
Liverpool FC 37–40, 65
Livingstone, Dugald 85–93, 112,
    132–3, 172
Ljungberg, Freddy 89
Lloyd, Cliff 149–50
London, Brian 78–81
Lord Palmerston (pub) 76
Louis, Joe 80
Lucio, Ferreira 26

Macdonald, Malcolm 113, 130–1, 135–6
Macedo, Tony 48, 104–8, 170, 172
McGhee, Frank 234
managership 131–5, 159, 191, 210–11, 284
Manchester City 129
Manchester United 39–40, 102–7, 129, 158
Mancini, Dennie 51, 75–6, 140–1
Mannion, Wilf 149, 164–5
Manor Place Baths 76
Manzie's pie and eel shop 58–9
Maradona, Diego 41
Marciano, Rocky 79
Marks and Spencer 256–7, 286
Marlet, Steve 158
Marsh, Rodney 113, 126–30
Mas, Oscar 220, 222, 227, 241
Mason, James 94
Mathias, Q.M. 316–17
Matthews, Stanley 103, 149, 164, 194
medals, sale of 18, 323, 340
Mee, Bertie 271
Mexican national football team 208–9
Middlesbrough FC 164
Milburn, Jackie 85
Miller, Sir Eric 135, 279–80, 326
The Mirror of Life 52–5

Mitten, Charlie 152
Montgomery, Bernard 60
Moore, Bobby 1, 10–11, 18, 21, 31, 97, 167, 182, 185, 188, 192, 196–9, 203, 207, 219, 221, 237, 245–7, 252–3, 257–60, 265, 270, 273, 315, 319–22, 329, 332, 341–2
Moore, Stephanie 319–21
Mortensen, Stan 164
Moscow Dynamo 73
Mosley, Oswald 61
Mourinho, Jose 44
Mullery, Alan 98–100, 115, 132–3, 169, 193
multiple sclerosis 318
Murphy, Edward 103
Murphy, Jimmy 117
Murphy, Tommy 53
Mutu, Adrian 44

National Health Service 316, 338
Neill, Bobby 77
Neill, Pat 87–8
Neville, Garry 42
Neville, Phil 28
Newcastle United FC 85
Newton, Keith 269
Nicholson, Bill 171
noise at football matches 243
Nolan, Bill 52
Northampton RFC 2, 13
Northover, John 332–5, 338–9

O'Neill, Martin 193
Osborne, Frank 93, 99, 102,
    104, 125, 148–9
Osborne, Harry 287
Osgood, Peter 129
Overath, Wolfgang 246–7, 252
Owen, Michael 25–6, 37–9

Paine, Terry 194, 206, 209–12
Pearson, Pancho 59–60, 259
Pele 41, 79, 196, 229, 231, 270
Penn, Frank 114
Peters, Martin 21, 74, 97, 116,
    194, 200, 204, 209–10,
    218, 223–4, 249, 275, 340,
    342
Phillips, Ted 191
Pires, Robert 42
Pizzagate affair 41–3
Pleat, David 284
Portuguese national football team
    27, 231–2
positional play 87–91, 258
Powell, Robert 287
Professional Footballers'
    Association 122, 147
Puskas, Ferenc 79, 114, 189–90

The Queen 17–19, 242–5

Ramsey, Alf 19–21, 24, 31–3,
    37, 45, 97, 116, 129, 131,
    171, 175, 177–254, 263–76,
    281, 341

Ramsey, Vicky 177–8, 184, 204,
    262, 272–4
Rattin, Antonio 220–2, 227
Real Madrid 37–8
Reaney, Paul 167
Rehaggle, Otto 36
Revie, Don 85, 130, 187, 212
Richardson, Ralph 94
Rivaldo 30–1
Robbins, Derek 156

Roberts, Mel 70–1, 86, 236, 284
Robson, Bobby 66, 68, 96–7,
    112–13, 133, 135
Rocha, Pedro 208
Roma, Antonio 224
Ronaldinho 26, 30–1, 34
Rooney, Wayne 28, 33, 38–41
Roque Junior 30
Rous, Sir Stanley 242
Rowe, Arthur 171–2, 192
Royal Marsden Hospital 316
Ruth, Babe 164–5

Saha, Louis 159
St Paul's School 60
Schnellinger, Karl-Heinz 29,
    250–1
Scholes, Paul 28, 30
Schoen, Helmut 248–9, 264–5
Schulz, Willi 251–2
Scottish national football team
    268

Seaman, David 33–4
Second World War 101, 186
Seeler, Uwe 247
septicaemia 334–5
Sexton, Dave 26, 114, 132, 134
Shankly, Bill 65, 118, 235, 238
Shellito, Ken 180–1
Shepherd, Ernie 67–8, 86–7, 236
Shepherdson, Harold 203, 212, 238–9, 267
Silverstein, Jack 54–5
Simoes, Antonio 230, 241
Simon, Jacky 213–14, 233, 275
Sinatra, Frank 140
6606 project 340
Slater, Bill 181
Smith, Norman 87
Smith, Tommy 243
Southend FC 258
speech-making 259–60
Speight, Johnny 94
Spinks, Leon 52
Spinks, Terry 77
sport in schools 70–1
Springfield, Dusty 94
Stapleton, Joe 104
Stevens, Arthur 105, 107
Stewart, Mickey 282
Stiles, Nobby 10, 17, 20–1, 24, 34, 45, 116, 193–4, 198–9, 207–8, 212–15, 228–30, 233, 247, 250–5, 259, 269, 275, 343–4

Stock, Alec 98
Strong, Les 282
substitutes 87, 195, 271
Summerbee, Mike 267
swivel defence 88

Tambling, Bobby 203
Tanfield, John 69, 71, 284
tax liabilities 261
Taylor, Ernie 33, 103, 106
Taylor, Tommy 102–3
television finance 159–60
Temple, Derek 166
Terry, John 44
Thompson, Peter 194–6, 277, 345
Tigana, Jean 158, 326–7
Tilkowski, Hans 246
Tottenham Hotspur FC 122, 136–7, 169–71, 286
Tour de France 239
training 94, 127–8, 141, 239
Trinder, Tommy 94–5, 111, 122, 136, 156, 236, 280, 286–7
Troche, Horacio 208

UEFA 44
Uruguayan national football team 204–8

values in sport 9, 64
Van Nistelrooy, Ruud 115
Viera, Patrick 42–3, 115

Vieri, Ondino 207–8
Villalonga, Jose 197

Wayne, John 254
Weber, Wolfgang 249
Webster, Colin 103, 108
Webster, Harry 52
Wembley Stadium 244
Wenger, Arsene 41–3
Wheatley, Dennis 233
White, E.E. 69–73
White's Hotel 184–5
Wilkinson, Jonny 5–6, 10–11
Wilson, Ray 17, 21, 191–2, 196–9, 207, 245–7, 268, 346
Wilson, Tom 157
wingers 194, 197, 204, 209–12
Winterbottom, Walter 68, 101, 153, 189, 266
Wolverhampton Wanderers FC 171
women and football 74

Woodley, Tom 52
Woodward, Clive 7, 12, 302
World Cup of rugby 1–2, 5–14, 331–2, 337
World Cup of soccer
1966 competition 1, 6, 10, 13–14, 18–23, 29, 34, 45, 175, 192, 199, 204–13, 217–57, 262, 279, 320–1
1970 competition 264, 267–79, 346
1974 competition 267
1990 competition 319
1998 competition 239–40
2002 competition 19, 24, 28–34, 36
2006 competition 23, 28
Wright, Billy 134

Yamasaki, Arturo 213
Young, Alex 166

Zidane, Zinedine 28

More Non-fiction from Headline

MY AUTOBIOGRAPHY

TOM FINNEY

'His humility shines through this warm,
nostalgic book' Chris Maume, *Independent*

'Fascinating and moving' Graham Kelly

Tom Finney was arguably the greatest footballer
England has ever produced, and a true legend of the
sport. In this autobiography, he recalls the golden era
of post-war football, when he played alongside and
against other all-time greats such as Matthews,
Mortensen and Lawton. His story not only reveals
the changing nature of the game, and the money
it attracts, but also provides a fascinating insight into
the state of the game today.

NON-FICTION / AUTOBIOGRAPHY / SPORT
0 7553 1106 X

Now you can buy any of these other bestselling
non-fiction titles from your bookshop or
direct from the publisher.

FREE P&P AND UK DELIVERY
(Overseas and Ireland £3.50 per book)